MW01712018

INSIDE ETHNIC AMERICA

An Ethnic Studies Reader

Robert L. Perry

Lillian Ashcraft-Eason

KENDALL/HUNT PUBLISHING COMPANY
4050 Westmark Drive Dubuque, Iowa 52004

Cover art by Leonard Gadzekpo.
Cover photo of Robert L. Perry
courtesy of Jose L. Munoz.

Copyright © 1996 by Kendall/Hunt Publishing Company

ISBN 0-7872-2098-1

All rights reserved. No part of this publication may be reproduced, stored in a retrieval system, or transmitted, in any form or by any means, electronic, mechanical, photocopying, recording, or otherwise, without the prior written permission of the copyright owner.

Printed in the United States of America

10 9 8 7 6 5 4 3 2 1

CONTENTS

FOREWORD

E. San Juan, Jr.
Ethnic Studies Department, Bowling Green State University

By the year 2050, according to census extrapolations, the population of the United States will be comprised predominately of people of color, mainly Latinos, African Americans, Asian/Pacific Islanders, other diasporic settlers, and Native Americans.[1] This would mean that the global majority of people of color in the continents of Africa, Asia/Oceania, and Latin America would become predominant in a polity that since World War II has symbolized Western hegemony over the planet. In the event that the former numerical minority becomes the majority, would the existing power relations and social divisions today be fundamentally changed? How would this affect the production, circulation, and allocation of material wealth and symbolic goods? How would this register in the struggle for popular empowerment, equality, and justice by those presently categorized as "ethnic" or "racial" minorities? In short, would such population shifts foreshadow the shape and substance of a genuinely multicultural, racism-free democracy in the United States in the next millennium?

These are some of the crucial and urgent questions this anthology seeks to foreground, clarify, address. What distinguishes this volume is that it gives us an idea of what it means to be members of "underrepresented," marginalized or subalternized communities. The individual chapters allow the voices of "insiders" to participate in the current conversation about "American identity," a colloquium on the commonality or incommensurability of values, principles and goals in our society.

This collection is thus intended not just for specialized students and scholars in Ethnic Studies but for all concerned citizens. The contributors believe that an enlightened citizenry needs to address questions of power, equality, and justice in relation to people of color not just as academic topics rendered innocuous in the cliches of pluralism, cultural diversity and tolerance, but as substantive issues for public debate. Such issues are central to the agenda of practical and moral education in a society constituted by heterogeneous groups—not just the 17th century immigrants from Europe but all the world's peoples colonized, enslaved, and subjugated by Eurocentric power—with distinctive traditions, discourses, memories and histories.[2]

Basic to the discipline of contemporary Ethnic Studies is its insight that the historical formation of American society is distinguished by a racial, not ethnic, pattern. (Here the terms "race" and "racial" should be construed as sociopolitical constructs, not biological or genetic signifiers whose scientific validity is nil.) In a well-known argument, Ronald Takaki has demonstrated that the inaugural doctrines on citizenship and national belonging drew sharp distinctions between "ethnicity" and "race."[3] A logic of exclusion and hierarchical segregation based on notions about "race," not culture, has prevailed since the founding of the nation-state. Influenced by a long tradition of European "racial" thinking, beginning from Linneaus and Cuvier up to de Gobineau, Knox, and Galton, the Euro-American ruling class has legislated and ruled on the basis of subsuming cultures into the hegemony of what can only be appropriately called "white supremacy."[4] Historian Alexander Saxton describes this genre of statehood as a "racially exclusive democracy—democratic in the sense that it sought to provide equal opportunities for the pursuit of happiness by its white citizens through the enslavement of Afro-Americans, extermination of Indians, and territorial expansion largely at the expense of Mexicans and Indians."[5] The cogency of this axiom has been aptly registered in this volume of essays on the American Indian, Puerto Rican, Mexican American, and African American historical experiences.[6]

The explosion of the Civil Rights struggles in the sixties was a milestone event in the transformation of an apartheid system. Segregation *de jure* was abolished, but *de facto* racial exclusion and various forms of covert and institutional discrimination persist in the face of popular challenge and resistance. Cornel West's recent remark is, indeed, a timely intervention that connects origin and goal: "To talk about race in America is not to talk about something you've picked up or something you've been socialized into. To talk about racism is to talk about what it is like to be modern and human and American."[7]

Beginning in the late seventies, a neoconservative counter-revolution intent on dismantling the gains of the New Deal "welfare state," chiefly programs of affirmative action, has culminated in the "Contract with America" and the reactionary onslaught against "political correctness," the code word for all liberalizing trends. In this political climate, we witness how the ideology of "race" has been revitalized with Murray and Herrnstein's *The Bell Curve* and the resurgence of sociobiology accompanied by "race-thinking" or neo-Social Darwinism. Sometime ago Leith Mullings pointed out how the mainstream doctrine of ethnicity formulated by Nathan Glazer and Daniel Patrick Moynihan obfuscated stratification by gender, class, residence, nationality, and so on.[8]

Above all, it cancelled the saliency of racism and theory and experience. Meanwhile, a new kind of racism has emerged that deploys "ethnicity" (in the guise of IQ, new versions of cultural deficit, family values, e.g.) to explain retrenchment in public spending and government social services in a time when the cause of U.S. economic decline due to a worldwide crisis in profit accumulation is being shifted onto the masses of working people, in particular impoverished people of color.[9]

The discipline of Ethnic Studies was born in the sixties as a response to the endemic crisis of the system. Now it has a responsibility to confront a crisis of greater proportion, this time involving the future of the ideal of an egalitarian, just, multiracial democracy. As various commentators (W.E.B. DuBois, Gustavus Myers, Oliver C. Cox, Stephen Steinberg, among others) have noted, the ideal of cultural or ethnic pluralism in the United States has always been inseparable from systemic inequality across race, gender, nationality, class. What used to be called "*Herrenvolk* democracy[10] may now be obsolescent, but its effects are still with us, as revealed by the circumstances surrounding the Rodney King trials, the O.J. Simpson affair and the "racism" of the Los Angeles police, Proposition 187, and the bid to scrap Affirmative Action in California. In the wake of such events, Gerald Horne reminds us that the "Euro-Afro-centrism" of our analysis of race prevents us from grasping the fact that "the genocide against Native Americans is an essential component for comprehending all forms of U.S. racism, including anti-black racism."[11] Recent discussions on the social construction of "whiteness" (examples being Theodore W. Allen's *The*

Invention of the White Race and David Roediger's *The Wages of Whiteness*) rearticulate the black-white grid to give proper weight to racial violence and exclusion against Latinos, American Indians, Arab Americans, and Asians/Pacific Islanders.

One response to the crisis of universal commodification is separatist or cultural nationalism, a politics of identity.[12] Postmodern intellectuals contend that the Enlightenment metanarratives of reason, progress, and self-mastery no longer hold amid the decentering of the Cartesian subject and the dissolution of all objective authority. We are all "insiders" bearing testimonies of local truths, simulacra, the hyperreal. The claim that the "insider's view" is a privileged one possessing equal if not more validity than the "outsider's view" has been debated by mainstream and oppositional social scientists.[13] Its philosophical legitimacy inheres in what Charles Taylor calls "the politics of recognition." This demand by marginalized or subaltern peoples for recognition that their culture is of equal worth or value as that of the dominant society—the rationale of multicultural pedagogy—seems to contradict the procedural model of liberalism premised on "equal protection" for all citizens. Since the liberalism of individual rights and judicial review underpins our business society, the hegemonic consensus cannot sympathize with the vision of the collective good in which people of color share equal power, equal dignity, equal wealth. This is beyond what the formalistic version of the recognition of cultural distinctiveness entails, and beyond what Taylor calls the utopian promise of a "fusion of horizons" that will reveal the "relative worth of different cultures" in some distant future.[14] The problem with this idealist-metaphysical reckoning of culture lies in its divorce from the concrete historical ground of culture with its infinite variety and mutations, in particular from the specificity of dynamic social processes in which racial/ethnic differences are articulated dialectically with political, ideological, and economic practices.

This volume endeavors to show that inquiry into ethnicity and associated themes of identity, power, and justice, cannot dispense with such complex articulations. The black/white paradigm of traditional research needs to be enriched if not displaced by the intercultural and multidisciplinary contributions from humanist scholars with Latino, Asian/Pacific Islander, Native American, and other communal perspectives. Above all, the critique of competitive market society and its utilitarian ethos needs to be launched from the engaged, committed sensibilities of people of color. This is not because they have a claim to privileged access to sacrosanct knowledge (Their king of knowledge-production needs to be subjected also to historical critique.) but because their participation in the shaping of a project called "multicultural democracy" is integral to resisting the commodity-fetishism, alienation, and racial exclusivism indivisible from the power of transnational capital accumulation that profoundly determines our everyday lives. To guard against any essentialist, nominalist or relativist excess that may generate counterproductive ethnocentrism, we need to keep in mind Ramon Gutierrez's timely observation:

> At a moment when nationalism is reemerging powerfully among students in the United States as well as [among those in] many other nations and states, . . . it seems imperative that we see that glorification of local systems of knowledge which are rooted in racial, religious, and ethnic distinctions, as fundamentally tied to the globalization, commodification, and massification of social life.[15]

Hence the need to maintain communication and solidarity with scholars from all communities and regions around the world.

Today more than ever, with our transnationalizing electronic network, we all inhabit one ecological space where the fate of peoples anywhere affects everybody's well-being and life-chances. we have finally become the "Others" whose recognition has become the collective responsibility of all humanity. This consciousness of global realities is also in keeping with the mission of the department of Ethnic Studies at Bowling Green State University, that mission charges us to inform our students of the nature and implications of the rapidly changing racial and ethnic composition of our society. This knowledge may help them understand their civic responsibilities as mature citizens in what may become a genuinely multicultural planet.[16]

---

[1] By that time, the state of Hawaii could well be an autonomous if not completely independent nation-state; while California, Texas, and Florida would be preponderantly Spanish-speaking.

[2] See Robert Blauner, *Racial Oppression in America* (New York: Harper and Row, 1972). For a discussion of racialization, see Robert Milse, *Racism* (London: Routledge, 1989).

[3] Ronald Takaki, "Reflections on Racial Patterns in America," *From Different Shores* (New York: Oxford University Press, 2nd Edition, 1944), 27.

[4] See Michael Goldfield, "The Color of Politics in the United States: White Supremacy as the Main Explanation for the Peculiarities of American Politics from Colonial Times to the Present," *The Bounds of Race,* ed. Dominick Lacapra (Ithaca: Cornell University Press, 1991), 104-133.

[5] Alexander Saxton, "Nathan Glazer, Daniel Moynihan and the Cult of Ethnicity," *AmerAsia Journal* 4 (Summer 1977): 145. See also Stephen Steinberg, *The Ethnic Myth* (Boston: Beacon Press, 1981).

[6] One contributor, Joseph Scott, captured the resonance of this persisting racial pattern in his statement: "Afro-Americans have been a captive people who still are under a colonialistic system of domination and exploitation."

[7] Quoted in Andrea Wood, "West: All Must Work to Improve Race Relations," *The BG News* (9 November 1995), 4.

[8] "Ethnicity and Stratification in the Urban United States," *Racism and the Denial of Human Rights: Beyond Ethnicity,* ed. Marvin Berlowitz and Ronald Edari (Minneapolis: MEP Publications, 1984), 22.

[9] I elaborate on some recent trends in two articles: "Reconstituting the 'American' Nation: The Politics of Racism and Nationalism in the United States," *Nature, Society, and Thought,* 5.4 (Sp[ring], 1933), 307-319; and "Can't We Get Along? The Politics of Racial Difference in an Age of Hegemonic Pluralism," *The Arkansas Quarterly* 2.3 (July 1993), 168-176.

[10] Pierre van den Berghe, *Race and Racism: A Comparative Perspective* (New York: John Wiley and Sons, 1967), 77-95.

[11] "Race Matters: The Trajectory of Anti-Racism," *Science and Society* 57.4 (Winter 1993-94), 441-445. Of extreme importance is the global perspective on U.S. racism proposed by Joy James in her essay "Racism, Genocide, and Resistance: The Politics of Language and International Law," *Marxism in the Postmodern Age,* ed. Antonio Callari, Stephen Cullenberg, and Carole Biewener (New York: Guilford Press, 1995), 115-125.

[12] On identity politics, see chapter V of my *Racial Formations/Critical Formations* (Atlantic Highlands, NJ: Humanities Press, 1992); and on the problems of multiculturalism and "common culture," see chapter X of my *Hegemony and Strategies of Transgression* (Albany: State University of New York Press, 1995). "Identity politics" becomes symptomatic of the hegemonic efficacy of inventing "model minorities," as manifest in Toni Morrison, "On the Backs of Blacks," *Time* 142 (Fall 1993), 57, quoted in George J. Sanchez, "Reading Reginald Denny: The Politics of Whiteness in the Late Twentieth Century," *American Quarterly* 47.3 (September 1995), 393.

[13] See the essays by Robert K. Merton, "Insiders and Outsiders: A Chapter in the Sociology of Knowledge," and Patricia Hill Collins, "Learning from the Outsider

Within: The Sociological Significance of Black Feminist Thought," in *Taking Sides: Clashing Views on Controversial Issues in Race and Ethnicity,* ed. Richard C. Monk (Guilford, Ct.: The Dushkin Publishing Group, Inc., 1994), 4-23.

[14]"The Politics of Recognition," *Multiculturalism: A Critical Reader,* ed. David Goldberg (Cambridge: Blackwell, 1994), 102.

[15]"Ethnic Studies: Its Evolution in American Colleges and Universities," *Multiculturalism: A Critical Reader* (Cambridge: Blackwell, 1994), 165. On present-day global trends, I recommend Harry Magdoff, *Globalization: To What End?* (New York: Monthly Review Press, 1992).

[16]Robert L. Perry and Susan Mae Pauly, "Crossroads to the 21st Century: The Evolution of Ethnic Studies at Bowling Green State University," *Explorations in Ethnic Studies* 11.1 (January 1988), 13-22.

PREFACE

Robert L. Perry, Ethnic Studies Department
Lillian Ashcraft-Eason, History Department
Bowling Green State University

At thirty-years-old ethnic studies is a young area of formalized study in the academy. Established in the postmodernist era, it is multi-disciplinary as well as multi-racio-ethnic. However, publications from ethnic studies suggest that, with few exceptions, scholars continue to perceive an uneasy fit among the methodologies drawn from the multiple disciplines. Consequently, the textbooks tend to demonstrate (or at least infer) that the methodologies of the several disciplines are more at variance with than complementary to each other. The product of a social scientist and a humanities-oriented historian, this reader is multi-disciplinary in that the six parts into which the twelve essays are divided represent fields of study in the social sciences and humanities. Marriage of the methods and approaches of these two theoretical orbits contribute to the import of the volume.

The reader is divided along ethnic groupings. In the context of the U. S. experience, ethnicity implies that "a group [is] socially distinguished or set apart, by others or by itself" on the basis of "a sense of common ancestry, a consciousness of shared experiences and of shared cultural patterns." The significance of differences in historical experiences between Europeans and peoples of color is not conceded by this definition. This reader acknowledges that the social privilege that generally is accorded to white Americans does not extend to Americans of color. Consequently, ethnics of color have experienced the democracy differently than their more privileged, white counterparts. For the most part, the ethnics represented in this reader fall within the peoples-of-color groupings.

The twelve essays pivot on themes that relate racio-ethnic diversity to power relations and allow for value analysis. "Pluralism," "diversity," "multiculturalism," "race," "ethnicity," all are terms connoting valuations of people, for they infer the positionality (marginality) of peoples of color in relation to white supremacy. As the essays will demonstrate, the privileged positionality resonates from the economic and political power dynamics commanded by privileged white Americans. Considering the real or imagined magnitude of white supremacy, one wonders whether ethnic and cultural pluralism can burgeon forth and whether diversity shall endure. This is a troublesome issue confronting the contemporary citizens of the United States, and it potentially impacts many other parts of the world.

Although ethnic diversity pervades most of the Western world, no other country is as truly a nation of immigrants and diversity as the United States. Diversity, resulting from the continuous influx of immigrants from abroad, has been the hallmark of the United States from its colonial beginnings to the present. It seems paradoxical, therefore, that in the contemporary moment of the postmodernist/decentrist global dynamic, the privileged white Americans assert that Eurocentric cultural traditions and values should be the established national norm in the United States. This faction would use its political and financial clout to preserve, or perhaps as some would say, to *cast* the national identity in its image.

The privileged, white Americans allegedly seek to keep the "nation of immigrants" (Read immigrants-of-color.) from imploding upon itself, dismantling national agencies with potential to support pluralism by funding projects in the arts and humanities. Although this minority-driven, anti-multicultural policy cannot eradicate diversity, underrepresented groups believe it threatens to thwart pluralism. The sociopolitical roots and moral and social ramifications of the Europhilic policy is a subject of heated discussion across the country.

Civic and business leaders, educators and other professionals have addressed issues of diversity and pluralism compellingly with reference to education, research, and literature. They properly view schools and universities as primary social institutions that are second only to the family in preparing the nation's diverse youth to be useful citizens dedicated to promoting the national welfare. How best to utilize educational institutions toward accomplishing these ends is a question that is intrinsic to the national discourse.

The heated dialogue that erupted when the National Endowment for the Humanities-sponsored *ad hoc* committee on History Standards issued its report highlighting the polarizing potential in the discourse over what should be the role of diversity in curricular development. There is to be sure little agreement on how the curriculum could be shaped to foster national unity amidst the multicultural identities. There is no *one* definitive answer to the questions implied by the discourse, but the essays in this volume inform us extensively about what it means to be a member of an unprivileged, politically underrepresented people within the United States.

These essays address various aspects of the diversity/pluralism issue. Six have not been published previously, and two ("Black Science, Black Self-Improvement and Nation-Building" and "Machismo: Meanings in the Mexican/Mexican American Experience") were revised by their authors from previously published essays specifically for this reader. Four parts present "insider" perspectives of four peoples of color, noting nevertheless the diversity (class, gender, sexual preference, and national origin) within the ethnic groups. With the exception of the Latino segment, which contains three essays, each group speaks through two voices.

The two introductory essays by Lonnie Kliever and James Banks provide the central themes for the reader by asking: *What core of values bind the diverse Americans together and can a moral education curriculum offer anything other than the dominance of one culture over others? Do the diverse peoples want a pluralistic society with dispersed power or is the latter a contradiction to E pluribus unum?*

The quandary over pluralism preceded the nation's constitutional republicanism, for the roots of discord over diversity stretch back nearly four hundred years into the colonial beginnings. Essays by Daniel Littlefield and by Linda Pertusati (who has Lakota ancestry) speak to this historical fact. They remind the reader of the Native American peoples' struggle for cultural survival and their bid for self-autonomy, i.e., the opportunity to control their own educational programs and to interpret and transmit their cultural traditions and histories.

In the African American section, the discourse over white privilege and cultural dominance is second only to issues of black cultural identity and economic concerns. It is in this vein that Joseph Scott asks: *What external factors legitimate the dominant scientific process as the proper method for studying black people?* Dorothy Denniston provides us with one of the few essays on black immigrants to the United States in the twentieth century—the Barbadians; she shows that they confront tensions between African-oriented communal values and American capitalistic, individualism. Both essays are concerned with identifying the essence of what it means to have a black experience.

Each of the three readings in the Latino section deals with themes of dominance as social constructions. Like Littlefield and Pertusati, Frances Aparicio and Lizabeth Paravisini-Gibert write about the impact of European American dominance on non-white culture(s) and social relations. Both essayists consider the factor of skin color in the U. S. Latino policy and wonder about its moral and sociopolitical implications for white and Latino Americans. Rolando Andrade provides a gender-focussed analysis of dominance as machismo, sketching its varied shades and meanings from a Mexican American perspective.

By drawing extensively upon the traditional cultural background(s) of the several Asian groups, writers in that section juxtapose the bi-cultural dimensions within which these most recent, immigrant peoples maneuver within the United States. The cultural influences on business and literature provide focus and context for the essays. Pyong Gap Min identifies several factors that make the Korean business experience in the United States unique and often productive as well. Cynthia Wong treats the issue of legitimizing a people's genre of self-study, asking *How authentic is a literary genre of peoples of color when it is legitimated from a Western perspective?*

Finally, Lorna Gonsalves-Pinto's essay speaks to how "insider" perspectives and knowledge about racial and ethnic groups can be conveyed effectively to students. Here the social sciences and humanities come together in a pedagogically useful way.

These essays articulate views representing perspectives from "inside" the communities of a range of racio-ethnic peoples in the United States. Thus, the histories, cultures, and aspirations of these peoples are expressed in this reader in a way that virtually no other ethnic studies textbook has set forth. Hear voices of these people via the narratives and analyses that social scientists and specialists in the humanities bring in the essays. Experience feeling and pathos, as well as cognitive awareness of and intellectual insight into issues and problems that confront these Americans.

ACKNOWLEDGMENTS

We express appreciation to the contributors. We thank several graduate students for their contributions to this reader: Roger Schmidt for initially researching and recommending ethnic essays, Wole Ife for research assistance, Jeff Sodergren and Kimberly Caldwell for reading and abstracting several of the essays, and Sharon Vriend for her help in word-processing and other aspects of manuscript preparation. Our sincere appreciation is extended to LaRouth D. Perry and L. Djisovi Eason—our wife and husband respectively, for good cheer that helped make the completion of this work possible as they both languished over the work of completing their Ph.D. dissertations.

PART I

PRUNING DIVERSITY INTO HEALTHY PLURALISM: TWO APPROACHES FROM THE ACADEMY

Commentary about the character of the nation inspired the recent NEH initiative for a national dialogue on multiculturalism and President Clinton's announcement that he would form a national commission on race. In the introductory essay to this volume, professor of religious studies Lonnie D. Kliever adds his voice to the discourse with the assertion that in a pluralistic society, national cohesion can best be promoted by a regimen of moral education. He cautions, nevertheless, that the promotion of morality as a national value in the pluralistic context necessitates a pedagogical system which fosters moral excellence rather than mere moral training. Kliever contends, that is, that the moral-education curriculum would promote private morality while inculcating the significance of a public moral order.

Thus, Kliever presupposes

1. that the diverse ethnic groups have a shared core of values and interests which would coalesce in a moral-education curriculum and
2. that moral education would benefit the nation by holding the potentially polarizing, individual ethnic-group interests in check.

Readers would be wise to ask what these shared values and interests are and how moral education would contribute to the social transformation from critical (a potentially disruptive) diversity to cohesive pluralism. The reader opens with this essay because, in one way or another, the moral value issues addressed by Kliever from his perspective as a European-American inside the academy permeate the eleven essays that follow.

James A. Banks writes about education's potential to help resolve problems associated with racio-ethnic diversity. Speaking of the moral, as well as of the cognitive dimensions of the diversity issue, Banks brings to this discussion both years of research and advocacy for multicultural education and the perspective of a marginalized American. He contends that the liberal arts curriculum should be multiethnic in order to help students develop cultural literacy, which—he asserts—will be attained when students are knowledgeable about and able to find value in the United States' diversity. Banks further argues that multicultural literacy would nurture the development of positive human interaction within and across racial and ethnic groups. The end-product would be the development of "a healthy nationalism" along with the preservation of the identities of individual racial and ethnic groups. His discussion extends beyond the United States to reflect on the ethnic diversity of other Western nations.

Lonnie Kliever expresses a Jeffersonian-like concern that the masses be contained. This position allows him to advocate that the predominantly white hegemony acknowledge and refrain from further stymying what could be a burgeoning pluralism. He implies that the judicious means to this end is to temper the disparate cultural and ethnic groups by teaching moral responsibleness from a ground of shared values. Banks begins where Kliever takes leave; that is, Banks assumes that the disparate racial and ethnic groups have a subliminal functional, if not consciously numbed awareness that it is morally imperative that they know more about each other. After reading the two essays in this section, how convinced are you that either author, or that both authors together, offer effective advice toward resolution of the United States' racio-ethnic and cultural divisiveness?

Moral Education in a Pluralistic World

Lonnie D. Kliever
Religious Studies, Southern Methodist University

Pluralism is in high vogue today, but the ease and enthusiasm with which pluralism is embraced suggests a widespread misunderstanding or naiveté about its meaning. Blithe pluralists often simply equate pluralism with the diversity of interest groups and the toleration of religious differences in modern democratic societies. But such political and ecclesiastical pluraformity is not pluralism. The dispersion of political power and the freedom of religious assembly within non-hierarchical societies usually represent differences and disagreements within a shared commitment to one nation under one God. Pluralism by contrast assumes no such overarching unity or loyalty. Pluralism is the existence of multiple frames of reference, each with its own scheme of understanding and criterion of rationality. Pluralism is the co-existence of comparable and competing positions which are not to be reconciled. Pluralism is the recognition that different persons and different groups quite literally indwell irreducibly different worlds.

Little wonder that virtually every study of higher education in the last five years has drawn attention to the lack of serious moral education in the undergraduate curriculum. Allan Bloom's celebrated

From *Journal of American Academy of Religion*, 51 #1 (Spring 1992). Copyright © 1992 by American Academy of Religion. Reprinted by permission.

jeremiad on *The Closing of the American Mind* and E.D. Hirsch's reader's digest of *Cultural Literacy* scold the academy for failing to deal with questions of moral value and civic virtue. The Association of American College's 1985 report on redefining the meaning and purpose of baccalaureate degrees identifies values as a necessary element in every student's undergraduate education. In the most recent study of the Carnegie Foundation for the Advancement of Learning, Ernest L. Bowyer insists that a coherent undergraduate experience must prepare students to maintain the necessary balance between private and public obligations in a participatory democracy. In short, these recent studies call on colleges and universities to confront directly the problem of moral education in a pluralistic world.

For the most part, religion scholars have been reluctant to take up this challenge, despite the obvious affinities between questions of value and the study of religion. This reluctance is deeply rooted in the recent history of Religious Studies as an academic discipline. Religious Studies has won a place in public as well as private universities by drawing very clear lines between descriptive and prescriptive approaches to religion. It is not that religion scholars have been timid about insisting on the centrality of religion in human affairs. Indeed, we routinely claim that religion is the source of everything political, social and personal. But our approach to religion has neither a determinative content nor a definitive history. Religion is reduced to a universal function of world construction and personal formation—a function that can be served by virtually anything that has *sacred* power and meaning for groups and persons. Even tentative judgments between various conceptions of the sacred are ruled out in the name of academic and constitutional scruples against religious indoctrination. Never mind that other academic disciplines routinely encourage normative approaches to other cultural symbol systems. Religion scholars typically treat the sacred as a neutral category rather than as an ultimate reality, thereby provoking Bloom's caustic comment that the typical religion scholar "is like a man who keeps a toothless old circus lion around the house in order to experience the thrills of the jungle."[1]

But religion scholars can and should play a key role in responding to the "crisis of values" in our pluralistic world. On the one hand, scholarly studies of religion have clearly contributed to the emergence of modern pluralism. During the last century, both the cultured despisers and the modern apologists of religion came together in their rejection of authoritarian and exclusivistic religion. Religion, whether finally judged destructive or constructive, was deemed to be historically and culturally relative. That remarkable consensus between religion's defenders and despisers gave scholarly impetus to the segmentation and privatization of human meaning and value so typical of modern societies.[2]

On the other hand, the academic study of religion can play a crucial role in maintaining the precarious balance between change and order that lies at the heart of modernity. Modern men and women are moved at once by a will to transform and a need to stabilize their environments and experiences.[3] People who are torn between these contradictory impulses are tempted to resolve the ambiguities of modern life by radical polarization—by either espousing revolution with uncritical enthusiasm or defending institutions with relentless determination.

But there are ways to hold these contradictory forces that inspire and torment us together—ways that accept the modern critique of religious traditions without abandoning the perennial quest for moral values. No academic discipline is better prepared to explore these ways of saving pluralism from its own revolutionary and reactionary excesses than the field of Religious Studies. There one can find resources both substantive and methodological for maintaining that dialectical "unity within disunity" which constitutes the central vision and values of modernity.

The peril of ethical pluralism is obvious when we recognize that such opposing moralities are based on mutually incorrigible aims and standards. What happens when these contrasting worlds collide? Can the relationships between contradictory visions of reality and schemes of meaning remain benign in a world of increasing population and decreasing resources? Can conflicts between such worlds be resolved in any way short of coercion or violence? What happens when the monopoly on world-definition is broken within a society? Can the common life survive without a common world view and moral system? Can the individual form a stable identity within a single life-world that guarantees order and meaning? In other words, the situation of pluralism not only jeopardizes international order and social stability, it threatens the very possibility of being a self and having a world. In a pluralistic world there are no uncontested systems of reality definition, social integration, and personality formation. Moreover, these tasks, which are interlocking in the traditional society, have been torn apart within the demythologized and historicized societies of the modern world. Precisely this separation must be grasped if we are to understand the character and the challenge of pluralism in our time.

Traditional societies combined the practical task of securing identity with the theoretical task of interpreting reality in a single world view.[4] Such interpretive systems dispelled chaos and guaranteed meaning by mastering the problems of survival in both nature and society. Of course, that mastery was always incomplete, and thus explanations, sanctions, and consolations for failure were built into those "nomizing" systems. In primitive societies the problems of survival *vis-a-vis* nature were so drastic that human ignorance and impotence were counterbalanced by a heavy overlay of mythic order. But increased control over nature gradually freed secular knowledge from dependence upon and loyalty to sacral world views, which in turn were increasingly restricted to functions of personality formation and social integration.

The natural sciences eventually established a monopoly on the interpretation and control of nature through standardized procedures of verification and technological conquests of nature. But the later-emerging social sciences have developed no comparable methods of confirmation or conquests of contingency in the social world. Indeed, the social sciences have intensified these problems of relativizing or dissolving the traditional world-views that deal with human loneliness and guilt, suffering and death. Consequently the sociocultural world, where fundamental questions of human worth and death predominate, has been rendered problematic by the separation of traditional interpretive systems of the social world from the consensus interpretive system of the natural world.

This separation has triggered a radical "legitimation crisis" in the life-worlds of modern societies.[5] This crisis is felt on two levels. The *life-legitimating* systems, which nomize the chaos and terror that threaten personal and social existence, have been decimated by the scientific erosion of mythic explanations and relativized by the scientific discovery of multiple world views. These disruptions have in turn generated a crisis at the level of system-legitimating arguments. Of course, "secondary legitimations" of a given life-world have always been required whenever challenges to the facticity or authority of the life-world have arisen. These arguments typically exhibit a wide range of theoretical completeness and sophistication. Justificatory appeals range from the customary (mythic narratives of origin) to the cosmic (metaphysical systems of reality). Such system-legitimating arguments were in the past thought to be universally compelling, but today we recognize that they are system dependent. This is the heart of the contemporary legitimation crisis.

Pluralism has put us in a situation where we do not know just which world we inhabit. Determining conclusively which world we are really in would require a means of arbitration that does not presuppose any of them. We have at hand, in scientific methods of verification, system-transcending criteria for adjudicating rival interpretations of the natural world. But appeals to publicly experienceable and repeatable evidence have not proven applicable to visions of human worth and duty in the sociocultural world. Thus we are confronted with a pluralism of life-worlds that are not legitimated by the cognitive content or criteria of scientific understanding. Shorn of demonstrably cognitive roots, religiocultural forms of life are without authority for those not predisposed to believe them.

But what is the future of such systems of personality formation and social integration in a pluralistic world? There can be no doubt that the traditional religions have undergone a serious erosion of belief and authority in modern societies. These religions have lost their monopoly on world-definition and world maintenance. But that loss has not signalled the end of religion. The massive debunking and dismantling of traditional religious world views at the hands of modern criticism has only loosed a new rage for order and meaning.[6] The persistence of religion should not surprise us. Skepticism and nihilism are after all philosopher's diseases and seldom if ever become epidemic among the populace. The human craving for meaning and order, which has the inexorable force of instinct, continues unabated despite the demystification and disenchantment of the natural world. Indeed, the persistence of religion has fueled the pluralism of our time by multiplying the religious options present *within* modern societies. Herein lies the real question of the future of religion. Can human meaning and order survive in a world and in society fragmented rather than united by religion?

Having thus clearly raised the problem of pluralism, I want to join the "blithe" pluralists in arguing that human meaning and order can not only survive but also can thrive in a pluralistic world. But the promise of pluralism will be reached only if the peril of pluralism can be avoided. And that will prove to be more difficult and costly than many enthusiasts for pluralism dare imagine. The promise of pluralism is a world and a society newly freed for diversity and even idiosyncrasy, newly flexible for experimentation and change. Out of pluralism's creative ambiguity and dissonance can come an enriched and enlarged sense of the possibilities of life here and now. Finally, the promise of pluralism is the dream of allowing each life to become a distinctive work of art—each person fashioning the materialism of his or her biological and cultural inheritance into a personal statement of reality. But this Nietzschean promise of a new person and a new world can be redeemed only if those diverse life forms are not allowed to overcome, dominate, and suppress one another.

Pluralism permits different groups and persons to create worlds unto themselves but they dare not become laws unto themselves. We must admit that forms of life are logically and psychologically self-legitimating. There are no external or neutral vantage points from which to confirm or commend a given vision of human order and meaning. But pluralism will surely self-destruct if accepting pluralism means *carte blanche* endorsement for any and all forms of life. The sophomoric argument against moral relativism, invoking the specter of the maniac whose "world-view" licenses mayhem, states the problem precisely if inelegantly because it recognizes the *social* solidarity of human existence and human meaning. Unfortunately that problem cannot be solved by the implied counter argument for moral absolutism. We can only solve the problem of pluralism from within, but solve it we must or whirl will truly become king.

In other words, the greatest peril of pluralism is that we will carry over into the pluralistic situation our centuries-old *authoritarian* habits of thinking and acting. These habits will not easily change because they are deeply rooted in *religious* cravings for absolutes to fend off death and all of its experiential counterparts—bafflement and impotence, suffering and evil, disorder and despair. Every religion and every sociocultural world is a pact with death. This pact takes the form of a system of death-defying and life-extending symbols and rituals, institutions and relationships which prescribe the patterns and dispense the assurance for heroic transcendence of death.[7] As such, these systems have traditionally claimed absolute devotion and exclusive deliverance for themselves alone. Such authoritarianism and exclusivism are highly effective instruments of integration and legitimations within a given group. But they are equally effective instruments of aggression and destruction against those beyond the group. This is doubly so when death is "fetishized"—located in alien places, powers, or persons.[8] Then the quest for heroic transcendence can lay waste to those actions and objects, peoples and cultures which are so identified as evil. This compulsive devotion to and defense of social and personal "immortality ideologies" are understandable, given the stark terror and sheer chaos of existence deprived of some such "sacred canopy." But just this compulsive power must be broken for a genuine pluralism to emerge and exist among us. Unless we reshape the pretheoretical depths of religious fears and hopes pluralistically, we will not avoid the kaleidoscopic violence of a world or a culture of multiple absolutisms.

Unlearning old habits of reflective and religious expectations will not be easy or automatic. The mere presence of multiple frameworks in our midst will not dispel the propensity for groups to make absolute and exclusive claims for their own life-world. The human hunger and search for absolute religious and moral claims must be combatted and negated—absolutely! This means that pluralism requires a legitimating principle that transcends all systems of thought without becoming a system in turn. Pluralism is possible only if conflicting frameworks that claim finality for themselves are relativized by some iconoclastic principle.

How, then can plural life-worlds be protected against all forms of absolutism? We may place competing and contradictory world-views within a context of radical transcendence or of radical relativism.[9] We may argue either that human order and meaning are grounded in a reality that radically transcends every historical concretion or that human order and meaning are adjustive responses to individual and social needs without grounds in any structure of reality. Either of these overviews of human value seems to offer a framework-transcending principle that relativizes all sociocultural systems of human order and meaning. As such, both are iconoclastic or empty principles of authority.

Radical transcendence as a normative overview of pluralism may be expressed in either monotheistic or mystic terms. A radically transcendent God can function as a permanent iconoclastic principle that not only relativizes all concrete world-views and life-styles but subjects them to perpetual revolution as well.[10] Such a "radical monotheism" centers in the Transcendent One in whom alone there is an ultimate good and from whom alone there are proximate goods. This radically transcendent God permits the construction and coexistence of many relative value systems—each of them tentative, experimental and objective. But these plural life-systems are possible only because the Transcendent One prevents any one of them from being erected into an absolute or even being elevated above others. In short, radical monotheism makes pluralism possible by freeing the world from idolatry.

The long tradition of divine sovereignty has always recognized that humankind are idolaters. Theologians of the sovereignty of God have known that human beings left to their own designs seek absolute security and significance by absolutizing finite things and groups, ideals and causes. To be sure, these theologians have not always perceived that the pursuit of cosmic heroism and the escape from cosmic dread are inseparable counterparts of the life-project of every human being. Nor have they discerned the ambivalence and danger in their own claims to absolute security and significance through their finite understanding and relation to the Infinite God. But the wisdom of this tradition can be carried over into a pluralistic situation by translating sovereignty into radical transcendence. This move runs counter to the reigning theologies of today, which stress the pervasive immanence of God. But stressing the indwelling presence of God too easily reinforces the human propensity to absolutize finite conditions and concerns. Only a God radically beyond yet universally related to the world can maintain the relative worth and well-being of all things. In a pluralistic world, the radically transcendent God is the experientially relevant God.

Non-dualistic mysticism offers an alternative conceptuality of radical transcendence. This type of mysticism conceives of the relationship between the everyday world and ultimate reality in a variety of ways, but all parties to the debate on the reality or the unreality of the world agree that the ground of all reality is an all-inclusive, unitary Absolute empty of all distinctions, qualities, and limits. The

Undifferentiated Absolute both relativizes the value of all things finite and shatters all attachments to particular things. Thus mysticism's Undifferentiated Absolute seems promising as an iconoclastic principle that continually breaks life open to variety and change. But this promise is often compromised by the tendency in non-dualistic mysticism to lose all interest in the finite and particular world. The quest to achieve oneness with the Absolute need not but often does end in negation of the empirical and social world.

The search for a transcendent iconoclastic principle that authorizes pluralism in a radically transcendent monotheism or mysticism runs into a common problem. Historically, the central principle in each is also the constructive principle of a traditional life-world. The Sovereign God or the Undifferentiated Absolute may keep symbolic and social expressions fluid within the general world view generated by each and may even facilitate conversation with and assimilation of alien world-views. In other words, a radically transcendent monotheism or mysticism may promote intramural ecumenism and benign evangelism. But as welcome as all such retreats from absolutism and exclusivism are, their historical elaboration in religious and cultural systems may stand in the way of legitimate pluralism.

What then of radical relativism as an authorization of pluralism? Radical relativism differs from all notions of "objective relativism" or "perspectival relativism." For objective or perspectival relativism, symbolic and conceptual constructs are relative, but they are relative *to* and relativized *by* an objective reality that in some way stands apart and over against all human knowing, doing and feeling. Systematic differences between human formulations of understanding and value reflect the inescapable limitations of one's stand point. Relativism lies in the eye of the beholder rather than in the beheld. By contrast, *radical* relativism assumes no such objective reality beyond our diverse interpretation of human order and meaning. Can such radical relativism sustain co-existence and cooperation between diverse and even contradictory life worlds? If so, how and why?

Once again there are, broadly speaking, two ways of articulating radical relativism—mystic and naturalistic. Certain forms of Tibetan, Chinese and Japanese Buddhism deny the reality of all unchanging absolutes, including the Absolute.[11] For these mystic traditions, the symbol of "emptiness" denies rather than describes the eternal, self-sufficient, Undifferentiated Absolute posited by other non-dualistic forms of mysticism. Such denial does not involve the annihilation or disconnection of all things but the discovery of the infinite relatedness and change of all things. This mystical way of seeing the familiar world "sees through" the "fabricated" character of all entities, qualities, and distinctions within the phenomenal world. It thereby diverts all religious craving for unchanging absolutes, whether temporal or eternal. Awareness that all entities visible and ideal are absolutely empty of self-sufficiency releases the individual from thirsting after ultimates and its accompanying anxiety and defensiveness. Thus released from attachments to false ultimates, the enlightened can live without pain or peril in the ordinary structures of existence by participating in their mutual dependence and co-origination.

The philosophies of empiricism and materialism offer an alternative version of radical relativism. These two traditions have typically argued that human values are relative to human needs—biological, psychological, sociological, and cognitive. As such there are no objective and necessary structures of reality that predispose or compel one way of realizing these needs over another. Neither tradition denies that human values have an air of objectivity. The facticities of embodiment in a world, the conventions of language in a culture, the persistence of institutions in a society place severe limits on freedom and innovation in need-fulfillment at any given time and place. Nor do these traditions necessarily deny that actual value judgments are subject to reasoned argument. Ultimate canons of value lie beyond all rational demonstration, but lower-level rational arguments over how and when these principles apply are certainly possible. But the "objectivity" of local standards and the "rationality" of lower-level arguments do not overcome the *radical* relativism of values.

Such comprehensive theories of radical relativism clearly offer an iconoclastic perspective over against all absolutized value-systems and life-worlds. Either the mystic affirmation of the radical emptiness of all things or the naturalistic denial of universal standards could provide a permanent check against all idolatrous attachments as well as the divisiveness and defensiveness that usually follow from such attachments. By the same token, these divergent views of radical relativism are open to an endless variety of tentative arrangements of human order and meaning. But the iconoclastic force of either version of radical relativism may be naturalized by the sheer negation of all historical order and meaning, in which case neither of these options is likely to prove attractive or workable for the masses. Radical world negation belongs to a madness or a saintliness that lies beyond most of us. But thoroughgoing skepticism and nihilism are certainly possible expressions of these forms of radical relativism.

We are left then with four distinct ways of legitimating pluralism, which divide in two over whether the grounds of value are radically transcendent or radically relative. Each of these ways offers an iconoclasm that relativizes all claims though perhaps not all cravings for the absolute. There is a tendency in all, especially monotheism and non-dual mysticism, to undercut a genuine pluralism of life-worlds by becoming the constructive principle of a distinctive world-view. The very fact that these iconoclastic perspectives have emerged out of *cultures*, whether ancient or modern, means that they are invested in unexamined values. Nevertheless, there are iconoclastic resources, both religious and philosophical, which can be construed in a manner that legitimates a genuine pluralism of intercultural and intracultural life-worlds.[12]

But even if we succeed in freeing such iconoclastic principles from the shape and sounds of their own heritage, we are still left with a problem. A truly iconoclastic principle may continually break open cultural forms of life, but it will not thereby automatically remake these forms. Relativizing all options does not necessarily solve the inevitable problems of co-existence in a pluralistic world. In a densely pluralistic culture or world, some way to shape and sustain orderly change and conflict must be found. Beyond an iconoclastic principle that legitimates pluralism we need an irenic pedagogy that will enable us to preserve pluralism. The openness and inventiveness of a pluralistic world will survive only if we find creative ways of resolving our disagreements while preserving our differences.

How then do we educate the young for life in a pluralistic world? Pluralistic no less than traditional societies must prepare children for full membership in a community that finally rests on shared moral values. But moral education in a pluralistic context must take a very different form than the moral training provided in traditional cultures or lifestyle enclaves within modern cultures. Such insular communities are built on moral values that are embodied in their institutions and internalized by their constituents. Moral *training* for them consists in authoritarian instruction in the rights and duties of those who are in good standing in the moral community. By contrast, moral *education* in a pluralistic society goes well beyond such indoctrination by raising questions about the ultimate grounds and exploring alternatives to the proximate forms of moral rights and duties within our society. Whether dealing with children or adults, the purpose of moral training is to produce moral conformity, whereas the aim of moral education is to foster moral excellence among its pupils.

For many, the central aim of moral education in a pluralistic society is teaching tolerance for differing world-views and life-styles. Indeed, producing such tolerance stands high among the goals of liberal education. Our central task as educators is liberating our students from their limited and limiting views of the world by immersing them in human otherness. The academy is built on an implicit assumption that understanding cultural diversity will produce social tolerance. Once students see that alien ideologies and institutions serve similar functions as their own, they will learn to accept if not cherish the myriad forms that human life can take and still be human. Activities as diverse as primitive human sacrifice and modern welfare programs can be seen as meaningful if not necessary within a given cultural system.

Underlying this approach to moral education is an unquestioned commitment to what can be called *private morality*—all those individual, interpersonal, and social actions that carry only personal moral sanctions of self-condemnation or self-congratulation. Our culture places a high value on freedom of conscience. Indeed, the self is defined by its ability to choose its own values. Each individual is entitled to his or her own "bit of space" and is utterly free within its boundaries. Of course, this ideal was originally built on Enlightenment visions of rational universalism and/or Romantic fantasies of pantheistic individualism. In affirming the inviolability of the individual conscience, it was understood that at the core of every person is a fundamental rational or spiritual harmony that links that person not only to every other person but to the cosmos as a whole. But, as we have seen, radical pluralism undercuts these notions of a seamless robe of rationality or intuition. Shorn of such overarching or underlying structures of being and value, each self constitutes its own moral universe. Little wonder that toleration is pluralism's *summum bonum*, since, on this reading, tolerance of human diversity and idiosyncrasy is all that really holds the line against social chaos.

This ideal of radical individualism has outlasted the collapse of its Enlightenment and Romantic underpinnings for two reasons. The autonomy of the individual is *socially* reinforced by the structural differentiation of modern society. Institutional segmentation and rationalization leave wide areas of life individually unstructured and culturally underdetermined. The interstices between society's functionally autonomous institutions create a "private sphere" of relatively autonomous action. Outside those areas that fall under the performance demands of the specialized institutions that regulate the legal and the economic orders, individuals are left largely to their own devices in choosing goods and services, careers and pastimes, friends and mates, even morals and religion. Indeed, within the private sphere individuals are free to construct their own identity so long as that identity does not encroach on the freedom of others or disrupt the performance of public duty. The fact that we are not as free as we imagine ourselves to be has little effect on our presumed autonomy because we can actually *see* the growth of our private freedom.[13]

The presumed autonomy of the individual is also supported by the *legal* expansion of the realm of private morality. As far as private morality is concerned, ethical pluralism raises no serious problems as long as we are willing to live and let live. Our society has capitalized on this tolerance by transferring a whole range of contentious and explosive moral matters to the private realm. Behavior that at times past was subject to public moral sanctions (e.g., consumption of alcohol, cohabitation outside of marriage) has been assigned to the realm of private moral judgment. Not surprisingly, such hotly disputed issues as legalizing contraceptives and abortion were settled under constitutional guarantees of privacy. Moreover, such much discussed matters as homosexual relations between consenting adults and pornographic materials for personal use are argued on the same grounds. The popular myth of individual autonomy has been greatly strengthened by legal expansions of protected and permitted behavior.

But the contemporary controversy that surrounds such celebrated issues as legal abortion and gay rights reveals the impossibility of solving all matters of moral disagreement by relegating them to the realm of private morality. There are whole areas of moral disagreement where we simply cannot agree to disagree, since the very foundations of social order and civil rights are the issues at stake. Moral tolerance will not save us in such explosive situations. Relegating such issues to the private realm would deprive us of those shared values and social institutions of conflict resolution which alone hold the forces of coercive violence and social chaos in check. Interpersonal and intercultural conflict resolution requires settlement by a *public morality*—all those individual, interpersonal, and social actions that carry communal moral sanctions of social condemnation or social condemnation.

Some would argue that we possess such a public morality in a shared religiosity that parallels but does not replace the traditional religions which are in our culture. This "civil religion" thesis insists that even highly differentiated societies rest on a religious basis. Such a civil religion transcends creedal, ethnic, and regional boundaries. It has its own collective representations by which the nation commemorates significant national events and confirms shared moral values. National shrines and holidays, patriotic symbols and gestures, national myths and heroes celebrate shared memories and exemplify shared values. The idealizations presented in American civil religion are a blend of ethical monotheism and enlightenment utilitarianism. But civil religion and church religions serve different functions. Civil religion regulates actions in the public sphere, while church religions are granted full liberty in the sphere of personal piety and voluntary social actions.

But this division between "civil" and "church" religion has become quite problematic in American society. As Robert Bellah has shown, the covenant between the people and the God of their civil religion has been betrayed by the people and their leaders. American civil religion has become an "empty and broken shell" that no longer provides the unified and unifying criteria for moral judgment and social change.[14] Shorn of its monotheistic moorings, utilitarianism has been reduced to a morality of self-interest. The rhetoric of a divine human covenant is still with us, as evidenced in pronouncements of our national leaders, but the binding power of a consensus morality is gone.

Others would argue that we possess such a public morality in the procedural methods and judicial pronouncements of our legal system. In describing America as a "nation run by lawyers," Alexis de Tocqueville put his finger on the distinctive problems faced by a society that weaves a plurality of religious systems into its basic social fabric. With the breakup of a religious monopoly on articulating the social order, the need for a single reality-defining agency and a single consensus building symbolic medium was transferred to the legal system. The history of the American legal system, most noticeably in the Supreme Court, can be seen as a halting, hesitant, but inevitable effort to provide a common moral architecture for American society. The result is a set of legal institutions with a decidedly religio-ethical character. Indeed, some have argued that these legal institutions are the primary bearers of America's "civil" religion. Legal institutions have not taken on the task of constructing and maintaining our moral architecture single-handedly. Public schools certainly play a crucial role in socializing children into the rights and duties of citizenship. But the legal system bears the responsibility for articulating and elaborating the "transcendence" of the law. Thus, as Phillip Hammond wryly observes, it might be said that public schools are the new "Sunday schools," while the courts are the new "pulpits."[15]

But the sweep and speed of changes in our society suggest that the problems of ethical pluralism cannot be solved by educational programs that emphasize respect for our heritage of civil pieties or our system of common law. While attention to both of these value-making cultural systems should have an important place in our education of the young, the aims of moral education for a pluralistic world must go beyond our traditional system of civic virtues and our procedural methods of conflict resolution. Moral educators must aim at teaching a morality that cultivates moral excellence—that produces adults who understand what morality is, why it is needed, and how it is grounded. In short, the aim of moral education, as opposed to moral training, is to produce adults who do not simply conform to the morality of their group but are able to justify and if necessary to challenge their public morality. The acid test of an adequate system of moral education is the moral possibility of civil disobedience—the ability to determine whether the morality required by one's group is morally required and, if it is not, whether to obey under protest, disobey and suffer, or contest and overthrow that public morality.

That such programs of formal education are scarce if not virtually nonexistent in today's educational system is evident to all who have thought about morality and education. We are besieged by calls on every hand to reintroduce ethics into the curriculum, but usually these calls are tied to requiring doctrinaire instruction in the majority's moral outlook or allowing the doctrinaire teaching of any subgroup's moral views. With only those options before us, we might be better off confronting students with the relativity of all moral systems, including our own public morality. In fact, a healthy dose of moral skepticism may free our students from their moral conservatism and intolerance, thus preparing the way for those moral changes that are overdue in our otherwise rapidly changing society.

But surely there are other options available to us than either consensus or parochial programs of moral training. While I confess that I remain unclear about how such a program in moral education should be structured, I am quite clear about what it should achieve. There are at least two goals that should be pursued in non-sectarian programs of moral education, whether or not these ostensible aims are ratified by the majority or are opposed by a minority. Morally speaking, these minimal educational goals *ought* not to be opposed by anyone or any group, since they interpret group morality as a rational strategy for self-fulfillment.

The **first aim** of a program of moral education is to convey a clear understanding of the need for some *public* moral order. In the absence of such justification in a pluralistic world, the members of an amoral community will rightly feel that the moral order is arbitrary or repressive. They will suspect that the group's morality imposes unnecessary restrictions on individual freedom or favors one or another class at the expense of the rest of society. The first step in justifying a common morality is to show that a compulsory social order holds self-interest in check. Thomas Hobbes and David Hume have presented classical demonstrations of this claim on the basis of very different philosophical anthropologies, and their arguments have been refined and expanded in many ways in recent years. The heart of their arguments is the natural scarcity of those things that human beings need for bare survival, to say nothing of the good life. The only known way of dealing with the problems of scarcity is to create a social order that limits rights and assigns duties to the mutual benefit of all. This assignment involves the establishment of clear rules for the distribution of scarce goods that are cooperatively produced and for the prevention of inflicting harm and suffering on others. Explaining the necessity and showing the advantages of some such compulsory social order should form part of a general moral education for all students. This demonstration shows that some social order that overrules mere class or self-interest is *rationally* necessary for any and all to achieve a life worth living.

But such a demonstration in and of itself is incomplete. It may show that any social order is better than none, but it does not discriminate between social orders that are unnecessarily harsh and precariously weak. The fact that a compulsory social order is necessary does not imply that all such orders are equally acceptable. It is clearly necessary that a social order should be acceptable to its members, or that order will collapse out of indifference or resentment. In short, a social order must be *moral* if it is to justify the sacrifice that it demands and deliver the benefits that it promises.

Therefore, a **second aim** of a program of moral education is to convey an understanding of the criteria of a *moral* public order. Those foundations of a society's moral architecture can be articulated in a variety of ways. In our society those foundations are contained in the natural rights guaranteed in the Declaration of Independence and in the "bill of rights" amending the Constitution. But the "ground-floor" or the "criterion of the criteria" or an acceptable public morality is justice. This fundamental moral value can be articulated in a variety of theoretical schemes—e.g., social utility or formal duty. But some fundamental sense of justice undergirds and overrides all systems of moral rules and is thereby substantially independent of particular styles of life and personal matters of taste. In this context, justice is more a methodological strategy than a metaphysical structure of practical reasoning.[16] Justice compels us to give *reasons* for revering or revising the public order that will prove broadly acceptable to any and all members of that community. Obviously, such practical reasoning will not carry the coercive authority of mathematical demonstrations or scientific proofs. But once moral issues are put on a rational slope, we have taken moral conflict out of the merely emotional and private realm of thought and action. Justice is a constitutive requirement for any moral public order that rationally regulates conflicts of interest while maximizing realization of interests.

In a real sense, I am calling for the kind of moral education that Emile Durkheim envisioned almost a century ago—a manifest and hidden curriculum that will both nurture the individualism and restrain the egoism that lie at the heart of modern democratized cultures.[17] The first task for this kind of moral education is to make the world safe for idiosyncrasy by dethroning all false and falsifying absolutes, especially the absolute of individual autonomy that claims the popular and educated imagination. However we ultimately legitimate such diversity, there must be no educational retreat from confronting students with the moral otherness of cultures and classes different from their own. Comparative and international studies, with special attention to racial, ethnic and gender issues, play an important role in educating young men and women for life in a diverse and changing world.

But having disabused our students of moral absolutes, we face the more difficult task of equipping them for responsible citizenship in this tumultuous world. A part of that task is uncovering all the shared values that are embedded in our common life as a diverse people. But the problems of ethical pluralism cannot be solved alone by educational programs that eulogize the civil pieties of our common heritage or that emphasize the binding power of our common law. Finally, we must arm our students for making rational choices in the arena of conflicting values and contested laws. We must help them develop that moral excellence which accepts the necessity while challenging the finality of every public moral order including their own. Unless I miss my guess, designing that kind of moral education may be the academy's great challenge and our society's greatest need.

---

[1] Allan Bloom, *The Closing of the American Mind* (New York: Simon and Schuster, 1987), 216.

[2] Lonnie D. Kliever, *The Shattered Spectrum: A Survey of Contemporary Theology* (Atlanta: John Knox Press, 1981), 187-205.

[3] Marshall Berman, *All That is Solid Melts Into Air: The Experience of Modernity* (New York: Simon and Schuster, 1982), 15-36.

[4] See Peter Berger, *The Sacred Canopy* (New York: Doubleday and Company, 1969), 3-104; Ernest Becker, *The Denial of Death* (New York: Free Press, 1973), 1-66; Joseph Campbell, *The Masks of God: Creative Mythology* (New York: Viking Press, 1968), 573-624.

[5] Berger, *The Sacred Canopy*, 29-51.

[6] See Andrew M. Greeley, *Unsecular Man* (New York: Dell Publishing, 1972).

[7] Ernest Becker, *The Birth and Death of Meaning* (New York: Free Press, 1971), 65-129; Becker, *The Denial of Death*, 109, 255-85; Ernest Becker, *Escape From Evil* (New York: Free Press, 1975), 146-79; cf. Berger, *The Sacred Canopy*, 53-80.

[8] Becker, *Escape From Evil*, 148-151.

[9] For a fuller discussion see Lonnie D. Kliever, "Authority in a Pluralistic World," in *Modernization: The Humanistic Response to Its Promise and Problems*, ed. Richard L. Rubenstein (New York: Paragon House, 1982).

[10] Richard H. Niebuhr, *Radical Monotheism and Western Culture* (New York: Harper and Row, 1966); Gabriel Vahanian, *No Other God* (New York: George Braziller, 1966); and Gabriel Vahanian, *God and Utopia* (New York: Seabury Press, 1977).

[11] Frederick Streng, *Emptiness.* (Nashville: Abingdon Press, 1967).

[12] Lonnie D. Kliever, "Radical Democratization and Radical Monotheism," in *Religious and Global Order*, eds. William R. Garrett and Roland Robertson (New York: Paragon House, 1990) and Lonnie D. Kliever, "Religion and the Democratization of Culture," in *Spirit Matters: The Worldwide Impact of Religion on Contemporary Politics*, ed. Richard L. Rubenstein (New York: Paragon house, 1987).

[13] Thomas Luckmann, *The Invisible Religion* (New York: Macmillan Press, 1967).

[14] Robert Bellah, *The Broken Covenant* (New York: Seabury Press, 1975).

[15] Phillip Hammond. "Religion Pluralism and Durkheim's Integration Thesis," in *Changing Perspectives in the Scientific Study of Religion*, ed. Allen Eister (New York: John Wiley and Sons, 1974), 134.

[16] Kurt Baier, *The Moral Point of View* (New York: Random House, 1965).

[17] Emile Durkheim, *Moral Education* (New York: Free Press, 1961).

Cultural Literacy, The Liberal Arts Curriculum, and the Human Condition

James A. Banks
Education, University of Washington

Be ashamed to die until
you have won some victory
for [Hu]mankind.
Horace Mann[1]

The theme of primary concern in this essay evolves about this pressing issue: Scientists and other educators must explore ways in which the liberal arts curriculum is to be reformed so-as-to prepare the nation's youth to deal effectively with cultural and ethnic diversity. Institutions that have the will and the ability to engage in critical self-examination are the ones most likely to adequately prepare our students for the challenges of the twenty-first century. Educators should be guided by these challenges when designing the liberal arts curriculum. The intent of the academic design should be to help students develop *cultural literacy* necessary for preparing them to act to improve the human condition.

We are living in times that try our souls. The gap between the haves and have-nots is widening within our society. We are rapidly

Reprinted by permission of the author.

becoming two nations—one rich and one poor. Growing numbers of homeless people are seeking refuge in our decaying cities. Fewer and fewer poor and ethnic youths are making it to our colleges and universities. The nuclear race escalates even though nuclear weapons threaten to destroy humankind. Despite these ominous developments, many Americans have little commitment to the public good and have retreated into a pernicious individualism.[2] Because of the serious human problems faced by our nation and the world, the liberal arts curriculum cannot afford to take a neutral position on the human condition. Educators must motivate students to care and to act to help solve our seemingly intractable human problems.

I believe individuals must be culturally literate in order to develop the commitment and skills to work for human betterment. Cultural literacy consists of the knowledge, attitudes, and skills necessary to function effectively within and across other ethnic and cultural groups, domestically and abroad. To help students attain cultural literacy, the liberal arts curriculum must help them acquire the knowledge needed to understand the changing characteristics of ethnic and cultural diversity. The changing ethnic texture of the United States is significant in as much as the white population of European ancestry and British influence, that dominated the culture for more than three centuries, is in substantial decline.[3]

A strong assimilationist idea has dominated American society since the British gained control of most American institutions early in the nation's history. The American assimilationist idea envisions a society in which ethnicity and race are not important identities. Group identities and affiliations would be based primarily on variables such as social class, politics, education, and other interests. The assimilationist idea that deeply influenced American life was symbolized by the melting pot concept. This concept was celebrated in Zangwill's play, *The Melting Pot,* which was staged in New York City in 1908.

While the strong assimilationist idea in American society contributed greatly to the making of one nation from disparate ethnic and immigrant groups, it has not eradicated ethnic and cultural differences and is not likely to do so in the future. Ethnic differences persist in American society for several important reasons. Discrimination prevents many individuals and groups with particular ethnic, racial, and cultural characteristics from attaining structural inclusion into the

American society. Ethnic cultures and communities often help individuals satisfy important human needs. Ethnicity also persists because of continuing immigration to the United States.

Immigration to the United States has grown by leaps and bounds since the Immigration Reform Act that Congress passed in 1965 and that became effective in 1968. Between 1971 and 1995, as many as seventy-nine percent of the new immigrants came from Spanish-speaking Latin American nations and from Asia rather than from Europe, the continent from which most American immigrants came in the past.[4] If current trends continue, it is projected that the Asian-American population will nearly double by the year 2000, while the total United States population will increase by only 20 percent.[5] The Asian (primarily Filipinos, Koreans, and peoples of Chinese ancestry) and Latina/o (most of them Mexicans, Puerto Ricans, and Cubans) populations are increasing greatly, partly because of a higher birthrate than most other Americans but primarily because of the large number of immigrants.

Some analysts think the Latinos will total 30 to 35 million by the year 2000.[6] If this happens, they will outnumber African Americans and every other ethnic group. However, it is misleading to view Latin peoples as a single ethnic group because they speak the same language (Spanish). There are tremendous cultural, ethnic, and racial differences between and within the various groups, such as those from Mexico, Cuba, Puerto Rico, El Salvador, the Dominican Republic, Columbia, and Venezuela. Most Latin peoples identify themselves by national origin, that is they think of themselves as having originated from a particular nation rather than as being generically "Hispanic" or "Latin."

The nation's present, largest non-white ethnic group—the African Americans—increased from 22.6 million to approximately thirty million between 1970 and 1990. They make up about 13 percent of the nation's population. Black population growth during the next few decades will outpace that of whites because the black population is relatively young. The median age of blacks was about 25 years in 1990 compared to 30 for the total U.S. population. While blacks had been moving North from the South in large numbers since the first World War, that trend was reversed during the last half of the 1970s. More than seventy percent of African Americans lived in the South in 1990.[7]

Ethnicity and ethnic affiliations will be perpetuated by discrimination and increasing segmentation (or balkanization) that prevents various ethnic and racial groups from fully participating in American society, that is by the growth of ethnic communities and identities and by the continuing immigration. Ethnic and racial variables and issues will continue to influence the lives of all Americans and will have a cogent impact on the nation's educational institutions. Public issues such as immigration policies, anti-Semitism, and the growing violence against Asian Americans require citizens to have sophisticated and accurate knowledge about various ethnic and racial groups. That knowledge would make it possible for them to participate in the making and implementation of enlightened, reflective public policies.

The United States received 808,000 immigrants in 1980, more than in any year since 1914, thus American classrooms are experiencing the largest influx of immigrant students since the turn of the century.[8] In 1984, ethnic minorities constituted the majority of school enrollments in twenty-three of the nation's twenty-five largest cities. More than fifty major U. S. cities will have a majority ethnic minority population by the year 2000 if current demographic trends continue. Interpreters of the census data correctly estimated that in the 1990s more than thirty percent of students in the public schools would be ethnics of other than European origins. These statistics describe documented immigrants only, for by some estimates there may be three- to six-million undocumented immigrants in the United States in a given year.[9]

Many Americans think ethnic and racial diversity are uniquely American. Yet, most Western societies are racially, ethnically, and culturally diverse. Since the 1960s ethnic revival movements have arisen in the United States as well as in other western nations such as Canada, the United Kingdom, Australia, and in several Western European nations.[10] Since World War II, the ethnic texture of western European nations such as the United Kingdom, France, and the Netherlands has been enriched greatly by immigrants from their former colonies. Many immigrants from southern and eastern Europe have settled in nations such as Germany and Sweden in search of jobs and upward social mobility. More than 405,000 foreign nationals were living in Sweden in 1983; the largest group consisted of 160,000 Finns and 38,000

Yugoslavs. Other groups included Turks, Greeks, Poles, Italians, Chileans, and Africans from several different nations.[11]

Australia also has become more culturally and ethnically diverse since the 1960s. Traditionally Anglo-Celtic with a ban on the immigration of non-white groups and a policy that discouraged the immigration of individuals from southern, eastern, and central Europe, Australia now has a large population of Greeks and Italians and a significant number of Indochinese.[12] Melbourne and Victoria have the largest population of Greeks of any city except Athens. Canada also is an immigrant society that is racially, culturally, and linguistically diverse.[13]

The kind of cultural, ethnic, racial, and religious diversity that the western nations are experiencing is both an opportunity for and a challenge to their societies and institutions, including educational institutions. It is a challenge because when groups with different cultures and values interact within a society, ethnocentrism, racism, religious bigotry, and other forms of institutionalized rejection and hostility result. There are ample examples of these forms of group hostility and rejection in each of the western nations today. In several nation throughout the world, the incidence of bigoted attacks on ethnic and cultural minorities is on the rise. This is true in both the United Kingdom and the United States. Some observers have linked the increase in overt bigotry to the serious economic problems that most of the western nations are experiencing.

Ethnic and cultural diversity can, on the other hand, enrich a society by effecting novel ways to view events and situations, to solve problems, and to assess the human relationship with the environment and with non-human life-forms. The exploitation of the environment is a serious problem in most of the industrialized nations, in part because of the way in which westerners traditionally have viewed their relationship with the earth. Traditional Indian cultures in North America, for example, viewed the earth as sacred and had deep reverence for other living creatures in contrast to conventions of European nations.

The challenge to western societies is to shape a modernized national culture that contains within it selected aspects of traditional cultures. In their, earlier singular quest for modernity and a technocratic society, the western nations tried to eradicate traditional cultures, repressing traditional practices by banning them through enforcement of legislation and by portraying them to be primitive and beastly. As a result, indigenes educated in European American schools often became alienated from their first cultures and mother tongues. This approach to shaping a unified nation has created anomie and alienation, and it has deprived individuals and groups of opportunities to experience important ways in which humans satisfy their needs for symbolic meaning and community. It has resulted also in the political and cultural oppression of racial and ethnic groups within modernized societies and has, consequently, caused them to focus on particularistic needs and goals rather than on the overarching goals of the larger nation. Westernized nations will be able to create societies with overarching goals that are shared by all of their diverse groups only when those so alienated feel that they have a real stake and place in their nation and that their nation mirrors their concerns, values, and ethos. A multiethnic curriculum that reflects the cultures, values, and goals of all the groups within a nation will contribute greatly to the development of a healthy nationalism and national identity.

A major goal of the ethnic revival movements of the 1960s and 1970s was not only to include more information about the cultures and histories of ethnic groups in the school and college curriculum, but to infuse the curriculum with new perspectives, frames of reference and values. However, in textbooks and in teaching, ethnic events and heroes often are added to the curriculum, but the interpretations and perspectives on these events and heroes remain those of mainstream historians and scholars.[14] When concepts, events, and situations in the curriculum are viewed only or primarily from the perspectives of mainstream scholars and historians, students obtain a limited view of social reality and an incomplete understanding of the human experience. As James Baldwin pointed out perceptively in several incisive essays, white Americans cannot fully understand their history unless they study black history from diverse perspectives because the history of blacks and whites is intricately interwoven.[15] The same insight should be applied appropriately to all ethnic groups when teaching the history of the United States.

In an important essay on the sociology of knowledge, published in the midst of the civil rights movement, Thomas Merton discussed *insiders* and *outsiders* and their competing knowledge claims.[16] Both claim that only they can obtain valid knowledge about the "insider" group. The insider claims that only a member can formulate accurate and valid knowledge about his or her group because of the special insights that result from being socialized within the group. The outsider claims that valid knowledge results only when groups are studied by outsiders because of the dispassionate objectivity that outsiders bring to the study of group life. Merton concluded that both insiders and outsiders can make important contributions to the understanding of group life, and that insiders and outsiders should unite in their quests for knowledge.

In an ethnically and racially stratified society such as the United States, ethnic and racial micro-cultures influence the formulation of knowledge. While social scientists and historians who are insiders in the black community and those who are outsiders are likely to agree on many observations about black life and behavior, they are likely to formulate some findings and interpretations that differ in significant ways. Many mainstream social scientists conducted studies of blacks prior to the civil rights movements of the 1960s that were strongly attacked by black social scientists in the 1970s.[17] Much of this controversy focused on historical interpretations of topics such as slavery and the Civil War, sociological interpretations of the black family, and descriptions and interpretations of black English and black culture. Black culture and life frequently were described as disorganized, pathological, and deviant by mainstream social scientists.[18] Black students were labeled "culturally deprived."[19]

Traditional research assumptions, methods, and conclusions of mainstream social scientists often differed sharply from those of the new black social scientists during this period. Prior to the 1960s, most mainstream social scientists viewed blacks as a "social problem."[20] They developed most of their concepts and theories from studies that compared blacks to middle-class whites and concluded that black life was deviant, pathological, and culturally deprived. Black social scientists in the 1960s and 1970s challenged the traditional conceptions of black life and formulated concepts and theories that viewed black life as different from middle-class white culture rather than deviant.[21] They also viewed black culture from the inside, saw it holistically, and described it as a viable and functional culture with tremendous strengths that had enabled it to survive against great odds.

While ethnicity and race often influence the knowledge claims, research, and perspectives of historians and other social scientists, these influences are complex and difficult to describe precisely. Individual white, Mexican-American, or black scholars may be influenced more by their class interests, commitment to scholarly objectivity, or other values than by race or ethnicity. The revisionistic and sensitive studies of blacks by white social scientists such as Baratz, Gutman, and Genovese,[22] during the 1970s are cases in point, as are the more conservative analyses of the black experience written by black scholars such as Wilson and Sowell.[23]

While the influence of race, ethnicity, and class on social knowledge is complex and difficult to describe precisely, it is nonetheless significant and far-reaching. Insider perspectives on important social and historical events such as the Holocaust, the internment of Japanese-Americans, and the civil rights movement provide students with insights, perspectives, and feelings about these events that cannot be gained from reading accounts by individuals who have experienced these events only from a distance of source materials.[24] Scholars who are socialized within ethnic cultures in which these events are important parts of the social and cultural history are likely to have perspectives on them that differ from those without that ethnic bonding.[25]

It is important for students to have a curriculum that presents the experiences of ethnic and cultural groups in accurate and sensitive ways. However, the teaching of courses in the curriculum also should enable students to see the experiences of both mainstream and minority groups from the perspectives of different cultural, racial, and ethnic groups. Such a curriculum would help students understand the complexities of the U.S. experience and the ways that the nation's various groups have interacted within the social structure and influenced each other culturally.

After more than two decades of debates and attempts to reform the school and college curriculum so that it reflects ethnic and cultural diversity in the United States, multiethnic reforms remain on the periphery of the mainstream curriculum in most U.S. schools and colleges. While most examples of blatant racism and stereotypes of ethnic groups have been deleted from textbooks and teaching materials, content about racial and ethnic groups is not thoroughly integrated into mainstream textbooks, teaching materials, or curricula. Instead, materials about racial and ethnic groups generally are relegated to special units, elective courses, and holidays and are appendages to the "main story" about the development of U.S. society.

Many reasons have been set forth to explain why the school and college curricula have remained mainstream-centric and euro-centric after more than two decades of attempted reform. I believe that the resistance to a multi-cultural curriculum is basically ideological. An ideology is a system of ideas, beliefs, traditions, principles, and myths held by a social group or society that reflects, rationalizes, and defends its particular social, political and economic interests. Dominant ethnic and cultural groups develop and support knowledge and curricula that defend, legitimize, and rationalize the current, dominant social structure or hegemony. The multicultural curriculum presents images, values, and perspectives that challenge the current, dominant social structure and call for its legitimization through reconstruction.

A major goal of education traditionally has been to socialize students so that they accept unquestioningly the existing ideologies, institutions, and practices within their societies and nations. Education within the U.S. traditionally has fostered political apathy rather than political action. Students are taught to vote and to participate in the political system in ways that will not significantly reform U.S. society. A major goal of the liberal arts curriculum should be to help students acquire the knowledge, values, and skills they need to participate in social change so that victimized and excluded class, ethnic, and racial groups can become full participants in U.S. society.

The major goal of research in the physical, natural, and social sciences is to build theoretical knowledge. In our quest to build knowledge and theories, we have devoted insufficient attention to how we can best use the knowledge we create for human betterment. We have too rarely asked the questions: "Knowledge for what?" and "What might or ought to be the uses for the knowledge we create?" Knowledge utilization has received insufficient attention in our colleges and universities.[26] Scientists frequently have failed to help students think about how knowledge can be used to improve or harm the human condition. They have given students the idea that knowledge can and should be pursued in a totally objective way with little or no attention given to its social consequences or to how it might or will be used.

Constructing and attaining knowledge are necessary but not sufficient. In addition to formulating and mastering knowledge, we should devote serious attention in the liberal arts curriculum. It must be reconstructed to show how it can best be used to improve the human condition. If we continue to accrue knowledge and devote little attention to its normative assumptions and possible uses, we not only will fail to solve our most intractable human problems but we may indeed destroy human civilization as we know it today. We now have more knowledge than any previous generation, yet we have created a proliferating nuclear technology that we do not have the will to control and that threatens to destroy humankind at the push of a button. We face the possibility of a nuclear holocaust today not because we learned how to obtain energy from atoms, but because the human intelligence and energy that went into determining how to release energy from the nuclei of the atom was not expended into conceptualizing and designing ways to use nuclear energy for human betterment.

We not only need to think about how knowledge can be used to improve the human condition, we also need to recognize that knowledge reflects the social context in which it is created and that it has normative and value assumptions. Both scientists and students need to be keenly aware of the values and assumptions that underlie their knowledge and research methods. Rather than acknowledging and making their value assumptions explicit, scientists often give the illusion of objectivity and fail to state how their knowledge can contribute to human betterment. Some scientists become apologists for and defenders of the status quo. Thus, they contribute to the victimization of the poor and the powerless. Some social scientists have developed intellectual justifications and arguments for national policies and actions that perpetuate inequality, homelessness, and the widening gap between the rich and the poor in U.S. society.[27]

The liberal arts curriculum should teach students how the work of social, natural, and physical scientists often reflects the biases and interests of those in power. It should inform them of how scholars and scientists often align themselves with those in power in order to obtain the symbols of power, such as research grants, publicity, and fame. Scholars like Jensen, Banfield and Shockley have developed research that reinforces the existing social structure and contributes to the victimization of powerless ethnic and cultural groups.[28] The liberal arts curriculum should help students become sensitive to the human frailties of scientists and researchers. It should teach them how to have intellectual confrontations with the work of these specialists by examining their biases and assumptions and by trying to predetermine the human consequences of their arguments and research.

In his plea to get social scientists involved in solving the urgent social problems of our times, Kenneth Clark—the noted psychologist—states that these scientists should become "involved observers." He explained like this:

> An important part of my creed as a social scientist is that on the grounds of absolute objectivity or on a posture of scientific detachment and indifference, a . . . serious social science cannot ask to be taken seriously by a society desperately in need of moral and empirical guidance in human affairs. Nor can it support its claims to scientific purity or relevance by a preoccupation with methodology as an end and by innumerable articles in scientific journals devoted to escapist, even quantifiable, trivia. I believe that to be taken seriously, to be viable, and to be relevant, social science must dare to study the real problems of men and society, must use the real community, the market place, the arena of politics and power as its laboratories, and must confront and seek to understand the dynamics of social action and social change.[29]

To use knowledge to improve the human condition, we must not only gather knowledge but must understand its normative assumptions, analyze and clarify the values of the multiethnic society regarding important social issues, use the most reliable knowledge to inform decision-making that is consistent with multiethnic values, and take action in the social and political arena so as to shape public policies that are consistent with multiethnic knowledge and values. Our greatest human problems—such as hunger, poverty, the denial of human rights, racism, sexism, and nuclear proliferation—will not be solved until compassionate individuals, with the best available knowledge, develop the will and the commitment to act to improve the human condition, not only for themselves but for peoples in distant lands and cultures.

We probably have the knowledge—but not the will—to solve our most intractable human problems, such as poverty and inequality. Despite the fact that we are the wealthiest nation on earth, 33.7 million Americans live below the poverty line. The gap between the rich and the poor in the United States is increasing rather than closing. We are not doing a better job of using knowledge for human betterment in part because scientists, in their quests to maintain objectivity, often remain detached and indifferent to our most serious human problems; or they study these problems in settings that are contrived and artificial.

Intellectuals and scientists—natural and social—need to be more concerned about and become more involved in the social problems of our time. They need to care more! Kenneth Clark explained it like this:

> Whatever might have been its historical significance or justification, the pretense that the scholar, the intellectual or the scientist could or should remain apart from the day-to-day problems of lesser men is no longer tenable. The German concentration camps and the atomic bomb attacks on a civilian population introduced a period of collective guilt, collective panic, and shared responsibility for resolution. The man of intellect cannot divorce himself from this new society. He cannot pretend that these crucial decisions must be made either by the masses or the elite of power.[30]

Despite the fact that our knowledge has grown by leaps and bounds within the last decades, it is astonishing how little we know about some of the most serious problems in our society. We have insufficient knowledge, for example, about why students from some social and cultural groups have achievement levels considerably below those of students from other social and cultural groups. It is true that we have a litany of folk explanations and several promising partial theories, but we are hard pressed to come up with explanations that provide useful guidelines for building educational programs that will help to eliminate the achievement gap.

We do a poor job in using knowledge to improve the human condition, in part, because knowledge in the university and scholarly community is highly specialized and fragmented. In order to become experts within our chosen disciplines, we develop highly specialized knowledge. In the process, we fragment knowledge! Yet the social problems in the real world are not divided into political science, anthropology, or psychology. Real social problems, such as the differential achievement of students from different social and cultural groups, involve political, cultural, and psychological factors. Individuals from each of the several disciplines need to get involved to help us find solutions to this and other difficult social and human problems.

There is another important reason that we do a poor job in using knowledge for human betterment. We have failed to develop *caring*—about social issues and problems—within the students we teach.[31] In our quest to make students knowledge specialists, we have neglected their moral education and moral development. As the research by scholars such as Lawrence Kohlberg and Carol Gilligan make clear, we must nurture our students' moral development just as we nurture their intellectual development.[32] We must nurture both the hearts and minds of students if they are to develop the skills and the will to use their knowledge to improve the human condition. If we succeed in nurturing both the hearts and minds of our students, that will make all the difference.

---

1 Commencement Address at Antioch College, 1859.

2 Walter C. Parker, "Constitutional Studies in the Strong Sense: Developing Civic Intelligence." A paper presented at the "Perspectives on Constitutional Issues" Symposium, Annual Meeting of the College and University Faculty Assembly of the National Council for the Social Studies, New York, November 1986. See also Robert N. Bellah, et al., *Habits of the Heart: Individualism and Commitment in American Life* (New York: Harper and Row, 1985).

3 Jamshid A. Momeni, *Demography of Racial and Ethnic Minorities in the United States: An Annotated Bibliography with a Review Essay* (Westport, Conn.: Greenwood Press, 1984).

4 U.S. Bureau of the Census, *Statistical Abstract of the United States, 1985* (Washington, D.C.: U.S. Government Printing Office, 1985), 86 and 1995 figures from the Center for Immigration Studies, which was established in 1985, and from the Population Studies Center, University of Michigan.

5 Robert W. Gardner, Bryant Robey, and Peter C. Smith, "Asian Americans: Growth, Change, and Diversity," *Population Bulletin* 40, No. 4 (Washington, D.C.: Population Reference Bureau, 1985) and 1995 figures from the Center for Immigration Studies and from the Population Studies.

6 "Hispanics: A Melting of Cultures," *Time* (July 8, 1985), 36 and 1995 figures from the Center for Immigration Studies and the Population Studies Center.

7 Equality and Excellence: The Educational Status of Black Americans (New York: The College Board, 1985), 5.

8 Gene I. Maeroff, "Rising Immigration Tide Strains Nation's Schools," *The New York Times Education Summer Survey* (August 21, 1983), Sec. 12, p. 1, ff. 37, 67.

[9] American Council on Education, "Minority Changes Hold Major Implications for U.S.," *Higher Education and National Affairs* (March 9, 1984), 8 and based on projections from the Center for Immigration Studies and from the Population Studies Center.

[10] James A. Banks and James Lynch, eds., *Multicultural Education in Western Societies* (New York: Praeger, 1986).

[11] The Swedish Institute, "Immigrants in Sweden," Fact Sheets on Sweden Series (Stockholm: The Institute, 1984).

[12] Des Storer, ed.-in-chief, *Ethnic Family Values in Australia* (Sidney: Prentice-Hall of Australia, 1985).

[13] John R. Mallea and Jonathan C. Young, eds., *Cultural Diversity and Canadian Education* (Ottowa: Carleton University Press, 1984).

[14] Jesus Garcia and Julie Goebel, "A Comparative Study of the Portrayal of Black Americans in Selected U.S. History Textbooks," *The Negro Educational Review* 35 (1985), 118-127.

[15] James Baldwin, *The Price of the Ticket: Collected Nonfiction, 1984-1985* (New York: St. Martin's/Marek).

[16] Robert K. Merton, "Insiders and Outsiders: A Chapter in the Sociology of Knowledge," *The American Journal of Sociology* 78 (1972), 9-47.

[17] Joyce Ladner, ed., *The Death of White Sociology* (New York: Vintage, 1973).

[18] Ibid.

[19] Frank Reisman, *The Culturally Deprived Child* (New York: Harper and Row, 1962).

[20] Charles A. Valentine, *Culture and Poverty: Critique and Counter-Proposals* (Chicago: The University of Chicago Press, 1968).

[21] Andrew Billingsley, *Black Families in White America* (Englewood Cliffs, N.J.: Prentice Hall, 1968); Robert B. Hill, *The Strengths of Black Families* (New York: Emerson Hall Publishers, 1972).

[22] Joan Baratz, "Teaching Reading in an Urban Negro School System," in *Language and Poverty: Perspectives on a Theme,* ed. Frederick Williams (Chicago: Markham Publishing Co., 1970); Herbert G. Gutman, *The Black Family in Slavery and Freedom, 1750-1925* (New York: Oxford University Press, 1964); Eugene D. Genovese, *Roll, Jordan, Roll: The World the Slaves Made* (New York: Pantheon, 1974).

[23] William J. Wilson, *The Declining Significance of Race: Blacks and Changing American Institutions* (Chicago: University of Chicago Press, 1978); Thomas Sowell, *Civil Rights: Rhetoric or Reality?* (New York: William Morrow, 1984).

[24] James Farmer, *Lay Bare the Heart: An Autobiography of the Civil Rights Movement* (New York: Arbor House, 1985); Takeo U. Nakano and Leatrice Nakano, *Within the Barbed Wire Fence: A Japanese Man's Account of His Internment*

(Seattle: University of Washington Press, 1980); Howell Raines, *My Soul is Rested: Movement Days in the Deep South Remembered* (New York: Putnam's, 1977).

[25] John W. Blassingame, *New Perspective on Black Studies* (Urbana: University of Illinois Press, 1977); Ladner, The Death of White Sociology.

[26] Donna H. Kerr, *Barriers to Integrity: Modern Modes of Knowledge Utilization* (Boulder, Colo.: Westview Press, 1984).

[27] Peter Steinfels, *The Neoconservatives: The Men Who Are Changing America's Politics* (New York: Simon and Schuster, 1979).

[28] Arthur R. Jensen, "How Much Can We Boost IQ and Scholastic Achievement," *Harvard Educational Review* 39 (Winter 1969), 1-123; Edward C. Banfield, *The Unheavenly City* (Boston: Little, Brown, 1970); William Shockley, "Dysgenics, Geneticity, Raceology: A Challenge to the Intellectual Responsibility of Educators," *Phi Delta Kappan* 53 (January 1972), 297-307.

[29] Kenneth B. Clark, *Dark Ghetto: Dilemmas of Social Power* (New York: Harper Torchbooks, 1965), xxi.

[30] Kenneth B. Clark, *Pathos of Power* (New York: Harper Torchbooks, 1975), 34.

[31] Nel Noddings, *Caring: A Feminine Approach to Ethics and Moral Education* (Berkeley: University of California Press, 1984).

[32] Carol Gilligan, *In a Different Voice: Psychological Theory and Women's Development* (Cambridge: Harvard University Press, 1982); Lawrence Kohlberg, "The Claim to Moral Adequacy of a Highest State of Moral Judgment," *The Journal of Philosophy* 70 (October 1973), 631-632.

PART II

THE NATIVE AMERICAN STRUGGLE FOR CULTURAL AUTONOMY IN EDUCATION AND LETTERS

In this section, two specialists in Native American studies document Kliever's point that the dominance of one cultural group over others in an ethnically diverse society eventually results in a social problematic that has moral implications. With the exception of Native Americans, all inhabitants of North America are classified as immigrants or as descendants of immigrants. Native Americans had lived in harmony with the natural order that nurtured them for millennia before the influx of European settlers. Although each group had its own indigenous name and cultural identity, Columbus who hoped he had reached the East Indies mistakenly called these diverse peoples Indians, and Europeans who followed in his wake continued that nomenclature.

When the English planted their first colony in North America in 1607, the nearly two million indigenes already had divided into several organized nations and hundreds of small clusters. The diseases and forces of settlement that the colonists brought with them decimated the Native American population. Demographers estimate that after one and a half centuries of colonial settlement, only 600,000 Native Americans had survived the onslaught, while the number of European settlers and Africans had risen to approximately 2.5 million.

Following their acquisition of independence, the European Americans' insatiable appetite for land led to a policy of westward movement and systematic removal of the indigenous peoples from their ancestral lands. This serialized event is symbolized in the Cherokee's "Trail of Tears" saga, an incident which might have been avoided had Cherokee males been more inclined to heed the wise counsel of their women. As the American migrants pressed further and further West to settle under the inspiration of "manifest destiny" sloganeering, the removal took its toll on the Native American population, eradicating all but 250,000 by the end of the nineteenth century. As a result of the holocaust that the removal policy unleashed upon them, the indigenous population never recouped its demographic losses. As recently as 1990, there still were less than two million Native Americans.

In the first essay, Linda Pertusati demonstrates how the United States' education policy contributed to the decimation of the indigenous peoples and destroyed their cultures. She employs methodologies from anthropology and sociology and uses a historical analysis to show that the intent of the policy was to destroy Native American traditional cultures by assimilating the children to the dominant white culture. One of the first means toward this goal was the removal of the children from their homes in order to isolate and break them from the aboriginal traditions and cultures. Pertusati explores the socio-political impact of the deculturating process on the Native Americans and discusses their attempts to create a liberatory curriculum in the twentieth century.

Pertusati initiates her discussion by reviewing characteristics of Native American traditional education, contrasting them with the alien educational practices imposed by European Americans. Finally Pertusati discusses the Native American struggle against the de-culturating processes of American education while reminding the reader that the struggle on this front continues.

Littlefield broadens the discussion on American education policy by extending it to include the academicians' research on and interpretation of Native American heritages. From the *emic* (insider-like) perspective of the academician, he analyzes the controversy between scholars in Native American studies and Native Americans over the interpretation of indigenous cultures and the too frequent misappropriation of indigenous orature and material artifacts. Littlefield expresses his concern that the tensions may cause the Native Americans to restrict outsiders' access to Indian communities and sources. He fears that the restricted access could diminish the place of Native American literature in both the curriculums of American schools and universities and the American literary canon.

Pertusati and Littlefield indicate the moral implications of European American educational practices and scholarship as they impact Native Americans. While Pertusati argues for a return to, or reintroduction of, education based on Native American traditions and values, Littlefield asserts that Native American leaders will assume a more determinative role regarding "outsiders'" appropriation and interpretation of indigenous traditions and artifacts. In any case, the reintroduction of Tradition and the assumption of a more determinative role in the exercizing of pedagogy and scholarship by Native Americans undoubtedly will lead to the sensitive retrieval and authentic interpretation of indigenous cultures.

De-(Culturating) *Qua* "Civilizing": The Perils of American Policy on Native American Education

Linda Pertusati
Ethnic Studies Department, Bowling Green State University

With only minor exceptions, the history of Indian education has been primarily the transmission of white American education to the Indian child. These educational institutions aimed at removing Indian children from their aboriginal cultures and assimilating them into the dominant white culture. Therefore, pedagogy and curriculum in these schools were imposed and controlled by the non-Indian society.[1] In effect, the system by which Native Americans purportedly are "educated" by European America has from the onset been little more than a means by which to supplant indigenous cultures. This has had, or at least has been intended to have, the predictable effect of demolishing the internal cohesion of native societies, thereby destroying the ability of these societies to resist conquest and colonization.[2]

The above insights summarize the imposition of European American educational ideology and practices upon the indigenous peoples of North America. And, they suggest the development of education within a complex and dynamic historical and socio-political context, which has in turn helped to shape the Native American condition. Those European Americans promoting assimilation into the dominant culture and the Native American cultural nationalists opposed to such

Reprinted by permission of the author.

goals both agree that this education system historically has been a means of indoctrination. It has been used to "civilize" and assimilate Native Americans into the dominant culture. Even today, with legislation in place to provide cultural continuity in the classroom, efforts to create a liberatory curriculum, or a curriculum grounded in Native American-centered beliefs and practices, have not really taken place. Despite the "good intentions" of multi-cultural reformers, what many of the Native American education programs have done is structured the dominant education curriculum and goals within a new colonialist pedagogical framework.

To understand the current state of Native American education requires a review of the history of that education and the struggles over what is important and meaningful knowledge. Therefore, this chapter will develop a chronological account of the history of education for the indigenous peoples of North America. First, this chapter will include an overview of the content and practice of Native American "education" (traditional indigenous teaching and learning) prior to the European American imposition. To this extent the first section will emphasize how traditional education reflected the "mythological" or cosmological perspective(s) of Native American society. Second, this chapter will examine and analyze the historical changes in the sociopolitical context of U.S.-aboriginal relations; it will discuss how those changes have affected the purpose and content of education for Native Americans. To this end, I will demonstrate that the purpose of the euro-centric education never has been value-free. Rather it has been a hegemonic activity intended to force the internalization of ideological repression, behavioral conformity, and political and economic acquiescence.

To illustrate my thesis, I will review briefly the traditional Native American teaching and learning practices. Next I will examine six periods in U.S.-aboriginal relations, showing that each period in U.S.-aboriginal relations epitomized a fundamentally distinct federal policy toward the education of Native Americans. The pertinent periods include the Treaty Period (1789-1870), the Reservation Period (1870-1877), the Allotment Period (1887-1934), the Reorganization Period (1934-1953), and the Termination Period (1953-1972). It will culminate with the Self-Determination Period (1972-present), which includes Native American resistance to the euro-centric education model. Specifically, I argue that Government policy-makers perceived and constructed Native American education as a solution to "the Indian problem" rather than as a process toward indigenous empowerment and collective liberation.

The processes of Native American teaching and learning traditionally have been informed by, and derived their meaning from, an indigenous cultural context(s) that was grounded in interconnectedness with the natural environment. "Education" involved acquiring the ways of teaching and learning via a "Nature-centered" philosophy.[3] Cajete outlined several indigenous cultural traits, which he depicts as characterizing traditional Native American teaching and learning. He contends that,

> a sacred view of nature permeates its foundational processes of teaching and learning; integration and interconnectedness are universal traits of its contexts and processes; . . . sources of knowledge are found within the individual and entities of nature; learning occurs through participation and honoring relationships in both the human and natural communities; . . . story, expressed through experience, myth, parables, and various forms of metaphor, is an essential vehicle of indigenous learning.[4]

Thus in this context, education essentially was holistic with emphasis on the importance of learning about everyday life through participation in and relationship with community, i.e., with plants, animals, and the people—both living and dead. In other words, traditional ways of teaching and learning sustained a life process that unfolded through mutual, reciprocal relationships between one's social group and the natural environment.

Informality characterized this process of teaching and learning, as most traditional knowledge was gained within the context of the day-to-day life experience of the people. Various ceremonial practices, rituals, myths, and customs founded upon experience and participation in indigenous culture(s) were used to integrate both the process and content of formal teaching and learning.[5] As elaborated on by Cajete,

> Traditional tribal education revolved around experiential learning (learning by doing or seeing), storytelling (learning by listening and imagining), ritual/ceremony (learning through initiation), dreaming

(learning through unconscious imagery), and tutoring (learning through apprenticeship).[6]

The context, or spiritual ecology, of traditional Native American teaching and learning included a three part, highly integrated educational process and content: the "Environmental," the "Mythic," and the "Visionary." The "Environmental" context afforded a process for integrating those cultural understandings, knowledge, and practices resulting from an interaction or relationship with the natural environment.[7] The process bonded the indigenous individual to the human and natural communities, allowing them to establish a sense of being and place. Thus, a reciprocal relationship between Native Americans and their environment was established.

The "Mythic" or cosmological context consisted of the stories that described the origins and significance of indigenous languages and traditions.[8] Through this process of storytelling, living and learning (education) were integrated. These narratives included creation stories that emphasized cultural norms and values and gave explanations and orientations of life. In other words, mythic lore made it possible for an individual and, indeed, an entire community to be socialized in the world view(s) of Native American peoples.

The "Visionary" context consisted of the spiritual experiences that led to, and/or resulted from the practices, rituals, and ceremonies of Native Americans.[9] The visionary approach provided a framework for teaching and learning through exploring the unconscious. This perception of education represents an anomaly for, and directly contrasts with, the dominant orientation of European American education, which emphasizes a process of education that is separated from the natural, social, or spiritual aspects of everyday life.

Traditional Native American education fully integrated living and learning. The extended family, the clan, and the entire indigenous nation provided the context and source for teaching. To attain such an integration of living and learning, required the knowledge, experience, and wisdom offered through the understanding and experiences of the elders and spiritual, or "medicine," people.

Perhaps the best way to understand the extent and form of the differences in the approach to learning and education between the two cultures is a visual device. The following chart illustrates the differences that exist between the traditional Native American approach to teaching and learning and the European American model of education.

A Comparison of Euro-Centric and Native American Education

Subject	Euro-centric Approach	Native American Approach
Cosmology	Man is separate from nature and exists to dominate nature	Man is part of nature and co-exists with and nurtures the natural world
Epistemology	All knowledge can be fragmented into parts: science, religion, history, and literature	All knowledge is part of an integrated, unified, and indivisible totality
Pedagogical Style	passive and direct learning often by repetition and in the form of abstractions	participatory and self-initiated learning by experience
Pedagogical Form	principally written, linear exposition	principally oral, circular exposition
Assumptions	rational, repetition, and purposeful or causal intent	unique, divine, mythical in origin and goal
Learning Context	mass grouping by age with socially-approved master	individual in context with tutoring by a student-selected master
Educational Practice	formal and standard in time, content, and duration for all	informal, intermittent, and continuous at the behest of the individual
Ideal Benefactor of Knowledge	The Individual Student	The Community

Seeing how different these two perceptions of education are, highlights the unique nature of Native American teaching and learning and anticipates the section to come on euro-centric education. Given the extent of this difference, the groundwork has been laid for an understanding of the political nature of European American educational ideology and practices and the Native American resistance to such a system of education. What is at issue in the educational struggle is nothing less than the meaning of the universe and how folk learn to conduct themselves within it.

From the beginning of contact with European culture, the issue of education has been a major area of conflict for Native American society. Education no longer was a cultural process rooted in indigenous philosophies and social values. Early efforts by the Spanish, French, and English were directed at transforming the indigenous culture(s) into replicas of European societies. Until the 1970s, then, Native Americans struggled to adapt to an educational process that was not their own.

As a result of European contact, Native Americans have been educated in federal, public, and church-run mission schools. Although the form and even the structure of education imposed upon Native Americans has changed over time, the purpose of such education has fluctuated between segregation and cultural assimilation of Native Americans into the dominant society. However, underlying this fluctuation in federal policy has been a continued dedication to a single goal. The government has attempted to use education to resolve the "Indian problem," in other words as a tool of domination and social control.

Education imposed upon Native Americans has been conceptualized based on:

1. European American values and ideology, and
2. the dominant relations of power in society.[10]

Because of the discontinuity between values embedded in the curriculum and those of the indigenous cultures, education becomes a source of cognitive dissonance for Native American children. The explicit biases (for example, referring to natives as savages and to their hunting methods and weapons as primitive) embedded within the hegemonic curriculum contributed to feelings of alienation and disempowerment among the native students.[11]

The "Indian problem," as it historically has come to be known, is a recurring theme throughout much of the historical literature on Native American issues. In 1939, Lloyd Blauch described the problem as "epitomiz(ing) the frustration that generations of western-oriented peoples have experienced in their relationships with the aboriginal peoples of the new world."[12] A more precise, cross-temporal definition of "the Indian problem" is the perception of European Americans (including the federal government) that the values and ideas of aboriginal culture are at variance with, and less valuable than, those of the dominant society in regard to cultural and political legitimacy.

In 1888, a member of the Board of Commissioners of Indian Affairs explained that "the Indian problem" is not a single problem but a threefold problem, related to land, law, and education; and with respect to the third aspect of the problem, education is the real crux of the Indian problem.[13] In 1928, the term "Indian problem" was again noted in relation to education. This time, in a comprehensive survey on aboriginal affairs, Lewis Merriam asserted that "the whole Indian problem is essentially an educational one."[14] Clearly, early analysts saw education as a method of getting Native Americans to assimilate to European American values and life-styles.

Over the years, the U.S. government formulated a number of policies in the attempt to resolve the so-called "Indian problem" by assimilating the Indian. Review of early federal legislation pertaining to aboriginal matters discloses the sentiment that nothing less than full assimilation of indigenous peoples into the mainstream of European American life would be an adequate resolution. This intent is striking when the six historical periods in U.S.-aboriginal relations are assessed.

The earliest period in formal U.S.-aboriginal relations is called the treaty period because all relations between the indigenous peoples of North America and the federal government were regulated by treaty negotiations. Treaties are agreements between mutually-recognized, sovereign political powers or nations. During this period, the government of the United States was preoccupied with territorial expansion. Each of the land gains during this period occurred at the expense of Native Americans. The "Indian problem" during this period involved major U.S.-aboriginal military conflicts over expansion. The sociopolitical ideology of the U.S. government was to seek to both pacify Native Americans and to exact acceptance of the new territorial realities and economic and political practices. While the U.S. military imposed the successive territorial conquests and domination, the Indian agencies and agents sought to culturally assimilate the indigenous peoples into the dominant society through a system of formal education.

The initial federal efforts to educate the indigenous peoples were made on an individual tribal basis. The first treaty which specifically committed the federal government to providing education was made with the Oneida, Tuscarora, and Stockbridge Nations in 1794. These aboriginal nations were singled out to receive education because they had loyally supported the U.S. against the British during the Revolutionary War.

In 1819, the federal government enacted legislation directed toward the education of larger numbers of indigenous peoples. This act represented the first expression of systematic, federal responsibility for the education of Native Americans. When Congress passed this act—known as the Indian Civilization Act—in 1819, the implication of the word "civilization" was primarily acculturation through formal education. The assimilative provisions of this act are obvious:

> Be it enacted by the U.S. of America that for the purpose of pacifying the Indian and resolving our Indian problem, it will be introduced among them, habits of civilization; the President of the U.S. shall be authorized to employ means of instruction for teaching their children in reading, writing, and arithmetic.[15]

This legislation authorized an annual appropriation of $10,000 for the "civilizing" of indigenous peoples. Specifically, provisions of the act were to be carried out through religious agencies already engaged in proselytizing among the aboriginals.

The government's policy reflected its belief that the indigenous peoples of North America were simple and child- like. For European Americans, the "Indian problem" was, in part, that Native Americans did not perceive the "superiority" and "legitimacy" of European American culture. From this European American perspective, education was both a reward for loyalty and an invitation to participate in the dominant society. But its primary aim was to displace all vestiges of aboriginal culture and belief.

That aim was reflected in two pieces of federal legislation—The Act of 1871 and The Reservation Act. The Act of 1871 provided: "that hereafter no Indian nation or tribe within the territory of the United

States shall be acknowledged or recognized as an independent nation, tribe, or power with whom the United States may contract by treaty."[16] Terminating aboriginal independence and abolishing the treaty system marked the official beginning of the adoption of indigenous peoples as "wards of the United States." Concurrent with the Act of 1871 was another piece of federal legislation, The Reservation Act. This legislation stipulated the government's plan to concentrate the indigenous peoples of the Great Plains on a vast reservation. It simultaneously removed them away from land marked for white settlement and segregated them away from the dominant society. This means toward resolving the "Indian problem" can be interpreted as a policy of ethnic and cultural segregation. Enactment of the 1871 legislation ending the treaty period and the establishment of the reservation system made indigenous peoples "wards of the United States." Consequently, the federal government designated itself as being responsible for the education of Native Americans.

As such, Congress passed the General Appropriations Act of 1874, also known as "An Act for the Support of Schools Among the Indians." This act appropriated $100,000 for the establishment of federally-operated boarding schools, giving control of Native American education to the Bureau of Indian Affairs.[17] These schools were designed to devalue and eradicate the traditional culture, language, and religion of indigenous peoples. Once again the hegemonic aim was to assimilate the indigenes into European American society. The aim behind the policy reflected in reports on the establishment of boarding schools for Native Americans. One Indian agent stated that, "The philosophy underlying the establishment of boarding schools . . . [was] to 'civilize' the Indian . . . [by taking] Indian children . . . as completely as possible away from their home and family life."[18]

Prior to 1871, Indian schools were maintained by religious agencies with the aid of government funds. Those schools had been almost exclusively under the control of missionary teachers. But from the date of the General Appropriations Act, the federal government began to control its own schools, to employ its own teachers, and impose its own curriculum. In his 1874 annual report, Commissioner Edward Smith commented on the thinking behind the preference for boarding schools:

> It is well-nigh impossible to teach Indian children the English language when they spend twenty hours out of twenty four in the wigwam, using only their native tongue. Irregular attendance at missionary schools for a few hours of instruction is inadequate to overcome cultural influences of the Indian child's home life. The solution to the Indian problem depends largely on the schooling given to the present generation of Indian children. We choose the boarding school because if it be admitted that education affords the true solution to the Indian problem then it must be admitted that the boarding school is the very key to the situation. Only by complete isolation of the Indian child from his savage antecedents can he be satisfactorily educated. The boarding school affords us education isolated from their primitive conditions and at the same time civilization and acculturation can be wrought into the Indian constitution.[19]

Commissioner Smith would like us to believe that the government was concerned with intellectual and social development rather than in undermining Indian authority on reservations. Jorge Noriega offers a more honest and accurate picture of the government's political goal for federally-operated boarding schools:

> In part, graduates from these institutions were groomed to comprise a "responsible leadership" among their respective peoples, offsetting and in many cases negating the authority and effectiveness of traditional national leaders who were far less compliant in regard to serving U.S. interests. More frequently, they were themselves deployed as teachers under the premise that Indians would be more credible than non-Indians in such capacities. In this way, Indian students targeted for training in the early stages of U.S. colonialist education were used essentially as a virus, a medium through which to hurry along a calculated process of sociocultural decay "from within" thus speeding the day in which Native America might be predicted to become fully integrated into the Euroamerican state structure.[20]

It is evident that these schools were dedicated to the eradication of indigenous political and cultural influence. Locating the schools at great distances from the reservation was an essential factor supportive of this general objective. Thus the General Appropriations Act of 1874 attempted to use formal education as the primary means of segregating the indigenous child in order to overcome cultural influences and wrest away Indian political autonomy.

An important piece of legislation during this period was the General Allotment (Dawes) Act of 1887, which sought to impose European American economic concepts upon native peoples in an effort to encourage their assimilation into dominant society. In so doing, the federal government undermined indigenous nations by forcing the breaking up and re-distribution of communally held-lands.[21] Its political intent is evident in the following statement composed by the Board of Commissioners of Indian Affairs, which states: "plainly [that] the ultimate purpose of the act [is] to abrogate the Indian tribal organization, to abolish the reservation system, and to place the Indians on an equal footing with other citizens of the country.[22]

From the perspective of European American Indian agents, at the crux of the "Indian problem" was communal life. The communal life of indigenous peoples was regarded by the federal government as the primary hindrance to their acculturation since their economic way of life was incompatible with that of a capitalistic culture. The reactive goal of the Indian Bureau was to make land and labor into commodities so as to undermine the sacredness of communal land. The means to this end was to break up communalism by offering economic incentives to nuclear families which individually cultivated their plots of land. Another was to confiscate communal land and redistribute it to white settlers.

Two decades later, in 1892, Congress passed an act that mandated compulsory education for all Native American children. Specifically, the latter act stated that: "In order to ensure the civilization of the Indians the necessity of education is admitted and therefore Indian children, male and female, between the ages of six and sixteen years should be compelled to attend school."[23] Thus began the trend of mass assimilation and the "final solution" to the "Indian problem"—the education of Native Americans in public schools.

In his 1892 annual report, Commissioner Price expressed the rationale behind compulsory education for aboriginal children, when he stated:

After observing that education is reaching only a small proportion of Indian children, we must place them all in school at a tender and impressionable age before the Indian cultural influences are set. Government education of the Indians must not be offered as a gift; it must be imposed by superior authority as a requirement. In other words, the education of Indian children must be made compulsory. We must establish compulsory education for the good of the lower race.[24]

For roughly one hundred years after the Indian Civilization Act of 1819, Native American education in the United States was almost exclusively under the direction of religious organizations. Even after the government enacted a policy of federally-operated boarding schools, sectarian schools predominated for a number of years. However, with the development of a public school system, the federal government positioned itself to administer federal public schools on the reservation; assuming complete control over Native American education. Federal education policy was individually focused; this promoted divisive concepts such as citizenship. It emphasized the "legitimacy" of land as commodity while denigrating aboriginal religion and culture.

Thus once again, the federal government attempted to use formal education as the primary means of culturally assimilating indigenous peoples into the dominant society. Only this time, they finally decided to take direct control of the education (and therefore the acculturation) process. And they decided to impose it on all indigenous students and not just the perceived leaders who were taken away to boarding schools. In line with Noriega's analogy mentioned earlier, the "virus," once incubated in isolation was reintroduced and exposure was compulsory.[25]

Another attempt to impose European American values upon Native Americans was manifested in the passage of the Indian Citizenship Act of 1924. This act imposed U.S. citizenship on the indigenous peoples of North America, making them subject to the governance of the dominant society.[26] Thus by imposing U.S. citizenship, this act authorized the termination of aboriginal sovereign status. By substituting elected forms of government for traditional forms of aboriginal organization, the federal government weakened and divided aboriginal peoples in terms of family structure and identity. The land and education policies contributed to the rapidly increasing settlement and development of aboriginal lands during this period.

Following the late-nineteenth–early twentieth-century period of U.S.-aboriginal relations, Native American education was reorganized. The federal government engaged in a new approach to Native American education, namely, decentralization. The Johnson-O'Malley Act of

1934 ushered in the reorganization period. Designed to limit the federal government's involvement in Native American education, the Johnson-O'Malley Act:

> authorized the government to enter into a contract or contracts with any State or Territory having legal authority so to do, for the education of Indians in such State or Territory, through the qualified agencies of such State or Territory, and to expend under such contract or contracts money appropriated by congress for the education of Indians in such State or Territory. In addition, all federally operated boarding schools with an average attendance of less than eighty pupils shall be discontinued and pupils transferred, where possible, to state public white schools. The work of Indian education shall be completely systematized, with a uniform course of study. The education of Indian children in state public white schools shall afford us [the opportunity] to educate Indian children as Americans, with other Americans in the instruction of rights, duties, and privileges of American citizens.[27]

Specifically, this legislation authorized appropriations of federal aid to state governments for the education of Native Americans in public schools. The purpose of these appropriations was to compensate and subsidize the states for the additional costs to them of enrolling and educating Native American students. As noted by Reyhner and Eder in 1992:

> Originally this money went into the general operating fund of the school districts and could in fact be used to support the education of non-Indian students. Today, much changed, the JOM Act still provides money to public schools educating Indian children. However, current JOM programs must be supplemental programs like special counseling, tutoring, or native culture programs.[28]

With the passing of the Johnson-O'Malley Act, the federal government attempted to enroll as many Native American children as possible in public schools. By 1940, over fifty percent of Native American children attending school were enrolled in public schools.

A serious hindrance to the education of Native American children in public schools was that insufficient attention was paid to their specific sociocultural needs. Certain legal conditions contributed to this neglect. No Native American influence was possible on boards of education because these indigenes were not taxpayers. As a result, Native

Americans could not vote for or serve on boards of education. Therefore, boards of education could act without fear of electoral response in their mis-dealings with Native Americans. Further, they could gain additional support from voters by re-allocating funds to non-Native students and therein could reduce the costs of, and taxes needed to support, the education of non-Native students and their voting parents. Thus locally, there was an incentive to ignore Native American youth and to use monies allocated for their education more broadly.

It is evident that the goal of the Johnson-O'Malley Act can be interpreted as intending to culturally assimilate Native Americans into the dominant society through formal education within white controlled schools. Implicitly, Native American students were to learn their minority status and to have their culture both minimized and denigrated within the curriculum. Each of these occurred within a forum in which Native American parents and elders had no representation and no influence.

Finally, the goal of education (consistent with the vocationalist focus of the larger education establishment of the era), was to prepare students for jobs in the dominant economy—jobs that did not exist on reservations. Thus again, the goal was to lure Native Americans from reservation areas, with an implied goal of eventually eliminating reservations. Thus, the federal government's attempt to "Americanize" the Native American student can be (mis)interpreted as being an attempt to resolve "the Indian problem" through education policy.

This post-1934 period in U.S.-aboriginal relations is referred to as the termination period because the federal government endeavored to terminate its trustee relationship with Native Americans. As part of this termination effort, state governments assumed responsibility for educating Native Americans via two 1953 federal initiatives—House Resolution 108 and Public Law 47.[29] The socio-political ideology marking this period was one of expediting the process of assimilation through formal education.

The first act of the termination period, House Resolution 108, held that:

> the federal government makes clear its intention to resolve the Indian problem as quickly as possible by disengaging itself from its guardianship status; to make all the Indian tribes and the individual members

thereof located within the territorial limits of the United States freed from federal supervision and control, and from all disabilities and limitations specially applicable to Indians; and to facilitate the full acceptance of Indians into the body politic.[30]

As such, this legislation reflected the government's emphasis on facilitating and accelerating the process of assimilation so that it might finally and completely resolve the "Indian problem." The effect of House Resolution 108 is reflected in the subsequent education legislation enacted in August of the same year (1953). Commissioner of Indian Affairs Myer made the following telling remark about the assimilative intent of the recent legislation in his report to the Board of Commissioners: "As part of the general pattern of withdrawal and acculturation, we must take additional steps to accelerate such acculturation and transfer responsibility for educating Indian children to the public school system of the country."[31] With the enactment of Public Law 47, the federal government conveyed to state government agencies and/or to local school authorities "all the rights, title, and interest of the United States in the education of the Indian."[32] Despite this transfer, the Bureau of Indian Affairs maintained a number of schools that were located on reservations. This was necessary to accommodate those Native American children who, because their homes were located in isolated areas, would have found it difficult to impossible to participate in public education.

Having expropriated aboriginal land, introduced and imposed European American economic and political values, and having begun the integration of indigenous peoples into the public schools, the federal government could begin terminating its responsibilities. More specifically, the federal government movement in this direction can be interpreted in the broadest sense as their termination of attempting to resolve "the Indian problem." In another sense, this can be interpreted as an attempt to transfer the solution of "the Indian problem" onto the shoulders of the state and local governments.

During this period in U.S.-aboriginal relations, the focus had been on indigenous cultural values and needs. The principal characteristic of this period had been a renewed emphasis on Native American self-determination. The socio-political ideology marking this period is an acknowledgment by the federal government of the relevance of aboriginal culture. At the same time, that acknowledgment had been framed in a manner which inferred that the European Americans perceived aboriginal culture to be a sub-culture within the dominant culture. It could be trivialized and reduced to a series of decontextualized arts and artifacts.

The education process experienced by Native American students during this period was directly impacted by the escalating confrontations and protests by Native Americans rejecting years of imposition of euro-centric educational ideology and practices. These activities, which included participation by the American Indian Movement (AIM), occurred during the late 1960s and early 1970s. Specifically, conflicts over curriculum content and community input vaulted the issue of education reform to the forefront of Native American protest. Once the hegemony of the dominant system was challenged by a resurgence of aboriginal cultures, Native Americans engaged in a partial rejection of the education constructs and values of the dominant society. This resulted in the rise of (alternative) Survival Schools on reservations, i.e., the Akwesasne Freedom School.

These alternative protests led to efforts purportedly designed to adapt curriculum content (cultural continuity) and instruction (pedagogy) to the cultural and practical needs of Native American students. An indication of this revised federal policy encouraged revisions in the courses of study Native American students received in public schools. This approach is best reflected in The Indian Education Act (Title IV of Public Law 92-318 of 1972). This legislation authorized the appropriations of federal aid for special programs for Native Americans attending school both on the reservation and in urban public schools.[33] Prior to this the only courses offered in the public schools had been oriented toward participation in the European American culture. Native Americans had appeared within that curriculum as naive impediments to nineteenth century progress; sometimes the texts portrayed them in caricature as the embodiment of modern social problems.

This 1972 federal legislation mandated (and provided funding for) the creation of classes that were supposed to stress culturally relevant and bi-lingual curriculum materials and emphasize instruction in aboriginal arts and crafts, history, culture, and language. Due to the variety of aboriginal cultures, each school district was encouraged to base its program on the cultural heritage of the Native American students in their district. Compared to the earlier omission and denigration of aboriginal cultures, this program promised to be and in part was a step forward. Yet, European American teachers continued to control the content of the curriculum and the pedagogical methods, as well as to de-contextualize and fragment knowledge.

In 1975, the 1972 legislation was amended to "promote maximum Indian participation in the education of Indian people and to support the right of Indians to control their own educational activities."[34] As such, the purpose of the Indian Self-Determination and Education Assistance Act, Public Law 93-638, was to insure the participation of Native American parents in the education process of their children.[35] Many of these parents are engaged in cultural preservation and have collectively moved to take community control of the education of their children. As a result of such parental efforts to develop an educational program that served specific Native American educational and cultural needs, a number of Native American communities began to control and run their own schools, distinct from the public schools.

Students attending these schools receive the full curriculum of "traditional" or European American academics as well as aboriginal language, history, and culture courses. In addition to these elementary and secondary community-controlled and run-schools, Native American studies departments at a number of universities and Native American controlled colleges resulted from this legislation as well.

On the surface it would appear that both the Indian Education Act of 1972 and the Indian Self-Determination and Education Assistance Act of 1975 implicitly recognize the pluralistic nature of the United States, and consequently they acknowledge the validity of aboriginal cultures. However, even with such legislation in place, critics of the current state of Native American education have called for a reevaluation of this "educational self-determination" legislation. They specifically argue that efforts to create a liberatory curricular structure have not really taken place and that they resulted in little more than a form of multicultural education within a colonialist pedagogical framework.[36] This is reflected in the following remarks by Reyhner and Eder on the current state of Native American education:

> Education as the great equalizer is a vision of education as a liberating force that empowers individuals . . . but education has not always served as a weapon for liberating American Indians. Previous federal policies of assimilation have used education as a weapon to annihilate American Indian cultures and languages. While the assimilation policies are no longer an official position of the federal government, the attitudes of teachers and administrators . . . as well as the teaching methods and textbooks used, still reflect the discarded policies.[37]

This assertion is supported by other scholars who rather forcefully and accurately point out the lack of cultural integrity in the current state of Native American education.

> Nothing really changed. . . . Aside from some cosmetic alterations like the inclusion of beadwork, traditional dance, basket weaving, and some language classes, the curriculum taught in Indian schools remained exactly the same, reaching exactly the same conclusions, indoctrinating children with exactly the same values as when the schools were staffed entirely by White people. Only now it was supposedly more credible to grassroots people, because people who were visibly Indian were doing the teaching and the administering. . . . It's really a perfect system of colonization, convincing the colonized to colonize each other in the name of "self-determination" and "liberation."[38]

Thus it would seem that little progress has been made toward a liberative education for Native Americans since the federal government enacted its first education provision for Native Americans in 1819.

Fortunately, efforts at ameliorating this pattern of colonization already has begun to take root. Native American scholars and activists are developing and implementing studies programs which offer a liberatory curriculum. Its intent will be to promote and preserve the cultural integrity of the indigenous peoples of North America. These programs train Native American students in the entirety of their culture, placing education within the "nationhood" context.[39] Hopefully, this will be the future of, and the next historical time period in, the state of Native American education.

Based on the findings of the research reviewed and analyzed throughout this essay, it is clear that while the methods of education imposed upon Native Americans have changed, the central functional dynamic motivating euro-centric educational ideology and practices has been an attempt to address "the Indian problem" in manners beneficial to the European American government and society. Also, the purpose of this model of education changed with the fluctuations in the socio-political ideology of U.S.-aboriginal relations. That recognition verifies critics who take the position that the structure and curriculum of education is not value free. It is part of a political, economic, and cultural battleground. As a result, the content of education has gone beyond the scope of teaching and learning..

Attitudes of European American superiority and aboriginal inferiority have influenced much of the federal legislation pertaining to the indigenous peoples of North America. Native American educational legislation has not escaped the influence of, and in fact has been a principle focus of, that ideological struggle. One of the basic assumptions of the European American educational system is that it prepares individuals to live in the dominant society. This assumption implies that if every individual receives enough education in the values and practices of the dominant society, he or she can function as a useful, or "civilized" citizen. Historically, euro-centric education imposed upon Native Americans was designed to create such "civilized citizens" without the recognition that maintenance of the indigenous cultural traditions was valid and desirable. Today there is the widespread recognition among ethnic Americans, including Native Americans, that a people have a right to choose their destiny.

The emphasis of the European American educational approach is uni-directional, a dynamic reflected in much of the federal legislation on Native American education. It implies that if the indigenous peoples could be educated and assimilated ("civilized") to accept the values and practices of the dominant culture, then the so-called "Indian problem" would by definition be resolved. In the final analyses, concerns about resolving "the Indian problem"—an issue of power, domination, and economics (property)—have overridden considerations of meaningful knowledge, educational effectiveness, value-continuity and self-determination, and the educational process itself is burdened by a value contra-position and by concerns with power and domination.

During the 380 years since the creation of permanent settlements in North America, traditional Native American teaching and learning have been all but eliminated in favor of institutions that adhere to a euro-centric orientation to life. Contemporary efforts to revive Native American cultural values and to improvise processes of education have in recent decades yielded a fundamental change in the substance of indigenous education. What is needed is a return to, or a reintroduction of, the traditional cosmological perspective that once was the ground of Native American "education" and tradition.

---

[1] Estelle and Robert Havighurst, *To Live on This Earth* (New York: Anchor Books, 1973), 19.

[2] Jorge Noriega, "American Indian Education in the United States," in *The State of Native America*, ed. M. Annette Jaimes (Boston: South End Press, 1992), 373-374.

[3] Jeannette Armstrong, "Traditional Indigenous Education: A Natural Process," a paper presented at the World Conference, Indigenous People's Education, Vancouver, B.C., June 1987.

[4] Gregory Cajete, *Look to the Mountain: An Ecology of Indigenous Education* (Durango, CO.: Kivaki Press, 1994), 29-30.

[5] P. V. Beck and Anna Walters, *The Sacred* (Tsaile: Navajo Community College Press, 1977) and Gregory Cajete, *"Science, A Native American Perspective: A Culturally Based Science Education Curriculum,* Ph. D. Dissertation (International College, 1986).

[6] Gregory Cajete, *Look to the Mountain: An Ecology of Indigenous Education,* 34.

[7] Ibid.; B. Devall & George Sessions, *Deep Ecology* (Salt Lake: Gibbs Smith, Inc. 1985); Donald Hughes, *American Indian Ecology* (El Paso: Texas Western Press, 1983).

[8] Kieran Egan, ""Literacy and the Oral Foundations of Education," *Harvard Educational Review* 57, No. 4 (November 1987); Kieran Eagan, *Teaching as Storytelling* (Chicago: University of Chicago Press, 1989).

[9] Beck & Walters, *The Sacred*; Jim Nollman, *Spiritual Ecology* (New York: Bantam Books, 1990).

[10] Jerome Buckanaga, "Inter-Racial Politics: The Pressure to Integrate an Experimental School," in *The Schooling of Native America, ed. T. Thompson* (Washington D.C.: American Association of Colleges for Teacher Education, 1975); T. Davis and A. Pyatskowit, "Bicognitive Education: A New Future for Indian Children," *Journal of American Indian Education* 15, No. 3 (1976); Vine Deloria, "The Indian Student Amid American Inconsistencies" in *The Schooling of Native America,* 1978; G. Heath, *Red, Brown, and Black Demands for Better Education* (New York: Westminster Press, 1972); M. Zintz, "What Classroom Teachers Should Know about Bilingual Education," in *Bilingual Education for American Indians* (New York: Arno Press, 1978).

[11] M. Annette Jaimes, "American Indian Studies: Toward an Indigenous Model," *American Indian Culture and Research Journal* 11, No. 3 (1987); M. Annette Jaimes & Ward Churchill, "American Indian Studies: A Positive Alternative," *The Bloomsbury Review* 8, No. 5 (1988); Noriega, "American Indian Education in the United States."

[12] *Educational Service for Indians* (Washington, D.C.: Government Printing Office, 1939), 4.

[13] Annual Report, Board of Commissioners of Indian Affairs, Supplement on Indian Education (Washington, D.C.: Government Printing Office, 1888), 50.

[14] The Problem of Indian Administration (Baltimore: The Johns Hopkins Press, 1928), 348.

[15] The Indian Civilization Act of 1819 in *U.S. Statutes at Large,* 3 (Washington, D.C.: Government Printing Office), 516.

[16] Act of 1871 in *U.S. Statutes at Large,* 16 (Washington, D.C.: Government Printing Office), 544.

[17] Jon Reyhner and Jeanne Eder, "A History of Indian Education," in *Teaching American Indian Students,* ed. Jon Reyhner (Norman, OK: University of Oklahoma Press, 1992.

[18] Merriam, *The Problem of Indian Administration,* 403.

[19] Annual Report, Board of Commissioners of Indian Affairs, Supplement on Indian Education (Washington, D.C.: Government Printing Office, 1874), 8.

[20] Noriega, "American Indian Education in the United States," 379.

[21] Reyhner and Eder, "A History of Indian Education."

[22] Annual Report, Board of Commissioners of Indian Affairs, Supplement on Indian Education (Washington, D.C.: Government Printing Office, 1887), 6.

[23] 1892 Act for Compulsory Education *U.S. Statutes at Large,* 11 (Washington, D.C.: Government Printing Office), 743.

[24] Annual Report, Board of Commissioners of Indian Affairs, Supplement on Indian Education (Washington, D.C.: Government Printing Office, 1892), cxiv.

[25] Noriega, "American Indian Education in the United States."

[26] Indian Citizenship Act of 1924 in *U.S. Statutes at Large,* 43 (Washington, D.C.: Government Printing Office), 253.

[27] Johnson-O'Malley Act of 1934 in *U.S. Statutes at Large,* 49 (Washington, D.C.: Government Printing Office), 328.

[28] "A History of Indian Education," 51.

[29] Ryhner and Eder, "A History of Indian Education."

[30] Find House Resolution 108 in *U.S. Statutes at Large,* 67 (Washington, D.C.: Government Printing Office).132.

[31] Annual Report, Board of Commissioners of Indian Affairs, Supplement on Indian Education (Washington, D.C.: Government Printing Office, 1953), 389.

[32] Find Public Law 47 in *U.S. Statutes at Large,* 67: p. 41.

[33] Ryhner and Eder, "A History of Indian Education," Margaret Szasz, *Education and the American Indian* (Albuquerque, NM: University of New Mexico Press, 1977).

[34] National Advisory Council on Indian Education, *Indian Education: America's Unpaid Debt*, 1982, 120.

[35] Reyhner and Eder, "A History of Indian Education," Margaret Szasz, *Education and the American Indian.*

[36] Jaimes, "American Indian Studies: Toward an Indigenous Model," Jaimes and Churchill, "American Indian Studies: A Positive Alternative," Noriega, "American Indian Education in the United States."

[37] Reyhner and Eder, "A History of Indian Education," 15.

[38] A quote from Noriega, "American Indian Education in the United States," 387.

[39] Jaimes, "American Indian Studies: Toward an Indigenous Model," Jaimes and Churchill, "American Indian Studies: A Positive Alternative."

American Indians, American Scholars and the American Literary Canon

Daniel F. Littlefield, Jr.
Department of English, University of Arkansas—Little Rock

As a member of the editorial board whose work culminated in the *Heath Anthology of American Literature,* I have watched with interest during the last two years the debate on the American literary canon and the related issue of political correctness. Heretofore, I have not publicly addressed the issues of the debate. My intention is not to rehash them here, for one additional statement more or less will not matter much. What I wish to address, instead, is a matter related to the debate on the literary canon: the growing controversy between American Indians and American scholars. Presented first are the broad outlines of the controversy and some of its causes, followed by an analysis of what implications the debate might have for American studies that deal with Indian matters, particularly for the American literary canon and those whose scholarship concerns it.

During the past twenty years, American Indians have been critical of American scholars, especially the anthropologists, for whom their criticism has been relentless. In recent years, with ever increasing intensity, their criticism has spilled over to other American scholars as well. Depending on the political stand of the person making the statement we have been naive, ignorant, racist, colonialist, or two or more of these

Copyright © 1992 by Daniel F. Littlefield. Reprinted by permission.

in combination.[1] In some instances, there is outright repudiation of our efforts. Oren Lyons, for example, "a runner for the Six Nations" and a member of the Onondaga council, has said to us, "We will determine what our culture is. . . . We are not going to be put in a museum or accept your interpretations of our culture."[2] Elizabeth Cook-Lynn, the Sioux scholar and writer, has asked, "Why should the university systems of this country and Indian studies units and publishing houses define who an Indian is?"[3] And Philip Deloria, the Sioux legal scholar, has put it more broadly:

> We exist in a distinct status in this society simply because we have a right to exist. Our rich cultural heritage is our own business and not the business of the federal government or the scholarly community. We do not owe an obligation—other than to ourselves—to preserve or not to preserve Indian culture.[4]

Finally, "It may be," as Roger Buffalohead has said regarding anthropologists, "the scholarly differences that we need to explore have more to do with our ways of thinking, our intellectual traditions, and our ways of perceiving than with deliberate exploitation of one group by another."[5] Whatever the cause of our differences, real or perceived, Indian intellectuals have a bone to pick with the American scholar, and not with just the anthropologists among us.

Despite our protestations against, and denial of our complicity in romanticizing the Indians, we have done so, they say. They say also that we simply replaced the old stereotypes with new ones, thus perpetuating paternalism. Deloria presents a good outline of the case against us. Much of what we have written, he says,

> [is] a simplistic good guys versus bad guys analysis resting on fundamental ideological criticisms of American culture and society. . . . These philosophical criticisms no doubt play an important role as scholarly commentary and for a larger social and ideological agenda, but they are of limited use as Indian tribes try to deal with their immediate problems.[6]

Because of our simplistic view, Deloria tells us that we missed the point of the Indian cultural awareness movement of the 1960s and 1970s. In the wake of that movement, our tendency has been to idealize the Indians. Our analyses of the failure of resource development policies of that era tended to place the blame on the federal government because we are "wedded to a method of historical analysis in which tribes are never responsible for their mistakes and the government never makes an honest mistake." In reality, though, he says, "There must have been at one point in history at least one Indian who did not know what he was talking about. There must have been at least one person who worked for the Bureau of Indian Affairs who had a good idea." Promoting the idea that policy failures rest solely with the government leads Indians to self-deception regarding their role in that failure. Promoting "the view that Washington is a monolith hostile to tribal interests" undermines tribal willingness or ability "to learn how to understand and manipulate" the political process. Thus we let the Indians down by not helping them clearly understand their position vis-a-vis the government. The result is "that tribal interests are not adequately articulated at key points in a federal process that is largely oblivious to Indians."[7]

Because of our tendency to idealize, thus stereotype Indians, we became sidetracked from what Dolor calls "the real issues of Indian cultural survival" and became intellectual peeping Toms and Tomasinas, prying into areas where we have no business. Though there are many issues of concern to Indians, what constitutes Indianness is a prime one. It is impossible to estimate how many pages of published academic prose and papers at professional meetings have been given to that debate.[8] Indians maintain that determining who is or is not one of them is their province, not ours, and that it is basic to tribal or Indian national sovereignty that they be free to do so. And they have done fairly well at policing their ranks. They have taken care, for instance, of books such as Ruth Beebe Hill's *Hanna Yo* and people such as Jamake Highwater, Princess Pale Moon and Harley "Swift Deer" Reagan.[9] And they are presently engaged in a debate among themselves that will profoundly affect our definition of what constitutes *Indian* art.[10]

Yet scholars are captivated by the question of Indianness and continue to intrude into what should be Indian business. In historical and Indian literary studies, we have been extremely concerned with the matter of authenticity. Rodney Simard has recently argued that we have been *overly* concerned with authenticity regarding texts, translations and authors.[11] While Simard challenges us to change our ways, his concern is with the directions of academic scholarship and not how that scholarship has affected the Indians. We have managed to make some scholars and Indian writers self-conscious, making them feel compelled to explain their subjects' or their own qualifications to speak as Indians. For example, the issue pervades recent collections of interviews with Indian writers, such as those put together by Joseph Bruchac and Laura Coltelli and autobiographical essays such as those collected by Brian Swann and Arnold Krupat.[12] If a writer is accepted by the community of Indian writers, who are we to question? I was honestly astounded when, in the manuscript stage of my recent biography of Alexander Posey (1873-1908), two of three reviewers complained that I had not addressed the issue of Posey's Indianness. Here was a man who was a member of the wind clan and of Tuskegee tribal town, who did not speak English until age fourteen, who was fluent in not only dialects of the Muscogee people but Choctaw as well, who spent very few days of his life outside the Creek Nation and fewer still outside a fifty-mile radius of where he was born. No one in his day would have thought to question whether Posey was a Creek. The Creeks certainly did not. To do so today can be nothing more than academic exercise.

Yet we have persisted, and some of us have built careers around this exercise. As a result, say the Indians, we have contributed, unwittingly in some cases and intentionally in others, to racism and polarization in American society. An example is James Clifton and his school of thought.[13] If we can believe Clifton and his followers, there is really no such thing as an Indian any more, and anyone who claims to be one has a political agenda or is looking for a way to feed at the public trough. They would have us believe that European diseases did not have the impact on native populations that we have been led to think they did, that the U. S. military did not engage in wars of extermination, that termination of tribal status was an enlightened federal policy, and that affirmative action for Indians is reverse discrimination. Any scholar who says differently either has a political agenda or is seeking a pay raise or tenure. It is no wonder that Indians consider Clifton a racist.[14] At bottom, Clifton's work gives scholarly sanction to the actions and rhetoric of Protect America's Rights and Resources and other anti-treaty and racist organizations in Wisconsin, the Citizens Equal Rights Alliance in Montana, the American Farm Bureau, and other groups whose goal is to dissolve tribal and Indian national status. Clifton's work contributes to the same type of polarization inherent in the politics of David Duke and the agenda of *The Journal of Historical Review*, which would have us believe that the holocaust did not occur.[15]

Despite Clifton's belief that Indians are stuff of the imagination, with the opening of the American canon and the ongoing debate on that issue and on political correctness, we can expect an increase of interest in American Indians in the context of American studies in general and, in specific, American Indian literature, one of the most rapidly growing areas of interest in literary studies. As that happens, we must consider how the growing controversy between the Indians and us will affect not only our scholarship but our teaching and the counsel we give our students who wish to pursue Indian subjects in their studies. We can expect Indians more and more, as they have been doing in recent years, not only to demand accountability from us but to attempt to shape the direction of scholarly research and writing.

In the long run, we can expect some important limitations on not only the amounts but kinds of information that will be available to us from the Indian community. Indians are beginning to say to us, "Since you have got it wrong all these years, we will develop strategies to squeeze you *out.*" An example is an interesting direction now being proposed for American Indian studies as an academic discipline. In the mid-1980s American Indian studies faculties went through serious evaluation of their programs. They concluded basically that they were "intellectually subordinate" to university administrations, that their curriculum was in the Anglo-American mode, that it appealed more to non-Indian students than to Indians, and that it constituted little more than "white studies." There was in addition an "ideologically motivated suppression of divergent Native American" thought on the part of scholarly journals, and the products of university presses, "even those with strong orientation toward Indian studies—the University of Oklahoma and the University of Nebraska?" were "actually non-Indian historical/anthropological undertakings rather than American Indian Studies efforts per se." As a result of this assessment, American Indian studies "practitioners" set out to make American Indian studies "an autonomous *Indian* tradition of intellectualism" and to develop alternatives to "white studies" by the end of the century.[16]

Some of those alternatives are now becoming clear. Some Indian scholars are calling for a shift in curriculum "from generic American Indian topics to the study of specific regions and cultural communities" that have a commonality based on "a shared history, a cultural unity, language, kinships and social organization."[17] Others call for "tribally described" models, "presuming to serve particular societies, nations, cultures within the state's borders, or within the university's regional perspective." These are "the most impervious to outside interests such as the popular culture" because "their faculties are generally made up of tribal intelligentsia, native language speakers, reservation based scholars, native poets and singers and dancers and writers." American Indian studies, then, would become the defender of the cultural and historical "parameters" of the discipline: the "spiritual and philosophical notions imbedded in language and literature and religion and mythology" and the "legal status of Indian nationhood and Indian citizenship, the mechanisms upon which all indigenous legal rights and political conditions are dependent." In the long run, these trebly specific disciplines would defend the Indians "from nefarious and dangerous pretenders who have become as numerous as flies in this modern valueless world, writing books and conducting workshops on everything from moon ceremonies for the middle-aged woman to religious freak pipe ceremonies to how to save the earth, Indian-style."[18] The idea is obviously aimed at restricting certain areas of research and writing to Indians or to non-Indians who have gone to the effort to learn a particular native language and at the same time train articulate Indian scholars equipped to challenge outsiders who happen to venture onto their tribal or cultural turf.

There are other, more immediate, evidences that information sources are becoming more restricted. Some tribes, for example, are moving toward control of what is written about them. A good example is the Hopi suppression of Ekkehart Malotki's book *The Hopi Salt Journey,* which had been scheduled for publication by the University of Nebraska Press in 1991. The Hopis argued that it struck at "the roots of Hopi religion" by "revealing what should remain closely guarded knowledge transmitted only to a *few* privileged religious initiates." In addition, Malotki, who had published other books with Hopi collaborators, was declared *persona non grata* on the Hopi Reservation. A Hopi spokesperson said, "Basically, we no longer recognize him as an expert.

If he was an expert on our culture, he would have known where to draw the line."[19] The Hopi leadership considers unsanctioned research "exploitative intrusions" which they will no longer tolerate. They deny that they want a moratorium on research in other aspects of Hopi culture, but the tribe is developing guidelines to govern whatever research is done.[20]

On a larger scale, political, economic and other forces are also conspiring to restrict the flow of information. Indian religious freedom is under attack. Recent Supreme Court decisions such as *Lyng vs Northwest Indian Cemetery Association (1988)* and *Employment Division of Oregon vs Smith (1990)* have begun to dismantle the Indian Religious Freedom Act of 1978.[21] Coincidental with the erosion of religious freedoms has been an increase in the number of the New Age followers, those "spiritual orphans" philosophically suspended somewhere between the Bagwhan and Black Elk. Groups like the Great Round, the Deer Tribe, and the Bear Tribe and writers like Lynn Andrews, the Indians charge, have become "spiritual hucksters," appropriating and selling Indian spiritualism for profit.[22] There is already evidence from sources as divergent as actor and entertainer Floyd Red Crow Westerman and Tim Johnson, editor of *Turtle Quarterly*, that Indians are becoming more careful regarding what they tell the public about their spirituality. Westerman says, for example, "We are being more careful nowadays with our spirituality and how much we divulge because more and more persons are practicing sacred ceremonies and we are trying to pullback and expose these 'shaman showmen' who charge for those ceremonies without sanctions." And in response to a New-Age inquiry about dreams, Johnson responded that the *Quarterly's* intent was to provide information that would help readers "seek out wisdom, expand their understandings of life or elevate their acceptance and appreciation of cultural diversity. . . without infringing upon the intimacy of Native American spiritual belief or by making profitable use of trends in popular culture."[23] As Indian communities become more assailed by legal challenges regarding such matters as sacred sites and trust status of Indian land, I foresee a reluctance to be forthcoming in other areas, too.

In addition, we have not yet seen the full effects of the decentralization of the Bureau of Indian Affairs that began in the late 1960s. As Indians have assumed more control over the delivery of many services formerly supplied by the Bureau, the flow of records back to Washington has decreased. Today, most records concerning such matters as health, housing, education and economics remain with the tribes and are unavailable to outsiders. The old days of going to the National Archives and ordering all we needed sent down from the Natural Resources Branch to the main reading room are gone. Meanwhile, the printing presses are at work in practically every community—urban or reservation—in Indian Country, publishing newsletters, newspapers and magazines on a weekly, biweekly, monthly or quarterly basis. Tribal historians are at work generating tribal histories. Much of what the outsider knows of Indian communities of the late-twentieth century will have to be drawn from such sources. Slowly but certainly, the Indians are taking care of one of their basic complaints about us: that our thinking is calcified regarding what constitutes legitimate resources for scholarly research. While we are making our adjustments, we can expect their criticism to be more open, more common, and more strident.

Those who believe that our Indian critics can be dismissed as a few outspoken ex-AIM militant types do not read what I read on a daily basis: the nuts and bolts news from Indian communities and analysis of the issues that concern them. Indian editors and columnists hammer away at our misrepresentations of the Indians, condemnatory reviews of our books are reprinted, and full-scale attacks on establishment scholarship are mounted through reviews and articles in Indian controlled scholarly journals like *American Indian Culture and Research Journal, American Indian Quarterly, Wicazo Sa Review,* and *Northeast Indian Quarterly.*[24] The leading Indian national weekly, to mark the Columbian quincentenary, is publishing reviews of books that present American Indians in a way the editors perceive is "calculated to retrieve the world" Columbus helped to destroy.[25] Indian broadcasters are buying in more frequently to public and commercial radio stations and increasingly view them as a means of empowerment.[26] Indian librarians are influencing collections development policies, and the journalism organizations are developing guidelines for non-Indian journalists who write about Indians.[27]

In the face of such trends, what are our possible modes of action? On the one hand, we can do nothing, try to ignore what the Indians say, and go on about our business as usual. However, unlike the past, when Indian opinion could be ignored effectively, it will not be so easy to do so in the future because of Indian information networks. We who like to be taken seriously but persist in our ways will have to adjust to being the object of ridicule in Indian cartoons and satire and in public debate.[28] Worse still, the Indians might simply ignore us. In the 1980s, when they realized that our promises to them in the 1970s were not being fulfilled, they began to avoid our professional meetings and until recently were rarely seen at them. Though the anthropologists still seem to be bearing the brunt of the criticism, the historians are next in line ahead of the literary scholars, and if we are standing in a crowd when someone delivers a broadside barrage of "editorial grapeshot," we would have to have the hide of a rhinoceros not to feel the effects.[29] As the criticism mounts, its delivery system becomes steadily more sophisticated. Attacks on American scholarship in Indian publications get to grassroots Indian country on a weekly, biweekly, monthly or quarterly basis. By the mid-1980s many Indian publishers were associated with the world-wide indigenous peoples' movement and since then have linked into information networks on national, international, hemispheric and global scales, hence creating a much larger forum for the expression of Indian opinion than ever before.[30] Everywhere, from reservation and urban ghetto to university campuses, Indians are being told to distrust us, our methods, and our findings. Everywhere, Indians are demanding that studies of the Indians' participation in American society be written or rewritten to account for the Indians' perspectives. A key to how effectively these demands are met is the native press. Like never before, it has the power to help force change, and, as I recently suggested to fellow members of the Native American Journalists Association, one important use of that power would be to turn critical attention to us scholars and our work.[31]

Whether we want to admit it or not, Indian opinion is being heard. It has forced the Smithsonian Institution and other museums closely allied with scholarly research to develop policies for the repatriation of human remains and sacred objects and has forced scholars and college administrators to confront the implications attached to holding in perpetuity the bones of Indians. Indian opinion has also had much to do with reshaping our thinking, however reluctantly we did it, about the American Constitution, just as it is presently helping to reshape how we think about the significance of the arrival of Columbus.[32]

There are other hopeful signs. According to Frederick Hoxie, director of the D'Arcy McNickle Center for the History of the American Indian at the Newberry Library, public sentiment favors setting the historical record straight, but he believes educators and politicians are lagging behind that sentiment. However, Hoxie cites as promising developments, among others, the Newberry Library's work in recent years with high school and college teachers and a new series of which he is general editor called New Directions in American Indian History to be published by the University of Oklahoma Press. Educators may be catching up, leaving only the politicians lagging behind, for in early July, the National Education Association adopted a policy to require textbooks to detail "the contributions and major roles of Native Americans."[33] If Hoxie's hope is well placed and if we can believe a recent article in the *Chronicle of Higher Education,* we are on the verge of a revolution in how our scholarship "characterizes" Indians. As evidence of change, the writer of the article cites "new scholarship" on the American Indian, mainly by ethnohistorians who are providing what he calls "fresh insights into broader questions with which social-science and humanities scholars have been grappling—including such questions as the nature of resistance to colonialism, the biases in traditional ethnographies, the use of oral histories, and the character of America's colonial period."[34] I am afraid, however, that something in the writer's language or the comments of some scholars who were interviewed will cause Indians to ask, "What do you mean by the American colonial period?"

How we respond to this question will determine in large measure how receptive Indian intellectuals are to these "new directions" in American Indian scholarship. We have steadily refused, they argue, to recognize Indians as colonized peoples. They see the strain on our relations as "a part of a worldwide phenomenon where tribal and other colonial people have challenged academic experts' role as interpreters of non-western culture" and they accuse us of "lowering an ivory tower curtain around the exploitation and injustice suffered by subject or colonial peoples."[35] Thus what we write has little to say about the realities of America as American Indians experience or have experienced them.

While there is reason to hope—and I believe it is genuine reason—that the American ethnohistorians are on the right track, I can not say as much for scholarship in American Indian literatures.

Unfortunately, since the Modern Language Association and the Association of Departments of English gave their sanction to the study of Indian literatures a few years ago, writers like Momaday, Silko, Welch, Erdrich and a few others have not been able to write fast enough to keep us busy with contemporary literature. Thus generally ignoring other contemporary Indian writers as well as writers before 1968, we turned to "the oral tradition," as we call it, and worked it hard as a subject, "to the detriment," says Robert Allen Warrior, "of serious engagement with more theoretical work by Native intellectuals."[36]

While there has been some excellent scholarship, especially concerning the forms of oral literatures and the influence of oral traditions in contemporary writing, some of us have gone some strange ways. The academy, for example, particularly the "ethnopoets" among us, still gives legitimacy to the activities of Gary Snyder and his white shamanist descendants. Leslie Marmon Silko and Geary Hobson have described their work as "cultural imperialism," while John Bierhorst, on the other hand, claims that Snyder and others contributed to the formation of "a permanent channel of influence from the Native literatures to the Euroamerican" and "were among the first to rescue" Indian narrative "from balladry."[37] At MLA in 1986 in a session called "Native Oral Texts: Interpretations and Transcriptions," I heard one presenter say that he did not need to know a native language to "translate" a text. At MLA in 1988 in a session on our responsibilities as scholars in dealing with sacred matters (whatever that means), I listened to a speaker for twenty minutes and heard no mention of a literary text, oral or written. If she had a prepared paper, she got sidetracked in a digression on her study of sand paintings and the weird experiences she began to have. I have to admit that I did not hear the end of the presentation, for I left when she got to the point where lightning struck her car. Such activities give credence to the charge by Elizabeth Cook-Lynn that "too many scholars seem to be intellectualizing their own personal traumas in search of recognition or integrity or, perhaps, a tenured faculty position."[38]

Another example is a project underway called "Contemporary Translations of Native American Literatures of North America," designed to produce an anthology to be published by Random House in 1993. The purpose of the book, we are told, is "to give a sense of variety, scope, excellence, and excitement of Native American literatures, scattering stereotypes, opening minds, expanding the meaning of 'literature.'"[39] It would be difficult, I think, to convince Indians that it will do all of those things and that it might not, in fact, do the opposite of some. The editor has called for submissions of translations or "re-translations." In many instances, this last term is a code word for a non-Indian's "proper" English rendering of a native translator's literal translation of an oral text dictated to a nineteenth- or twentieth-century non-Indian ethnologist by an Indian who may or may not have had the authority to divulge the text and who may or may not have known all parts of it. Of late, it has also come to refer to a "re-translation," as poetry, of an earlier non-Indian's prose rendering of a native translator's literal translation, etc.[40] One certainly does not need to know the native language to do that sort of "translating." As Leslie Marmon Silko has written, "White poets use the term 'translation' very loosely when applied to Asian or Native American material; few, if any of them, are conversant in the Asian or Native American languages they pretend to 'translate.' What they do is sit down and rearrange English transcriptions done by ethnologists and then call this a 'translation.'" Silko would have "songs and stories which were taken by ethnographers" considered in the same light as "religious objects and other property" that rightly belong to native peoples.[41] Brian Swann, editor of the newly released *On the Translation of Native American Literatures,* acknowledges the "moral and political dimensions" of "translation" as well as the implications of cultural appropriation. He also acknowledges scholarly criticism of the "translators'" activities. Then he writes, "On a related issue, I regret not having any Native American scholars represented here. I contacted all I knew, but no one had any work appropriate for this volume."[42] That statement has probably caused no surprise in American Indian circles.

Unfortunately, with the opening of the American literary canon, we can expect more "translating." No wonder American Indians say that what we do has little or no relation to them, the texts in many cases being removed at least two, and sometimes three or more times, from contextual reality. They would probably say that much of it would be silly if it were not so dangerous. The danger in anthologies of such "translations" is that they can not account sufficiently for cultural and linguistic differences. Anthologies, by their nature, provide limited explanations of contexts because of limited space. A quick survey reveals a chilling sameness about the pieces commonly reprinted in anthologies of American Indian literatures. Readers with little experience in such literatures may read a "translation" or "re-translation," thinking they have a genuine work, not realizing it may be several steps removed from the native teller. Thus we become guilty of the Indians' charge of contributing to stereotyping. Indeed, Swann writes of his collection,

> I set out to include essays from and on all the Americas, for there is only one native America, one thought, one spirit, from Tahuantisuyo and points south, to Hochelaga and points north, and all points in between. And there is a unity to the literatures, from the 'literary' tradition of the Aztec Brotherhood's great court poetry and other Central and South American 'high art' to the four-line chants of the Midewiwin or the complex Navajo Chantways.[43]

So much for cultural, social and historical differences in peoples.

Relieving readers of the burden of accounting for the literature in a cultural context makes it easier to discuss it in what the Indians call the "lit-crit speak tropes" of Western literary criticism.[44] We also relieve the reader of the burden of tribal or Indian national history. Thus it is easy to force the literature into traditional Western historical constructs so that it becomes what we want it to be or think it should be. For Indians, the spectre of appropriation remains. Simon Ortiz has said in relation to ethnopoetics,

> There are a number of people who are utilizing indigenous cultures, not just Native American cultures but African cultures. They use themes or characters, Coyote, or Native American images which have particular reference to philosophical and religious ceremonies which are very visual and so easily used, and often times wrongly. And if it's wrong, it's probably exploitative. . . . And there has to be waged a struggle, and a very serious concern about misinformation and exploitation; exploitation means discrimination, racism, and domination over subject people, subject culture, and language.[45]

Indian writers are confronted by a dilemma: should they seek admission to the American canon or not? Our efforts to bring American Indian literatures into the canon are viewed by some Indian intellectuals as an ultimate act of colonialism because those efforts smack of appropriation. However, opinion varies widely among Indian writers on the matter. Louise Erdrich and N. Scott Momaday, for instance, have no difficulties viewing American Indian literatures as a part of American literature. Others are not willing to go that far. Most readily acknowledge a debt of literary influence to American, European, Asian and Third World writers, yet they believe that their literature is distinct in, the use of language and the themes it portrays. Most believe that those themes, which make publishers uncomfortable because of guilt or a lack of understanding, have made it difficult for them to find outlets for their work. They acknowledge that critical reviews and literary scholarship are a vital gear in the machine that drives the publishing industry. And, as Andrew Wiget has pointed out, they must deal with the realities of Anglo publishers and audiences, whether they admit it or not. They want their works debated and analyzed, yet most feel that we have in large measure misread and misinterpreted their works because of our ignorance of American Indian cultures.[46]

Now that we are debating the issue of canon, they grow wary because it appears that if we are finally to admit American Indian literatures, we will insist that it be done on our own terms. In early July, the University of Oklahoma was host to "Returning the Gift," the largest gathering ever of indigenous writers from Canada, the United States and Middle America. In a plenary session titled "Entering the Canons—Our Place in World Literature," certain allegations recurred: American scholars are engaged in "intellectual elitism;" canon as we refer to it in current scholarship is the "official line," a gauge used to exclude Indian writers because we do not like the message they deliver; and words like *center* and *margin* are earmarks of colonialist criticism. Robert Allen Warrior has responded to Arnold Krupat's *The Voice in the Margin,* one of the best-known arguments for opening the canon to American Indian literatures, this way:

> We need scholars to respect the integrity and continuity of American Indian literature, both historical and contemporary, as a literature of resistance to colonialism, and to compare it to other literatures of resistances, whether African-American, African, or Arab. We would learn a tremendous amount about our own literature by doing so, but not as long as Native American literature "belongs" to the national literature of the United States."[47]

When some of my writer friends told me a few years ago that they did not want American Indian literatures considered a part of American literature, I did not fully understand why. I do now. As long as we can appropriate Indians as subjects and deal with them on our own terms, we can effectively avoid explaining the extreme unemployment and poverty at Pine Ridge or the Indian bars on Franklin Avenue in Minneapolis. One of the demands that Indian intellectuals are making not only of us but of each other is that scholarly work need not be divorced from, but rather should be relevant to, the writers' contemporary conditions and should address issues concerning them.[48] As Warrior says,

> In spite of a general acceptance among American Indian scholars and non-Native Americanists that various research enterprises involving American Indians make little sense outside a wide interdisciplinary purview, few critics have connected the written creative output of their subjects with those subjects' concomitant specific relationships to Native political, cultural, and social history.[49]

"Returning the Gift" reiterated this demand through its consensus that the work of indigenous writers of America must contribute to the ongoing worldwide struggle against racism and economic, political, educational and literary colonialism. The literature they produce does not "belong" to America. It belongs to them and has its rightful place among other literatures of the world, including American. What M. Annette Jaimes wrote in 1985 is being reasserted today in louder, more insistent voices. What American Indians insist upon, she said, is "the articulation of native American perspectives *vis-a-vis* the content of various disciplines and without adherence to the academic structures specific to those disciplines (e.g., Native American philosophy is philosophy in its own right, and not by virtue of a juxtaposition to the philosophy of Plato or Hegel)."[50] Thus American Indian literature is literature in its own right, not by virtue of its juxtaposition to American literature. Persistence in this direction, however, has its dangers. As Kenneth Roemer has said, "A consistent emphasis in the separateness—the differentness—of Indian literatures can lead to equally serious academic and ethical problems: forms of literary ghettoization and tokenism, or, to borrow Peter Carafiol's phrase, transformations of tokens into totems."[51]

The future for scholarship concerning American Indians promises to be interesting. Those of us involved in American Indian literary studies can not expect our paths to be as smooth as they have been. Indian critics no longer hesitate to write devastating reviews of our work as Ward Churchill has done of Clifton's and Gill's works, calling them, respectively, "pseudo-scholarship in the guise of legitimate academic exposition" and "one of the shoddier historiographical exercises in living memory."[52] The Hopis have demonstrated that they can do considerable damage to a scholar's reputation by simply declaring that he is no longer an authority on their culture. How many of us could withstand this kind of devastating criticism or that which has been turned on the anthropologists and historians? It appears that our time has come, and we shall find out Churchill, for example, has asked about Michael Castro's *Interpreting the Indian*—whether Castro "was in fact even conversant enough with the topic to presume the writing of a book on it."[53] The only good thing William Willard could find about Andrea Lerner's *Dancing on the Rim of the World* was its title. To his review the editor of the journal added this note: "This anthology comes from the highly touted 'SunTracks' series, University of Arizona, Tucson, which gives rise-to further speculation concerning the responsibilities of university publishing houses."[54] *Wicazo Sa Review,* in commentary on Hertha Wong's *Sending My Heart Back Across the Years,* charged that Wong's claim to Indian heritage was "wannabe sentiment which clutters an otherwise tolerable piece of redundant scholarship."[55] We can expect not only continued but increased monitoring and response to our scholarly efforts. One of the missions of the American Indian Professoriate, established in February 1992, is to "serve as a resource, clearing house, evaluative body for scholarly work, text books, trade books, and other media that relate to American Indians."[56] Other Indian watchdog groups as well have been established recently to monitor what is written and said about Indians.[57]

We can also expect to be engaged in debate on issues relating to American Indian literatures. American Indians are experiencing a sense of empowerment through their scholarly journals, popular print and other media, and literature. Robert Allen Warrior has called on American Indian intellectuals to commit themselves to a struggle for "intellectual sovereignty." That sovereignty will be achieved in part, he says, through the study of Indian writers:

> Though the production of critical literature about these writers remains overwhelmingly the domain of non-Native critics, a growing number of American Indian intellectuals are realizing that American Indians must produce criticism as well as literature if the work of Native poets and novelists is not to become merely one more part of American Indian existence to be dissected and divvied up between white "experts."[58]

The "good ol' girl" and "good ol' boy" system has prevailed too long in academic scholarship regarding American Indian literatures. Too often, we look for complementing, not conflicting, ideas in formation of panels at conferences, thus reducing debate. Too often, we let jargon-filled, poorly reasoned presentations go unquestioned. This system may change if Indian intellectuals take up Warrior's challenge and return to our meetings. As Warrior has said elsewhere, "Anyone who has been part of an academic society that includes study of American Indian cultures is acquainted with the tensions and sometimes outright hostility that the growing number of American Indian scholars in such societies has produced."[59]

Warrior's statement might be seen as further evidence of what others have called "the growing movement among American Indians to wrest control of their cultural identity and history from non-Indians."[60] In a review essay on books by and about American Indians, James R. Kincaid recently raised an important question, "Who gets to tell their stories?"[61] But to reduce the controversy between Indian intellectuals and American scholars to a question of race is unfair to Indian intellectuals. They simply appear more willing than in times past to engage in scholarly debate. The question is not who tells the stories but *how* the stories are told. The latter, at least, has been the crux of complaints that Indian intellectuals have had against us. We must respond.

The focus on our points of difference will be more defined, I believe, as the debate on the American literary canon and political correctness continues. Therefore, I welcome the debate. It will force each of us, as it has in the past, to take stock and reconsider what we do. For one thing, each of us must decide if we care what opinions Indians have of what we write or say about them. I do. As one involved in creating the *Heath Anthology of American Literature,* I must ask myself if, despite our best intentions in creating the anthology, we were not guilty of some of the charges the Indians have made against us. I must wrestle with myself on this issue as I work with the other editors on a second edition. I wonder, for instance, if we should not change the first two sections, which we have designated as the colonial period to 1700 and to 1800, to *European* colonial period to 1800. Then, if we must keep such historical organization, perhaps we should add somewhere in the anthology two more sections, *American* colonial period to 1900 and American colonial period since 1900 and put American Indian and, possibly, Chicano/Chicana literatures in those sections. While we may be uncertain about the directions the debate on the canon may take, we can be certain of one point. We will never return to where we were in American Indian scholarship before the debate began. Those of us who remain in the field of Indian studies, and those who consider entering it, should understand that the game we are now playing is a new one with rules that are constantly changing, that the Indians expect to be players, and that they know as much about the rules as we do.

---

[1] By *we*, here and below, I mean American scholars, American Indian as well as non-Indian, who are products of Western educational philosophies and whose scholarly research and writing and teaching relate to American Indians.

[2] Oren Lyons, et al., "Traditionalism and the Reassertion of Indianness," in *Indian Self-Rule: First-Hand Accounts of Indian-White Relations from Roosevelt to Reagan*, ed. Kenneth R. Philp (Salt Lake City, 1986), 244.

[3] Elizabeth Cook-Lynn, "The Radical Conscience in Native American Studies," *Wicazo Sa Review* 7 (Fall 1991), 12.

[4] Phillip S. Deloria, "The Era of Indian Self-Determination: An Overview," in *Indian Self Rule*, 206-207.

[5] R. Robert Buffalohead, "Self-Rule in the Past and the Future: An Overview," in *Indian Self-Rule*, 276.

[6] Deloria, "The Era of Indian Self-Determination," 203.

[7] Ibid., 195-196, 202-203, 205.

[8] Some good examples, however, are W. David Baird, "Are There 'Real' Indians in Oklahoma? Historical Perceptions of the Five Civilized Tribes," *Chronicle of*

Oklahoma 68 (Spring 1990), 4-23; William T. Hagan, "Full Blood, Mixed Blood, Generic, and Ersatz: The Problem of Indian Identity," *Arizona and the West* 27 (Winter 1985), 309-26; Terry P. Wilson, "Osage Oxonian: The Heritage of John Joseph Mathews," *Chronicles of Oklahoma* 59 (Fall 1981), 264-293; James A. Clifton, ed., *Being and Becoming Indian: Biographical Studies of North American Frontiers* (Chicago, 1989); James A. Clifton, ed., *The Invented Indian: Cultural Fictions and Government Policies* (New Brunswick, New Jersey, 1990).

9 See e.g., Bea Medicine, "*Hanta Yo*: A New Phenomenon," *Indian Historian* 12 (Summer 1979), 2-5; "*Hanta Yo*: A Gross Insult Offered to Indian People," *Wassaja/The Indian Historian* 13 (Fourth Quarter 1980), 15-23; "Pale Moon Gets the Boot, Can't Prove She's Indian," *Lakota Times* (March 11, 1992); "Time to Clip Wings of False Shamans," *Lakota Times* (April 15, 1992).

10 See e.g., Ward Churchill, "American Indian Art and Artists in Search of a Definition," *Spirit of Crazy Horse* (December/January 1992); Churchill, "Nobody's Pet Poodle. Jimmie Durham: An Artist for Native North America," *Indigenous Thought* 1 (October 1991), 9-11; Lee C. Woodward, "Who's Protecting Who from Artist Impostors?" *Muscogee Nation News* 20 (April 1991), 2.

11 Rodney Simard, "American Indian Literatures, Authenticity, and the Canon," *World Literature Today* 66 (Spring 1992), 243-248.

12 Joseph Bruchac, ed., *Survival This Way: Interviews with American Indian Poets* (Tucson, 1987); Laura Coltelli, ed., *Winged Words: American Indian Writers Speak* (Lincoln, Nebraska, 1990); Brian Swann and Arnold Krupat, eds., *I Tell You Now: Autobiographical Essays by Native American Writers* (Lincoln, Nebraska, 1987). See also Terry Wilson, "Osage Oxonian," 267-268; Geary Hobson, "Remembering the Earth," in *The Remembered Earth: An Anthology of Contemporary Native American Literature*, ed. Hobson (Albuquerque, 1979), 8-10; Matthias Shubnell, *N. Scott Momaday: The Cultural and Literary Background* (Norman, Oklahoma, 1985), 3-11.

13 See Clifton, "Alternative Identities and Cultural Frontiers," in *Being and Becoming Indian*; Clifton, ed., *The Invented Indian*.

14 Ward Churchill, "The New Racism: A Critique of James A. Clifton's *The Invented Indian*," *Wicazo Sa Review* 7 (Spring 1991), 51-59.

15 "Remarks made by Doug Olson, P.A.R.R. Convention, 28-29 March 1987," and "Comments from the PARR Conference, March 28-29," in PARR file, American Native Press Archives, University of Arkansas at Little Rock; "Congress Draggin' on Treaty Decisions" and "Treaty Supporters Pickett PARR," *Wausau Daily Herald* (March 29, 1987); "Anti-treaty Group to Fight 'Discrimination,'" Ashland, Wisconsin *Daily Press* (March 30, 1987); James H. Schlender, "Treaty Rights in Wisconsin: A Review," *Northeast Indian Quarterly* 8 (Spring 1991), 4-16; "American Farm Bureau Votes to Eliminate Native American Rights," *News from Indian Country* 6 (Late June 1992), 7; Ellen K. Couglin, "Historical Association Issues Statement Deploring Efforts to Deny Holocaust," *Chronicle of Higher Education* 30 (January 8, 1992), A6.

16 M. Annette Jaimes, "American Indian Studies: An Overview and Prospectus," *Wicazo Sa Review* (Fall 1985), 15-18.

[17] William Willard and Mary Kay Downing, "American Indian Studies and Inter-Cultural Education," *Wicazo Sa Review* 7 (Fall 1991), 6.

[18] Cook-Lynn, "The Radical Conscience in Native American Studies," 11-12.

[19] Chris Raymond, "Dispute Between Scholar, Tribe Leaders Over Book on Hopi Ritual Raises Concern about Censorship of Studies of American Indians," *Chronicle of Higher Education* 37 (October 17, 1990), A6, A8; the Hopi spokesperson is quoted from A8.

[20] Raymond, "Dispute Between Scholar, Tribe Leaders Over Book," A8, A9.

[21] See e.g., David Wilkins, "Who's in Charge of U.S. Indian Policy? Congress and the Supreme Court at Loggerheads over American Indian Religious Freedom," *Wicazo Sa Review* 8 (Spring 1992), 40-64; Mark A Michaels and Tonya Gonella Fricher, "War Declared on Religious Freedoms," *Native Nations* 1 (February 1991), 30-31; Vine Deloria, "Sacred Lands and Religious Freedom," *NARF Legal Review* 16 (Summer 1991), 1-16; Walter Echo-Hawk, "Loopholes in Religious Liberty: The Need for a Federal Law to Protect Freedom of Worship for Native People," NARF *Legal Review* 16 (Summer 1991), 7-21; Henrietta Mann, "Indian Religious Freedom Under Attack," *Indian Affairs* 124 (Summer/Fall 1991), 1-3; Dean Chavers, "Protecting Indian Religions," *C'oeur d'Alene Council Fires* (November 27, 1991); Patricia Locke, "A Human Rights Crisis," *News from Indian Country* 6 (Late January 1992), 18.

[22] See e.g., Avis Little Eagle, "Lakota Rituals Being Sold," *Lakota Times* (July 2, 1991); Little Eagle, "Medicine Men for Rent," *Lakota Times* (July 9, 1991); Little Eagle, "Sacred Pipe Keeper Fears Feds Will Step In," *Lakota Times* (July 17, 1991); Little Eagle, "'False Prophets Will Suffer,'" *Lakota Times* (July 31, 1991); Little Eagle, "Oh Shinnah; Prophet for Profit," *Lakota Times* (August 7, 1991); Little Eagle, "Paid Ads Call Her 'Medicine Woman,'" *Lakota Times* (August 14, 1991); Little Eagle, "Sun Dances Take Place on Artificial Turf," *Lakota Times* (August 21,1991); Little Eagle, "Is Lame Deer Society of Europe Real?" *Lakota Times* (August 28, 1991); Little Eagle, "'Spiritual Orphans' Peddle Religion in Great Round," *Lakota Times* (January 21, 1992); Larry Cesspooch, "It's Popular to Be 'Indian' Nowadays," *Bah-Koh-Je Journal* 3 (December 1991), 5; Ward Churchill, "Spiritual Hucksterism: The Rise of the Plastic Medicine Men," in *Anthology of HONOR* (Milwaukee, 1992), 27-31.

[23] Edward M. Savilla, "An Interview with Floyd Red Crow Westerman," *News From Indian Country* 5 (Mid-December 1991), 8; "Letters to the Editor," *Turtle Quarterly* 4 (Spring/Summer 1991), 56.

[24] See e.g., Tim Giago, "Ignorance Follows Indians Everywhere" and "Columnists Should 'Dance with Facts!'" *Char-Koosta News* (January18,1991 and April 12, 1991), respectively; Tanis Thorne's review of Calvin Martin, *The American Indian and the Problem of History in American Indian Culture and Research Journal* 11 (1987), 131-135; Thomas Biolski, "Review Article: 'The American Indian and the Problem of Culture'" on the same work in *American Indian Quarterly* 13 (Summer 1989), 261-269; Ward Churchill, "Sam Gill's *Mother Earth*: Colonialism, Genocide and the Expropriation of Indigenous Spiritual Tradition in Contemporary Academia," in *American Indian Culture and Research Journal* 12 (1988), 49-84; Churchill, "Interpreting the American Indian: A Critique of Michael Castro's Apologia," *Wicazo Sa Review* 1 (Fall 1985), 24-31.

[25] Lakota Times (February 26, 1992).

[26] See e.g., "15 New Native American PTV Projects Funded by NAPBC," *Winds of Change* 6 (Fall 1991), 10; Avis Little Eagle, "KILI Celebrates 9 Years," *Lakota Times* (March 4, 1992); "New Center Set Up in Rio," and "Native Radio Station Planned in Anchorage," *Medium Rare* (Spring/Summer 1992); "Plans Laid for Native Radio Network," *News from Indian Country* 6 (Mid-July 1992), 8.

[27] See e.g., Beverly Slapin and Doris Seale, eds., *Books Without Bias: Through Indian Eyes* (Berkeley, 1988); Slapin, ed., *Through Indian Eyes: The Native Experience in Books for Children* (Santa Cruz, CA, 1991); Slapin, et al., *How To Tell The Difference: A Checklist for Evaluating Children's Books for Anti-Indian Bias* (Berkeley, 1988); Doug Ferguson, "Harjo: 'Stereotypes Must End,'" *News from Indian Country* 6 (Mid-July 1992), 3; Cynthia-Lou Coleman, "National Conference Focuses on Stereotypes and Media," *News from Indian Country* 6 (Late July 1992), 4.

[28] For examples of cartooning, see *Akwesasne Notes* 21 (Spring 1989), 18, 25, and "John Kahionhes Guilty of Stereotyping Eurocentric Scholars," *Indigenous Thought* 1 (October 1991), 27. A recent example of sophisticated satire is Beverly Slapin's *Basic Skills Caucasian Americans Workbook* (Berkeley, 1990). An example of what might be in store for American scholars in a public forum occurred on the Oneida Reservation in Wisconsin on April 30, 1992, when Wilcomb Washburn defended Columbus as a national hero before members of Native American Journalists Association. He was given a blistering response by Suzan Shown Harjo, whose best line perhaps was "Older white males are afraid of the 'browning of America." She could well have substituted "American scholars" for "older white males."

[29] I am indebted to Creek writer Alexander Posey (1873-1908) for the grapeshot-rhinoceros image.

[30] Jaimes, "American Indian Studies," 19.

[31] Daniel F. Littlefield, Jr., "The Native Press as History," Native American Journalists Association, Green Bay, Wisconsin, April 30,1992.

[32] See e.g., "Stanford Anthropologist Claims Possession of Indian Remains," *Akwesasne Notes* 21 (Summer 1989), 22; "Repatriation Act Protects Native Burial Remains and Artifacts," *NARF Legal Review* 16 (Winter 1990), 1-4; Madeleine Jacobs, "NMAI's New Repatriation Policy," *Smithsonian Runner* 91 (May/June 1991), 1,4,6; Robert McC, Adams, "Cultural Patrimony," in *Anthology of HONOR*, 14-15; "Repatriation = Protection of Our Ancestors: Interview with Michael B. Haney, United Indian Nations of Oklahoma," *Spirit of Crazy Horse* (December/January 1992); Jose Barreiro, ed., *Indian Roots of American Democracy* (Ithaca, New York 1988); "Williamsburg Conference Anthropologists Challenge Confederacy," *Akwesane Notes* 21 (Spring 1989), 18; Donald A. Grinde, Jr., "Iroquoian Political Concept and the Genesis of American Government: Further Research and Contentions," *Northeast Indian Quarterly* 6 (Winter 1989), 10-21.

[33] 1Robert Chadbourne, "Native Americans Revisited," *Wilson Library Bulletin* 65 (June 1991), 22-23; Pamela Stillman, "Educators Demand History Be Rewritten," *Lakota Times* (August 12, 1992).

[34] Chris Raymond, "Growth of Scholarship on American Indians Brings New Insights about Native Cultures," *Chronicle of Higher Education* 38 (January 15, 1992), A8, A10; the quote is from A8.

[35] Buffalohead, "Self-Rule in the Past and the Future," 276.

[36] Robert Allen Warrior, "Reading American Indian Intellectual Traditions," *World Literature Today* 66 (Spring 1992), 239.

[37] Leslie Marmon Silko, "An Old-Time Indian Attack Conducted in Two Parts. Part One: Imitation 'Indian' Poems; Part Two: Gary Snyder's Turtle Island," in *The Remembered Earth* 211-216; Hobson, "The Rise of the White Shaman as a New Version of Cultural Imperialism," in *The Remembered Earth*, ed., Hobson, 100-108; John Bierhorst, "Incorporating the Native Voice: A Look Back from 1990," in *On the Tradition of Native American Literatures*, ed. Brian Swann (Washington, D.C., 1992), 53, 54.

[38] Elizabeth Cook-Lynn, "Commentary," *Wicazo Sa Review* 8 (Spring 1992), 104.

[39] See "Calls," *ASAIL Notes* 9 (November 1991), 10.

[40] Brian Swann, "Introduction," in *On the Translation of Native American Literatures*, ed. Swan (Washington D.C., 1992), xix, n. 3.

[41] Silko, "An Old Time Indian Attack Conducted in Two Parts," 212.

[42] Swann, "Introduction," xiv-xvii, xix.

[43] Swann, "Introduction," xvii.

[44] Willard and Downing, "American Indian Studies and Inter-Cultural Education," 6.

[45] Coltelli, ed., *Winged Words*, 111-112.

[46] For comments on one or all of these issues, see e.g., Coltelli's interviews with Paula Gunn Allen, Louise Erdrich, Joy Jarjo, Linda Hogan, N. Scott Momaday, Simon Ortiz, Wendy Rose, 95-96, 98, 114-116, 130-132, 177-178, 196; Andrew Wiget, "Identity, Voice, and Authority: Artist-Audience Relations in Native American Literature," *World Literature Today* 66 (Spring 1992), 260.

[47] Warrior, "A Marginal Voice," *Native Nations* (1991), 30, quoted from Willard and Downing, "American Indian Studies and Inter-Cultural Education," 2.

[48] See e.g., Philip Deloria, "The Era of Indian Self-Determination," 207; Willard and Downing, "American Indian Studies and Inter-Cultural Education," 5; Owanah Anderson, "Squanto...Tonto...and Geronimo," in *Anthology of HONOR*, 9-13; Tim Giago, "The Hard Poetry of Reservation Living," *Lakota Times* July 29,1992.

[49] Warrior, "Reading American Indian Intellectual Traditions," 236.

[50] Jaimes, "American Indian Studies," 18.

[51] Kenneth M. Roemer, "The Heuristic Powers of Indian Literatures: What Native Authorship Does to Mainstream Texts," *Studies in American India Literatures* 3 (Summer 1991), 8.

[52] Churchill, "The New Racism," 53; Churchill, "Sam Gill's *Mother Earth*," 58.

[53] Churchill, "Interpreting the American Indian," 31.

[54] William Willard, "Review: *Dancing on the Rim of the World: An Anthology of Contemporary Northwest Native American Writing*," *Wicazo Sa Review* 7 (Spring 1991), 63-64, 65.

[55] Cook-Lynn, "Commentary," 104.

[56] "Mission Statement of the American Indian Professoriate," *Wicazo Sa Review* 8 (Spring 1992), 103.

[57] "Accuracy in Textbooks Demanded by Natives," *New from Indian Country* 6 (Late July 1992), 3; "Indian Anti-Defamation Council Formed," *Notes From Indian Country*, 5 (Mid-December 1991), 1.

[58] Warrior, "Intellectual Sovereignty and the Struggle for an American Indian Future," *Wicazo Sa Review* 8 (Spring 1992), 9.

[59] Warrior, "Reading American Indian Intellectual Traditions," 239.

[60] Raymond, "Dispute Between Scholar, Tribe Leaders Over Book," A6.

[61] James R. Kincaid, "Who Gets to Tell Their Stories?" *New York Times Book Review* (May 3, 1992).

PART III

AFRICAN AMERICAN IMAG(E)ING IN SCIENCE AND LETTERS

Essays in this section are about the only population forced to migrate to the Americas to be servants and slaves. When they reached these shores, members of the varied African ethnic groups had bound within them memories of the traditions and values of the respective societies from which they originated. Scholars of the African Diaspora have conducted extensive studies documenting the continuing influences of African cultural traditions among Africans in the British North American colonies. Thus, the myth of the *tabula rasa* effect on the beleaguered African captives has been negated. This makes it normative for one to ask, as has been done in the Native American essays, about the impact of the eurocentric culture on the traditions and values of this non-European people, who experienced America differently than did their white counterparts.

In the first essay in this section, Joseph Scott—an African American sociologist—makes the interesting assertion that that different experience has made "mainstream" scientific method of research and analysis irrelevant when appropriated for the study of black peoples. He raises and addresses questions that give his essay an Afrocentric focus: What is the relevance of the scientific method for black research conducted on the black experience? What have been the limitations of the application of the scientific method when applied to Blacks in the past?

Scott answers these questions by analyzing several "white-expcrience" models, showing their irrelevance to Blacks and proposing alternative models based on the black experience. In addition, he analyzes the black experience with the scientific establishment. Given the present status of race relations, many of these theoretical and clinical concerns still confront professionals who set policies which affect the more than thirty million African Americans who presently live in the United States. His essay is particularly compelling because Scott argues that the social policy derived from scientific studies impacts black self-improvement and nation-building.

Scott's images of black folk experiencing America provides a useful background of perspective for the second essay, which is a humanities-oriented analysis by Dorothy Denniston of Paule Marshall's novel, *Brown Girl, Brownstones.* Denniston provides a feminist (womanist) perspective on the saga of black immigrants (Barbadians) whose traditional social values are tested in the European-centered culture of the United States, despite benefits of Barbadian-group solidarity. It is particularly fitting to include an essay on the Barbadian-immigrant community. Of all American Diasporic blacks, they have the longest association with Africans in North America. This is particularly so of descendants of the earliest Africans, for Barbados was the primary source of slaves for Virginia, South Carolina and other early, seventeenth-century English colonies, although the masses of Barbadians and black Americans outside the academy may not be apprised of this fact. The significance of the Barbadian presence in the United States is even more telling when one realizes that these folk comprise only part of a larger West Indian-immigrant population that presently numbers more than 350,000.

In this essay, Denniston enables us to understand what Marshall has to say about the lives, culture, and aspirations of Barbadian, female immigrants and their descendants in the United States. Fittingly, Marshall is the daughter of Barbadian immigrants. As Denniston presents her analysis of Marshall's insider's view of the Barbadian immigrant community, she reminds us that class and other variables contribute to the diversity among Afro-Americans.

When compared, what do these essays suggest about differences in how native-born Blacks and immigrant-Blacks, such as Barbadians, experience life in the United States? What, if anything, do these differences infer about the value systems and diversity in the historical experiences of these two peoples? Do these essays indicate that one group is more assimilated than the other? Can/How can these groups be factored into a pluralistic mode within the United States?

Black Science, Black Self-Improvement and Black Nation-Building

Joseph Scott
Department of American Ethnic Studies & Sociology, University of Washington

The Afrocentrizing of scientific methods in the interest of the black American's future is inescapable, if these folk are to achieve some degree of control over the physical and social forces that determine their life-chances and quality of life. Their individual betterment and community development require that they use scientific methods. To exploit the natural resources of their territories and manage the economic, social, political, and psychological forces that make the American Dream possible, they must use science.

Science has been defined in two ways:

1. as a set of methods and techniques and
2. as a body of facts, theories and models.[1]

In methodological terms, science has been one of the essential ways human beings have come to know about the empirical world when they find it oppressive or unhealthy. What makes scientific knowl-edge different from intuitive knowledge is scientific knowledge supposedly is objective and verifiable. To this end, social scientists use random sampling techniques, experimental designs, and inferential statistics to reach their generalizations. The body of knowledge derived by these

---

Reprinted by permission of the author.

methods is supposed to be empirical and value-free. If this were true, Blacks would have to move quickly to use all available scientific methods and knowledge to advance themselves. But, the foregoing is not true.

There is a big problem with the wholesale adoption of current scientific methods and models. Today when Blacks apply these theories and models, they are finding that they have been developed exclusively out of the white experience and that they do not illuminate the black experience. In fact, they often make Blacks look bad and explain neither black advancement nor the lack of it. Using these white-experience norms leads to denigrating conclusions about Blacks. To be specific, these methods and models presume that Blacks lived in a racially open society rather than a racially closed one. Thus, the methods and models invariably conclude that the lower achievement of Blacks is a function of either less effort, or less innate capability, or cultural deficits. This conclusion is a self-perpetuating one promulgated by white behavioral scientists through their methods and models.

What usually is hidden is the fact that this pool of so-called scientific knowledge is disproportionally about the male, white, and middle-class experience. For example, most "attitude" tests, "intelligence" tests, health-quality tests, and public opinion polls have been exclusively "developed," "normed," and "validated" on white people—particularly white males. Even white women complain about the continual gender bias of the scientific establishment. Statistical curves, like the bell curve, which supposedly "represent" the response patterns of all human beings really are representations of white people's responses. Current, social science theories of government, economics, education, personality, and intelligence almost exclusively describe the dominant white culture and experience.

Given that this is true, black people should treat the current tests, theories, and models as either invalid or as scientifically limited in that they have applicability to white people only. Black people should understand that the scientific establishment of the United States has not stood apart from the politics of racial exclusion and bias of this society. The scientific establishment's claims that it uses value-free methods and that it gathers unbiased facts are contradicted by the facts. Take the Tuskegee Syphilis Experiment for example.[2] This is an irrefutable case in point: The American medical science establishment wanted to learn about the natural history of syphilis. So a group of medical scientists selected two hundred poor, black male sharecroppers and deceived them into believing that they had "bad blood."[3] They carried on this experiment from 1932 to 1972. The scientists deliberately neglected to treat and cure the Blacks so the scientific establishment could obtain information about the development and ravages of syphilis in the human body. The result was that the black men suffered needlessly, died agonizingly, and transmitted to others a disease that was treatable.

Is the scientific establishment behind other genocidal studies? Consider the recent published bell curve study that stereotypically suggests the intellectual inferiority of Blacks. This study that one of its investigative principals, Charles Murray, purports to be scientifically and objectively based could have genocidal ramifications in the black communities, for it contains theory for social engineering that would further marginalize and disadvantage Blacks. Accordingly, black people have no other choice but to take an extreme skeptic's view of any so-called scientific methods and knowledge derived by the current scientific-research establishment. Black people must realize that any scientific methods and knowledge which harm and kill black people exclusively have to be morally bankrupt and just plain biased.

Eurocentrically-oriented science derives from the white historical experience, which has been at variance with black reality. In the United States, Whites have been neither slaves nor peons for more than three hundred and seventy-five years as Blacks have been. Whites have not been statutorially disfranchised for hundreds of years as Blacks have been. Whites have never been legally defined as chattel, commodified, bought and sold as Blacks have been. Whites have never been subject to state-sponsored terrorism, exploitation, and denial of life, liberty, property, and happiness as Blacks have been. In short, since the white experience and the black experience have been polar opposites, how could white-experience theories, models and generalizations about government, economics, education, personality, or intelligence be applicable to black Americans? White-experience concepts and models might be heuristic, but they can hardly be "good-fits" for the black experience. White-experience behaviors may parallel in form behaviors of the black experience, but that fact alone does not say they mean the same thing and are "caused" by the same social, economic, political, or racial experiences. Blacks can truly say that "their Blues ain't like our Blues." What this indicates is that "Blues" as metaphor for Whites is quite different from "Blues" as metaphor for Blacks. The metaphoric meanings and functions of the "Blues" are very different.[4]

To claim that the white-experience models are good models for the black experience is fraudulent science. Theories and models which apply to Blacks must of necessity be representations of the perceptions and behaviors of Blacks. Take the O.J. Simpson case, for example: By and large, Blacks and Whites have diametrically opposed perceptions of his guilt and the possibility that former detective Fuhrman planted the bloody glove to frame Simpson. Take the claims that the past U.S. foreign wars have been fought "to preserve freedom and democracy for all Americans." No matter how often Whites say these wars were intended to secure freedom and democracy for all Americans, Blacks know that these claims are vacuous. Blacks know that throughout all of these foreign wars (World War I, World War II, the Korean War, and the Vietnam War), they experienced the continued abridgment of their freedoms and opportunities all the while they were fighting. To this day, black folk know that their opportunities for advancement in the military, and in society in general, were curtailed for racial reasons.

Right now, as I write this essay, cadres of white political and civic leaders are rolling back Affirmative Action legislation and the civil rights gains of the 1960s and 1970s for racial reasons. Right now Blacks know that virtually every such policy change that maximizes the jobs and profits of Whites diminishes the same for Blacks. Blacks also know that shrinking the number of government employees disproportionately disemploys black people while disproportionately retaining white people. Blacks are correct when they say: "Their Blues ain't like our Blues."

If the research that has been conducted on white people and interpreted from the white-experience viewpoint was conducted on blacks and interpreted from the black-experience viewpoint, almost every contemporary model and theory in the behavioral sciences would have to be modified. Let me give you a few examples of white-experience theories and models which are inapplicable to the black experience. Consider first an assimilation theory. Robert Park, a white sociologist, believed his claim that the white-experience model properly reflected race relations in the United States. He perceived U.S. race relations to be a process evolving through five states, beginning with first contact and ending with assimilation, i.e., his model of successive stages and change included:

Contact ... Competition ... Conflict ... Accommodation ... Assimilation.[5]

Presumably, assimilation refers to full integration into the organizations, agencies, corporations, and institutions of "the mainstream." Park's model, however, was conceived out of the white-immigrant experience.

A black-experience processual model would be quite different from Park's in that it would reflect the fact that Africans did not choose to come here. They were captured and brought to these shores and then enslaved under a colonial system of European-centered, political domination and economic exploitation. The black-experience model would reflect never-ending black revolts and rebellions against the policies of white supremacy, which still are entrenched among the American power elite.

I conducted a study of social, cultural, legal and economic history of black Americans and found that a processual model reflecting their experience would be derived from eight epochs:

White Supremacy Strategies	**Black Liberation Strategies**
1. Despotism (Slavery)	2. Abolitionism
3. Jim Crowism	4. Neo-Abolitionism
5. Integrationism	6. Communal Separatism
7. Containmentism	8. National Separatism

In short, from the beginning of this republic until now, the relationship between Blacks and Whites has been one of continuous action and reaction, of overt and covert conflict. There has not been any historical epoch without racial conflict.

Consider next how the consumer-sovereignty economic theory[6] is inapplicable to the black experience. This theory posits the assumption that the consumer enjoys the privilege of making highly rational distinctions between products and prices in the marketplace. Second, it asserts that individual producers-retailers have virtually no control over consumer choices, product prices, and specific demand. The third postulate holds that the consumer induces the producers-retailers to price products close to the costs of manufacturing or processing them or/and close to prices of competitors; the suggestion here is that producers-retailers operate independently of each other. Thus, proponents of this theory assert that the consumer is sovereign in the producer-retailer-consumer exchanges.

An economic model reflecting the black ghetto experience would show that by and large the producers-retailers are truly sovereign due to the fact that they frequently have a monopoly on business.[7] That model would demonstrate that the black consumer is managed and manipulated by a group of marketplace actors—producers, retailers, advertisers, bankers, financiers and salespersons.[8] The black ghetto-economic model also would indicate that the producers-retailers generally do not wait for instructions from black consumers because they have few competitors. Thus, they can produce or offer products, which they in turn market and promote via a number of mechanisms, on their own terms. An example is the "buy-now-pay-later-arrangements" and advertising. Retailers can set exorbitantly high prices because they have no or few competitors.

Moreover, the black-ghetto model demonstrates how financiers and bankers routinely consider black consumers "poor credit risks" and systematically redline the predominantly black-populated areas of cities. This causes black consumers to be denied low-interest loans and to be forced to pay exorbitantly high interest rates and service charges to get credit. Those who cannot afford this exorbitance accruing from credit arrangements are forced to overpay in cash for low-quality goods sold as high-quality products because ghettoized Blacks have virtually no alternatives. Evidence shows conclusively that the consumer-sovereignty model definitely is invalidated by the black experience.

White social psychologists Albert Cohen and Marguerite Levy have designed a model of deferred-gratification based on middle-class white children. These psychologists claim that middle-class white children in particular are taught to delay immediate gratification for greater future rewards. Thus, they tend to be inhibited rather than hedonistic and future- rather than present-oriented. By contrast, these social psychologists argue that black children have not internalized the deferred gratification pattern and that they, therefore, are more impulsive and non-rational than white children. Thus, Cohen and Levy have concluded that Blacks (and lower-class white children) have not been taught by their parents to delay immediate gratification by engaging in long-range planning, which is required for socioeconomic advancement.[9] As this deferred-gratification theory indicates, high aspirations and achievements require the kind of futuristic-orientation that social psychologists associate with the ability to defer immediate gratification. They further argue that the ability to defer immediate gratification leads to antisocial behavior and underachievement.[10]

Those who have lived the black experience in America are very aware that the ascribed lower-class status of Blacks have been tantamount to being relegated to a life of either unemployment, underemployment, or forced low-wage labor. The conditions generally result in scarcity of food, clothing, shelter, health care, and private education. In short, the socially underprivileged are relegated to a perpetual, deferred-gratification pattern. This perpetual way of life is not a matter of personal preference but is rather a fact of life necessitating that black children learn to defer immediate gratification and to expect very little future reward for their perpetual self-denial. Unlike white middle-class children, black children cannot reasonably expect the same future rewards from the same amount of long-term deferred gratification and impulse inhibition.

I have seen black children respond to poverty in two ways: to sanctify it or to profane it. When they sanctify it, they wear it as symbol of honor. When they profane it, they engage in antisocial behavior and use it as justification. When some black children act in profane ways, it is often a direct result of their experiences with imposed deferred gratification rather than a lack of experience with it. The deferred-gratification theory as presently popularized is obviously a middle-class white experience theory. It is a theory based on the reasonable expectations of future rewards inherent in white middle-class life rather than in the experiences of the majority of black children.

Black scholars have long realized the inapplicability of white-experience theories and models and have called for the use of an Afrocentric perspective in the conduct of social science. Robert Chrisman, former editor of *Black Scholar* and professor of English, proposes that "the vanguard of black intellectuals, artists, and behavioral scientists" address themselves to the development of revolutionary values and resources latent among black Americans.[11] He further suggests that these professionals develop standards for assessing the fine arts and research techniques for the behavioral sciences based on black values and resources. Chrisman believes that the present cultural schemes, concepts, and theories, such as functionalism for example, emanate out of the European-American experience and cannot address needs of African Americans. To be specific, contemporary Anglo-Americanism is largely a culture of racial oppression. When we consider that that culture was weaned and nurtured on slavery and other socioeconomic exploitations of Blacks, why would anyone look to it as a liberative rather than oppressive source for Blacks.

Black professionals cannot rely on white-experience culture for liberation. They must analyze the black class structure, black economic conditions, and "the psychology of blackness, and [they must] translate that analysis into practical formulas of revolutionary action." Chrisman calls for them to develop a black propaganda system, a revolutionary esthetic, and a mechanism for mutual criticism between the vanguard and the black community.[12]

Political scientist James M. Jones argues that "Black politics is the art and science of moving Black people from a present, objective reality which is oppressive to a new reality, which is . . . liberation from that oppression."[13] The liberation of black people requires knowledge of the oppressor and knowledge of his techniques of oppression. "Knowledge," Jones observes, "Is relevant because knowledge . . . [has a controlling potential], and control is what . . . [black people] need, what we must have."[14]

Black political scientists must be about the business of black culture, black ideology, and black revolution, which has only one objective—liberation for black folks.[15] Jones proposes that in order for black politics to become a liberating force for black people, black politicians must wrest "control from the hands of . . . powers [alien to the black community]" and put the control of black behavioral and value systems back in the hands black people.[16]

Psychologist Joseph White speculates that black psychologists still are operating with a lot of "assumptions . . . developed by white psychologists primarily for white people."[17] He suggests that as an alternative black psychologists legitimize the black experience by conceiving psychological models based on the black experience. He further notes that black psychologists should view the behavior of black children as positive responses to a "complicated and hostile environment," for example. What eurocentric, scientific norms deem to be pathological behavior among black children must be re-evaluated and contextualized for the likelihood that it is "mental toughness," "survival skills," and "cleverness and originality" rather than pathological deviancy. In other words, White concludes that black psychologists "must . . . develop a model of black psychology which is free from the built-in assumptions and values of the dominant culture."[18]

Robert C. Vowels, a black economist, has charged that "In the real world, where the political economy of American racism holds indisputable sway, nonblack decision-making within nonblack organizations poses a formidable barrier to black aspirations and upward mobility.[19] He adds that contemporary economics "tend to deemphasize racial economic discrimination as a factor in the economic problems of minority groups."[20] Yet all sorts of private, white agencies, corporations and organizations use race as a factor in economic policy-making; often that policy forces Blacks to pay more for goods and services and receive less for their monies than Whites. More importantly, Vowels contrasts the black economic reality with the white as follows: "When everyone is poor, black people are even poorer. And when everyone is prosperous, black people are still poor."[21]

Black economists must include the factor of racial discrimination in their economic analyses and models. If the dynamics of racial discrimination are included, a new economics might emerge with different types of supply-and-demand relationships. Since racial discrimination is such an important market force in the lives of Blacks, and since it is not factored into major economic theories and models, it is logical to conclude that the present white-oriented theories and models do not apply to Blacks.[22]

Recently, in regard to the need for more revolutionary components in black scholarship, Molefi Kete Asante suggested an Afrocentric mode, when he wrote: "Afrocentric interpretation introduces a new, critical perspective into the nature of human discourse, especially when that discourse emerges from the cutting edges of rejection and resistance."[23] The Afrocentric approach necessitates placing African ideals at the center of any analysis that involves the culture(s) and behavior of black people. This means scholars must embody the icons, symbols, and signs of the cultural language of black peoples. By coining the term "afrology," Asante makes a strong statement on behalf of an Afrocentric study of the concepts, issues, beliefs, sentiments, norms, values, and behavior of black peoples in Africa and in the African Diaspora.[24]

The black experience itself in the United States is in essence a multifaceted experience, neither primarily economic, political, psychological, nor sociological. It is all of these and more; for it is also historical. The white supremacists have not only institutionalized economic barriers to black advancement but also social, political, and psychological ones as well. To better themselves, then, African Americans must take a multifaceted attack on these barriers.

Let me offer a metaphor for these barriers.[25] They can be likened to row upon row of intertwined barbed-wire fences surrounding black populations which are comparatively, young, eager, talented, idealistic and energetic. The first row of fence could be thought of as the judicial and legislative barriers to protection from racial discrimination. The second row is analogous to economic barriers that preclude black ownership and leadership of multinational and other major commercial ventures. The third row would bar black attainment of equitable education, and the fourth would deny them equal access to membership in private clubs and organizations which are arenas for networking among the privileged, who make political and economic policy that impacts the underprivileged. Finally there is the barbed wire of racism which ties all the rows upon rows of barriers together in mutually supportive ways. The ties of racism guarantee that no social institution operates in isolation, indicating that no meaningful social change can be effected without prior eradication of racism.

Given the barriers-situation just described, it is understandable that Blacks currently are pursuing a variety of liberation and betterment strategies simultaneously. Given the interrelatedness of the racial barriers which contain and constrict them, Blacks are correct in using several different strategies of self-improvement toward eradicating the systemic dimensions of racism. They should indeed use their unique strategies of litigation, legislation, demonstration, assimilation, separation, migration, coalition, commercialization, and education.

Social scientists must follow this lead. They must also use a multidisciplinary perspective, and they must construct multidisciplinary theories and models which help extricate Blacks from the interrelated political, economic, social, and psychological bondage just described. The new social science must offer new and not yet conceived theories and models for black self-betterment.

From the foregoing analysis, it is concluded that in order to realize their scientific goals black researchers should adhere to the following: First, they should be Afrocentric in problem selection, data gathering and concept building. Second, they should perceive, record and theorize from black people's points of view. Third, they should be black value-oriented instead of white value-oriented in their interpretations of data. Fourth, they should apply black-experience explanatory models and theories to understanding black people. Fifth, they should expose the inapplicabilities of all white-experience theories and models when they are used to explain the lived experiences of Blacks. Sixth, they should draw conclusions from data analysis which further the individual self-improvement and the collective nation-building of black people.

---

1 William J. Goode and Paul K. Hatt, *Methods in Social Research* (New York: McGraw-Hill, 1952).

2 Vanessa N. Gamble, "A Legacy of Distrust: African Americans and Medical Research," in *American Journal of Preventive Medicine*, 9, no. 6 (Suppl. November-December 1993), 35-38.

3 James Howard Jones, *Bad Blood* (New York: Free Press, 1993).

4 Henry Louis Gates, Jr., *Figures in Black* (New York: Oxford University Press, 1987).

5 Robert E. Park, *Race and Culture* (New York: Free Press, 1950).

6 John Kenneth Galbraith, *The New Industrial State* (New York: The New American Library, Inc., 1967).

7 William K Tabb, *The Political Economy of the Black Ghetto* (New York: W.W. Norton & Co., 1971).

8 David Caplovits, *The Poor Pay More* (New York: Free Press, 1967).

[9] Albert K. Cohen, *Delinquent Boys* (Glencoe, Ill.: Free Press, 1955) and Marguerite F. Levy, "Deferred Gratification and Social Class," *Journal of Social Psychology* 1 (October 1976).

[10] Ibid.

[11] "The Formation of a Revolutionary Black Culture," in *The Black Scholar* 8 (June 1970), 2-9.

[12] Ibid., 8.

[13] "The Political Dimensions of Black Liberation," *The Black Scholar* 1 (September 1971), 76-75.

[14] Ibid., 73.

[15] Ibid., 67.

[16] Ibid., 69.

[17] Joseph White, "Guidelines for Black Psychologists," in *The Death of White Sociology,* Joyce Ladner, ed. (New York: Random House, 1973).

[18] Ibid.

[19] "The Political Economy of American Racism—Nonblack Decision-Making and Black Economic Status," *The Review of Black Political Economy* 4 (Summer 1971), 28.

[20] Ibid., 4.

[21] Ibid., 24.

[22] Henry A. Coleman, "Student Symposium-Economics, With or Without Color?" *The review of Black Political Economy* 4 (Summer 1971), 142.

[23] *The Afrocentric Idea* (Philadelphia: Temple University Press, 1987).

[24] *Afrocentricity* (Trenton: African World Press, 1988).

[25] Joseph W. Scott, *The Black Revolts: Racial Stratification in the U.S.A.* (Cambridge, Mass.: Schenkman, 1967).

Glimpses of Barbadian-Immigrant Heritage in Paule Marshall's *Brown Girl, Brownstones*

Dorothy L. Denniston
English Department, Brown University

A 1992 recipient of the John D. and Katherine T. MacArthur Award, Paule Marshall is one of the finest contemporary writers of fiction. What makes Marshall's fiction especially compelling and provocative is her thorough allegiance and uncompromising responsibility to a cultural base which originated in West African traditional societies. For example, she includes in her fiction sounds and patterns of music (syncopation, repetition, improvisation), as well as rituals and elements of dance associated with West Africa. She appropriately, incorporates the notion of cyclical as opposed to linear time. Indeed, as I point out later, both structurally and thematically, Marshall re-creates the traditional West African view of the world which affirms a fundamental dualism in life; that is opposites simultaneously co-exist and the acceptance of paradox leads to wholeness.[1]

Perhaps most notably in Marshall's fiction is the author's mastery of the art of story-telling. She not only presents interesting tales but, as in the African oral-narrative tradition, she also provides important instruction. Finally Marshall makes us aware of folk traditions which include myths, tales, proverbs and riddles. In her first novel, *Brown*

Reprinted by permission of the author.

Girl, Brownstones, which is the focus of this essay, she presents as well a number of proverbs and sub-tales to reinforce her several messages.

Brown Girl, Brownstones is an important novel for several reasons. First, it describes the experience of a black immigrant (Barbadian) family and community in the United States. Second, *Brown Girl, Brownstones* foregrounds Marshall's individual identity as an artist who is conscious of the necessity of moving beyond the prevalent construction of identity within the United States. Third, this novel—which is dedicated to Marshall's mother and focuses primarily on black female characters—signals the author's artistic destiny to depict full portraits of black women. Here she portrays them not simply as "product[s] of America, but . . . [as those] whose story is [as] . . . tied and bound to the West Indies as it is to its primal source—Africa."[2] Finally, this novel launches the author on her journey through the Diaspora and toward an Afrocentric sensibility.

On one level, *Brown Girl, Brownstones* concerns the coming of age of Selina Boyce, for Marshall describes the physical and emotional growth of this central character. But on another broader level, the novel becomes a dramatization of cultural history in the making as the United States-born Selina searches for the meaning of her West Indian heritage and her place within that heritage. Like most creative artists concerned with cultural history, Marshall writes from a base that is essentially personal. Not surprisingly, then, *Brown Girl, Brownstones* presents in realistic detail the Barbadian or Bajan-American community in which the author grew up. But the personal need not be strictly autobiographical. The novel's characters are composites of people Marshall knew or imagined during her youth. Of the protagonist, whom many critics believe to be Marshall as a young girl, the author explains:

> If anything, she's a kind of idealized image of myself. The kind of person I would have liked to have been: assertive, forthright, taking life in hand. Those marvelous qualities she has were not me at all. I was always so retiring, with my books all the time, and terrified of life. But that force Selina has is, I suppose, a kind of wishful thinking on my part.[3]

Wishful thinking notwithstanding, the novel represents a type of thought that may have been functionally therapeutic for the author in that it allowed her to consider the cultural values which influenced her personal development. Marshall admits that as a child, she tried to deny her West Indian heritage:

> I went through torture as a girl growing up in Brooklyn, going to school with those heavy silver bangles on my wrist, and when we went to the West Indies and came back with heavy West Indian accents, the kids used to laugh at us. It was dreadful. So I went through a whole period of rejecting that part of myself.[4]

Brown Girl, Brownstones, then, can be interpreted as the artistic rendering of personal issues paramount to the author's internal and external dilemma of connecting her identity to its proper ethnic source. Ultimately, however, it provides the opportunity for the author to explore the complexity of the psychological and cultural displacement which blacks may experience in many other parts of the world.

That displacement becomes apparent in this novel as we travel the world of the Bajan-American community in Brooklyn. Working day and night, saving every penny to purchase property, seemingly undaunted by racial slurs and prejudice, these Barbadian immigrants banded together in tightly-knit neighborhoods to form a formidable social and economic power of their own. They like other immigrants, chose to leave their homelands to escape conditions of poverty and exploitation. But unlike other immigrant groups, Bajan-Americans also left their native land to escape the historical effects of slavery and colonialism. The United States, especially New York, was the symbol of wealth and opportunity, and Brooklyn became the nesting spot for most of these first-generation black immigrants.

Marshall's parents were part of the wave of Caribbean immigrants who came to the United states after World War I. Always mindful of the poor economic conditions of their homelands, the West Indians believed that with persistent determination and close scrutiny of even a limited income anyone could eventually "buy house." And the Barbadians, especially "[those] who had never owned . . . but a few poor acres in a poor land, loved the houses with the same fierce idolatry as they had the land on their obscure islands." In neighborhoods once dominated by Jews and Italians, "the West Indians slowly edged their way in. Like a dark sea nudging its way into a white beach and staining the sand, they came."[5] By 1939, when *Brown Girl, Brownstones* begins, the white exodus is nearly complete, and the neighborhood of Stuyvesant Heights (now Bedford-Stuyvesant) takes on a colorful, distinctively African-Caribbean dimension.

One of those distinctive dimensions is language—the round of voices and stories that reflect specific cultural elements. Most important is the juxtaposition of contrary terms, which suggests that in the West Indian view of the world, like that of the African, opposites or contradictions make up the whole. African Americans may be familiar with the adage, "God don't like ugly and He ain't stuck on pretty." In the Caribbean a similar construction of contrarieties describes both situations and people as "beautiful-ugly" or "poor-great" to underscore the integrity of both characteristics. Deighton, Selina's father, describes Barbados as "poor-poor but sweet enough." In keeping with the belief that the body and spirit are one, given names may be replaced or followed by such terms as "faith" or "soul." "Silla-soul," for example, not only becomes a name of address, but it further indicates a merging of the physical, visible self with the spiritual.[6] In such examples, woven throughout the novel, we see the importance of language in defining an epistemology which has a dialectic nature. Characters also make use of double adjectives to make a statement emphatic. Someone who is deceased is "dead-dead" or when the temperature is high, the sun is "hot-hot."

The language is peppered with proverbs which succinctly express an idea. Referring to the disciplining of children, one character cries, "Hard ears wun hear, own ways you'll feel." This may be interpreted as a loose equivalent of "Spare the rod, spoil the child." No explanation seems necessary for the following proverb which Silla, Selina's mother, cries out: "Two head bulls can't reign in the same flock." In addition to biblical allusions which abound in the speech, hyperbole and metaphor help us to visualize a given image. Miss Mary, the aging white tenant in the brownstone, provides a case in point. She is not merely old, but has "been down here since they said 'Come let us make woman'" (p. 19).

All of the above confirm Marshall's unmistakable exposure to the sounds and meanings of the Barbadian vernacular, and we conclude that before the words were even transcribed to the page, she had learned about the potential power of the spoken word. Verbal articulation, she came to understand, so vividly activated human experience in all its moods that the expression became inseparable from the experience.

As the title of the novel suggests, architectural imagery cements the novel together. In fact, the novel is built upon blocks (books) which are tiered. Book One, "A Long Day and a Long Night," introduces the major characters. Book Two, "Pastorale," engages us with the girl who is becoming a woman. Book Three, "The War," describes the on-going battle between Selina's parents within the larger battle of World War II. Book Four, "Selina," portrays the heroine's growth toward her own personal and cultural identity.

Nevertheless, the very first paragraph provides the blue print for marshall's artistic construction and her conception of place and values:

> In the somnolent July afternoon the unbroken line of brownstone houses down the long Brooklyn street resembled an army massed at attention. They were all one uniform red-brown stone. All with high massive stone stoops and black iron-grille fences staving off the sun. All draped in Ivy as though mourning. Their somber facades, indifferent to the summer's heat and passion, faced a park while their backs reared dark against the sky. They were only three or four stories tall-squat—yet they gave the impression of formidable height (p. 3).

Marshall indicates that while each house had some distinctive architectural feature (Gothic, Romanesque, Baroque, or Greek), "they all shared the same brown monotony. All seemed doomed by the confusion in their design" (p. 3). The successes and failures of the characters are motivated by the most noble of human concerns—love and survival with dignity, but the materialistic values the brownstones represented spelled the destruction of both.

Selina's presence is felt throughout the novel and her characterization as the brown girl of the novel's title lends superficial unity to the narrative, but an omniscient narrator firmly guides and modifies our impressions as we delve into the minds and hearts of several other complex characters. We learn, for example, that despite her father's apparent avoidance of Ina, Selina's older sister, the former is the symbol of the love that Deighton and Silla experienced during the early years of their marriage. The narrator states, "She was lovely as it had been lovely, and fragile as it had been found to be fragile" (p. 26). Although Ina's characterization reflects unquestioned acceptance of her immigrant community's mores and values and Selina is bent on rebellion and defiance, both girls generally remain in the background to augment a notion important to both Caribbean and African -American cultures: "A child is to be seen, not heard."

Nevertheless, the imaginative and impetuous Selina captures and sustains our attention. When we first meet her, she is alone with her daydreams touring the brownstone her family leases. Note how she prepares to descend the stairs:

> She rose, her arms lifted in welcome, and quickly the white family who had lived here before, whom the old woman upstairs always spoke of, glided with pale footfalls up the stairs. Their white hands trailed the bannister; their mild voices implored her to give them a little life. And as they crowded around, fussing with her, she was no longer a dark girl alone and dreaming at the top of an old house, but one of them, invested with their beauty and gentility. She threw her head back until it trembled proudly on the stalk of her neck and, holding up her imaginary gown, she swept downstairs to the parlor floor (p. 5).

Architecture comes into play as the narrator continues:

> At the bottom step she paused in the entrance hall, which was a room in itself with its carpet, wallpaper and hushed dimness. Opening off the hall was the parlor, full of ponderous furniture and potted ferns which the whites had left, with aged and inviolate silence. It was a museum of all the lives that had ever lived there. The floor-to-ceiling mirror retained their faces as the silence did their voices.
>
> As Selina entered, the chandelier which held the sunlight frozen in its prisms rushed at her, and the mirror flung her back at herself. The mood broken. She was only herself again. A truculent face and eyes too large and old, a flat body perched on legs that were too long. A torn middy blouse, dirty shorts and socks that always worked down into the heel of her sneakers. That was all she was. She did not belong here. She was something vulgar in a holy place. The room was theirs, she knew, glancing up at the frieze of cherubs and angels on the ceiling; it belonged to the ghost shapes hovering in the shadows. But not to her (pp. 5, 6).

Cultural conflict, alienation, displacement—all these are apparent in this brief passage that so forcefully employs architectural place as a trope. The architectural imagery may indicate a suggestion of self-hatred which many blacks, not all of them children, experience in a white dominated society.

Conversations between the women reveal West Indian cultural mores and beliefs while exposing spousal conflict that sometimes center on the Bajan-American women's acquisitive nature. In one passage, Deighton Boyce inherits a "piece of home ground." He plans to return to Barbados to build his dream house—one "just like the white people there own; a house to end all house!" Silla insists that he sell the land and use the money to purchase the brownstone in which they currently reside. This difference of opinion provides the fuel for the developing controversy between the parents, but it also creates a clear demarcation between land and house, between Barbados and Brooklyn, between humanism and materialism.

The question of where to live turns into the more penetrating question of how to live,[7] which leads Marshall into a critique of both the "American Dream" and the "Dream of the Return [to Barbados]." Only his dream of returning to Barbados to live in high style allows Deighton to suffer the indignities of gossip and isolation. Consequently, when his wife betrays him by fraudulently selling his piece of "home ground," he is left with virtually nothing. He enacts his revenge by squandering the proceeds from the land on gifts for himself and his family. Silla, livid with angry contempt, becomes even more determined to buy the Brooklyn brownstone. An almost Satanic presence fills the room when she vows not only to get the house but Deighton as well.

As a child, Selina cannot understand the layers of historical, cultural and social biases which mount to create intolerable pressures upon her immediate family and the surrounding community. Silla Boyce figures prominently and, for artistic purposes, she represents most of the Barbadian women. Marshall chooses to focus on women in this novel to correct the usual presentation of the black woman as a one-dimensional sexual being. She also wishes to present these women as self-propelled, assertive women who are active in controlling their own separate spheres of meaningful existence. It is significant that Selina never refers to Silla as "my" mother; rather, Silla is "the" mother:

> It was always the mother and the others, for they were alike—those watchful, wrathful women whose eyes seared and searched and laid

> bare, whose tongues lashed the world in unremitting distrust. Each morning they took the train to Flatbush and Sheepshead Bay to scrub floors. The lucky ones had their steady madams while the others wandered about those neat blocks or waited on corners—each with her apron and working shoes in a bag under her arm until someone offered her a day's work. Sometimes the white children on their way to school laughed at their blackness and shouted "nigger," but the Barbadian women sucked their teeth, dismissing them. Their only thought was of the "few raw-mouth, pennies" at the end of the day which would eventually "buy house" (p. 11).

Readers cannot help but marvel at the phenomenal strength of these women in the New York setting and wonder about its source. In fact, they seem so invincible in the novel that critics have erroneously charged that Marshall perpetuates the myth of the emasculating black women. Although the author is concerned with the sexist nature of fixed-gender roles, the novel revisits and revises Selina's initial impressions to uncover cultural and racial conflicts that lead to certain behaviors. She chooses to highlight the female struggle because it is the one with which she is most familiar. Perhaps most importantly, Marshall chooses to make the black woman representative of the larger, collective black struggle for survival.

In contrast to the romantic Deighton who is associated with springtime and sunshine, Silla is the stern pragmatist whom Selina associates with winter and darkness. The Mother is a formidable and tenacious woman who, because of her far from idyllic life in Barbados, is determined at any cost to "make it" in America. She recognizes, all too painfully, the realities of racist exploitation in their new environment and, unlike her husband, is willing to sacrifice pleasure for security and economic advancement. Also, unlike her husband, she believes in her ability to succeed, to provide a better life for herself and her family in America, where ostensibly "one has a chance."

The novel, of course, provides information which reveals a historical background of exploitation and suffering to help the reader begin to understand the drive and determination of the several female and male characters. Very importantly, passages of the novel devoted to revealing the women's multi-faceted personalities are invariably made in Selina's presence. This suggests that early on and without her knowledge, Selina is joined in a pact which later will define her indisputable inclusion in a powerful, black sisterhood.

Silla's initiation into this sisterhood, which had its beginnings in Barbados, was especially harsh. She tells of her membership in the "Third Class" in the hills of Barbados. Contrary to Selina's innocent assumption, the "Third Class" had nothing to do with school. Rather it was "a set of little children picking grass in a cane field from the time God sun rise in heaven till it set. With some woman called a Driver to wash yuh tail in licks if yuh dare look up. Yes, working harder than a man at the age of ten."[8] As she continues with her diatribe over her lot as a worker, Silla's images parallel the lot of slaves in North America. "And when it was hard times, I would put a basket of mangoes 'pon muh head and go selling early-early 'pon a morning. Frighten bad enough for duppy and thing 'cause I was still only a child." Alluding to the commonality of Silla's experience, Marshal writes in summation: "She became the collective voice of all the Bajan women, the vehicle through which their former suffering found utterance" (pp. 45, 46).

That suffering remains in the forefront of Silla's mind. Speaking to one of her woman friends, she recalls the poverty and exploitation of her homeland:

> "Iris, you know what it is to work hard and still never make a headway? That's Brimshire. One crop. People having to work for next skin to nothing. The white people treating we like slaves still and we taking it. The rum shop and the church join together to keep we pacified and in ignorance. That's Barbados. It's a terrible thing to know that you gon be poor all yuh life, no matter how hard you work. You does stop trying after a time. People does see you so and call you lazy. But it ain laziness. It's just that you does give up. You does kind of die inside" (p. 70).

Silla comes to America to keep from dying and, given the back-breaking work she has already experienced, nothing in America seems insurmountable. It is with tragic awareness that she admits to her daughter: "I come here and pick up with a piece of a man and from then on I has read hell by heart and called every generation blessed" (p. 46).

The hell to which Silla refers is a combination of a deep and complex love countered by an equally deep and complex resentment toward her husband (Deighton Boyce). If she is to achieve her dream, she feels that she needs the help of an equally ambitious mate. Deighton, however, refuses to concede to her expectations of him, leaving

Silla to assume the dominant role. The rapaciousness of American society only exacerbates the predicament, as Silla indicates as she muses over the situation: "It's not that I's avaricious or money mad . . . or that I's a follow-pattern so that everything they do, I must do. But c'dear, if you got a piece of a man you want to see yourself improve. Isn't that why people does come to this place?" (p. 174) Silla admits that black people "catch H— in this man's country," but it is still a place where working diligently together, she believes that she and Deighton could at least make a headway.

Through the architectural imagery so important to the novel, we are alerted early on that the "whiteness" of the larger world impacts quite differently on Silla and Deighton. Deighton, for example, pauses uneasily before the kitchen, "shaken as always by the stark light there, the antiseptic white furniture and enameled white walls. The room seemed a strange, unfeeling world which continually challenged him to deal with it, to impose himself somehow on its whiteness." Silla, on the other hand, "stands easily amid the whiteness . . . in the relaxed unselfconscious pose of someone alone" (p. 22). As the complexities of personality and psychological motivation are revealed, the reader is hurled into a world of fluctuating tensions: violence and calm; turmoil and peace; practicality and romanticism; conformity and rebellion. Much like the antonymic adjective, "beautiful-ugly," Marshall does not privilege one as more realistic or noble than the other. Instead she leaves Selina to establish her own values, her own traditions, her own homeplace. Before Selina's destiny can be named, however, she must under the cultural conflict which shapes her in an almost allegorical way as her parents battle each other in their contrasting responses to America.

Her "aloneness" stems from the conflict between her and Deighton, and it is this conflict that makes up the core of the novel.

Via her placement of the characters, Marshall provides the reader with more information than any single character within the novel has, thus enabling readers to understand the conflicting forces at hand. In the process, she unveils her broad insight into the development of the African-Caribbean/African-American psyches. Hers is an insight not marred by the acknowledgment of American racism. Rather it is enriched as she shows that in its umbrella-like dimensions, American racism makes no distinctions in culture. The issue of Deighton's citizenship, for example, is never questioned as he seeks employment early in the novel. "These white people here does think all colored people is from the South," Deighton comments (p. 82).

Because of her romantic and imaginative bent, Selina often is associated with her father. In fact, she repeatedly is referred to as "Deighton's child." She is drawn to her father not only because of his affable and carefree personality, but also because his favorite room, the sun parlor, which she associates with his idyllic memories of his native land. It is important that the narrator tells us that Selina, vaguely but surely, carried the impression that the differences between her parents stemmed from their very dissimilar childhood experiences. Deighton himself explains:

> I's a person live in town and always had plenty to do. I not like yuh mother and the 'mounts of these Bajan that come from down some gully or up some hill behind God back and ain use to nothing. 'Pon a Sat'day I would walk 'bout town like I was a full-full man. All up Broad Street and Swan Street like I did own the damn place (pp. 9, 10).

While certainly not well-to-do, Deighton lived a life of relative, middle-class comfort. According to Virgie Farnum, a Barbadian immigrant who was reared near him, his mother was a kind and forbearing woman; she went beyond her means to rear her children. Deighton, the only boy, was gladly indulged. His mother sacrificed nearly everything to finance his college education with the hope that he would become a schoolmaster, one of the few professional options available to blacks in Barbados. However, Deighton sought the prestige and glamour of the white world. When his mother died, he left for Cuba as his father had done, then jumped ship to America where he met and married Silla.

Although Deighton, too, wishes to acquire property as an important sign of personal and economic independence and as an indication of upward social mobility, two important distinctions guide his thinking. First, he wants to build his dream house on "home ground." He thinks of Barbados as "poor, poor, but sweet enough." Through such descriptions, Barbados takes on an uncomplicated, relaxed, and romantic image both in contrast to Silla's memory of the island and in contrast to the fast-moving, competitive pace of Brooklyn. This consideration is directly related to the second distinction: Deighton will not be made to sacrifice all of his pleasures to work. "A man got a right to take his ease in life and not always be scuffling" (p. 31). Part of that ease is reflected in his stylish, meticulous dress (He loves the feel of silk.) and in his extra-marital affairs.

It is significant that his wife's objections stem not so much from sexual jealousy as from economic factors. "Who in the bloody hell cares how many women he got," she grumbles. "Those women got nothing but a man using them. But his own got to come first" (p. 31). Here, Silla voices the Bajan immigrants' attitude toward thrift. Whatever extra money one earns should be set aside to "buy house." Deighton is by no means disdainful of work, for in addition to his correspondence studies, he holds down a full-time job in a mattress factory. His sense of style, however—his culturally derived definition of manhood—dictates something more lavish and a life which is certainly less restrictive than his fellow Barbadians accept in America.

A minor character speaks for the black immigrant community when she says of Deighton:

> I tell you those men from Bridgetown is all the same. They don't know a thing 'bout handling money and property and thing so. They's spree boys. Every last one of them. . . . There ain nothing wrong with wanting piece of ground home but only when you got a sufficient back prop here. I tell you, he's a disgrace! (p. 55).

Marshall may here be comparing class attitudes toward labor as they exist between the city folk and those who have a rural background; but more important seems to be her exploration of how personal and cultural values may become subsumed or obliterated in the push toward assimilation. Deighton not only refuses, but perhaps is unable, to submit to a devaluation of his Bajan-made identity. Of course, he is aware that racism exists back home. Fleetingly he recalls,

> Those white English faces mottled red by a sun in the big stores in Bridgetown and himself as a young man, facing them in his first pair of long pants and his coarse hair brushed flat, asking them for a job as a clerk—the incredulity, the disdain and indignation that flushed their faces as they said no (p. 39).

Although he dreams of a different answer, they also said "no" in the United States.

The "glitter and tumult" of Fulton street on a Saturday night becomes for the author an avenue to describe Deighton's zest for life. It provides as well a vehicle through which Marshall can explore, if only momentarily, "the beauty and desperation and sadness" of the African-American experience.

> [Fulton street was] a whirling spectrum of neon signs, movie marquees, bright-lit store windows and sweeping, yellow streamers of light from the cars. It was sonorous voices, hooted laughter and voices ripping the night's warm cloak; a welter of dark faces and gold-etched teeth; children crying high among the fire escapes of the tenements; the subway rumbling below; the unrelenting wail of a blues spilling from a bar, greasy counters and fish sandwiches and barbeque and hot sauce; trays of chitterlings and hog maws and far back in the meat stores; the trolley's insistent clangor; a man and woman in a hallway bedroom, sleeping like children now that the wildness had passed; a drunken woman pitching along the street; the sustained shriek of a police car and its red light stabbing nervously at faces and windows (p. 37).

This snapshot of black American poverty reflects precisely what the black immigrant population wishes to avoid. Literary critic Deborah Schneider comments:

> As blacks, they have been forced by white society to live in restricted ghetto neighborhoods; as Barbadians with a middle-class tradition, such as Deighton came from, which they are eager to defend, they wall themselves off from contacts with American blacks, contacts which would mean to them a drop in status as well as a blurring of their special ethnic identity.[9]

For those like Silla, who came to America from an economically lower-class background, the poor living conditions of many black Americans is a vivid reminder of what the immigrants left behind. As Rosalie Troester says, they shun those black Americans "whose lives mirror conditions [they] dare not bring to consciousness."[10]

The "beautiful-ugly" wedding scene foreshadows Deighton's destruction. Marshall describes the extravagant wedding in minuscule detail to show the success of the Bajan community in their total imitation of white America, but she also criticizes this success by revealing that no real joy accompanies the occasion. The bride (forced to marry a West Indian instead of the southern American black whom she loves) walks toward her groom. With the guests of the bride and groom seated on either side of the center aisle of the church "like two warring camps," the mood of combat is created anew.

This mood underscores the escalating tension between the major characters. It also serves to underscore the community's support of Silla, who becomes the center of attention. Everyone has heard of Deighton's shameful waste of the money; they alternately commiserate with Silla, then praise her stamina. Marshall illustrates in this pivotal scene the notion of supportive kinship relations so critical to corporate life in African and, by extension, West Indian societies. Since the social order and peace are "conceived of primarily in terms of kinship relations," any offense against an individual member of the community becomes an offense against the whole group.[11]

Communal support for the individual is symbolically rendered through the ritual of dance, which becomes both a form of entertainment and a form of social commentary. With the lilting sounds of the calypso, everyone is caught up in an infectious wave of movement and flow. The dancers form a tight, symbolic circle which, with centrifugal force, holds the participants together. Selina, pressed to the edge, glimpses her father at the door of the reception hall and, as she tries to pull away to greet him, the dancers keep her bound to the group. They all are singing loudly, "Small island, go back where you come from," a refrain which strikes a parallel with the West Indian community's attitude toward Deighton. Collier rightly observes:

> In this scene Selina sees herself first as an integral part of the community, reveling in a new sense of wholeness, then imprisoned by that same community, helping it to persecute her most beloved person. She has experienced two poles of belonging; the community as completion of the individual self, the community as control.[12]

Deighton is excommunicated symbolically from the circle as Marshall goes on to describe the dancers closing "protectively around Silla and Ina; someone pulled Selina back. Then . . . the dancers turned in one body and danced with their backs to him" (p. 150). The entire community condemns the offender and, with their song, drives Deighton away. Selina, on the other hand, is initiated now into the group, is governed by its dictates, even against her will."[13]

Excluded from the Barbadian-American community, Deighton seeks another in the Father Divine Peace Movement. In this section of the novel, Marshall makes an important historical reference to Father Divine (aka George Baker) who, in the 1920s and 1930s, organized a social and religious movement which spread to many eastern and mid-western communities in the United States. Divine claimed to be God incarnate and, recognizing the spiritual as well as the physical needs of his followers, he espoused an ideology of peace in the here and now, as opposed to the more common religious theme of peace in the hereafter. He opened buildings which he called "heavens," and there he fed thousands of the dispossessed, the disillusioned, the disenchanted—black and white.[14]

When Deighton joins Father Divine's movement, he literally abdicates his responsibilities as husband and father. Love, combined with anger, guilt and envy, lead Silla to initiate deportation procedures against him. Shortly thereafter (on the day WWII ends), she receives a cable announcing that Deighton had either jumped or fallen overboard and drowned within sight of the coast of Barbados. Selina reacts violently in a memorable scene in which she repeatedly calls her mother "Hitler." Quite understandably, she deplores her mother's actions. Initially in quiet desperation but later in open defiance, she rejects what she considers the acquisitive and selfish values of her mother in particular and the Barbadian immigrants in general.

To Miss Thompson, a U.S.-born woman, Selina reveals her feelings of confusion and anger. This woman who, by day is a beautician and by night a cleaning woman, mirrors the strength and endurance of the West Indian women. Here Marshall seems to be pointing to their common experiences. Marshall also may be alluding to their common primal ancestry when she describes Miss Thompson's face as resembling "an African wood carving: mysterious, omniscient, the features elongated by compassion, the eyes shrouded with a profound sadness" (p. 41). Though culturally "outside," Selina's immediate world, her experience in the American South has clearly taught her the subtle and overt manifestations of racial and gender oppression. Thus, she can authoritatively caution Selina to try to understand her people before making judgments.

That understanding comes through Selina's gradual appreciation of the Barbadian Homeowners' and Businessmen's Association, a self-help organization committed to the cultural and economic advancement of its members. It is as well a testament to the dawning political consciousness of a small black community determined to make its presence felt. One character refers to it as "the biggest thing since Marcus Garvey."

Garvey was the Jamaican leader who founded the widely supported Universal Negro Improvement Association and brought it to New York in 1916. Convinced that the United States was unwilling to accept blacks on equal terms with whites, he advocated that black folk with skills should "return to Africa" to help establish a superior and independent black civilization. While Marshall deliberately includes this historical reference as a noteworthy contribution of the West Indian people to the progress of blacks all over the world, she also suggests the early influence this legendary hero exerted over the formation of her own African sensibility. She remembers that during her own childhood, her mother's women friends spoke of Garvey with pride:

> His name was constantly being invoked, for he had been their leader in the early twenties, the revolutionary who had urged the black and poor like themselves to rise up: "Rise up you mighty race." Who had declared black is beautiful to women like themselves who had been brainwashed into believing they did not possess beauty. Garvey who had said economic self-sufficiency and black nationhood. Who had said Africa . . .[15]

In the novel, the Association illustrates not only the ethnic cohesiveness of the Barbadian immigrants, but also the dawning political consciousness of a marginalized community. Its members clearly support the American myth of assimilation despite, or perhaps in spite of, the racial discrimination imposed upon them. However, their experiences remain paradoxical. On the one hand, the Barbadian-Americans want and deserve economic success as their reward for hard work, and they strive collectively in their resistance to the hostility and resentment of those in the larger society. On the one hand, the Barbadian-Americans want and deserve economic success as their reward for hard work.

On the other hand, in order to improve their economic standing, they adopt the same single-mindedness and selfishness of their detractors who are born in the United States and nurtured on acquisitive and materialistic values. Consequently, not only is the integrity of the individual Bajan-Americans maligned, but they also are prevented from relating their circumstances with those of the larger black-American community.

Marshall briefly touches on this dissociation from the black community, when a member of the Barbadian Homeowners' and Businessmen's Association proposes that the name on the banner be changed to Association of Negro Homeowners:

> "We got to stop thinking about just Bajan. We ain't home no more. It don matter if we don know a person mother or his mother mother. Our doors got to be open to every colored person that qualify. . . . I know it gon take time. Wunna gon have to ruminate long, but I ain gon return till I see that word *Barbadian* strike out and *Negro* put in its place. I thank you!" (p. 222).

Association members agree that the business of renting rooms in their homes to increasingly greater numbers are African Americans is a nuisance. "Even though they ain Bajans," she explains, "they's still our color." Another member's response is harsh but real:

> "Sorry! . . . Sorry for roomers? Sorry? But God-blind yuh, Iris, who did sorry for you? I ain sorry for a blast. I had to get mine too hard. Let the roomers get out and struggle like I did. I sorry for all the long years I din have nothing and my children didn have and now I got little something. I too fat and old to enjoy it and my only son dead in these people bloody war and he can't enjoy it. That's what I sorry for." (p. 224).

Silla helps to clarify these feelings when she proclaims, with painful awareness, that Florrie's move to the more prestigious neighborhood of Crown Heights would not have been possible without the exploitation of others. "We would like to do different. That's what does hurt and shame us so. But the way things arrange we can't, if not we lost out." Power, she explains, has nothing to do with color:

> "It's true the roomers is our own color. But if they was white or yellow and cun do better we'd still be overcharging them. Take when we had

> to scrub the Jew floor. He wasn't misusing us not so much because our skin was black but because we cun do better, and I din hate him. All the time I was down on his floor I was saying to myself: 'Lord, lemme do better than this. Lemme rise!' No, power is a thing that don really have nothing to do with color. Look how white people had little children their own color working in coal mines and sweatshops years back. Look how those whelps in Africa sold us for next skin to nothing." (p. 224).

Silla concludes in proverbial fashion: "What's that saying about the race is not to the swift? You best be swift, if not somebody come and trample you quick enough" (p. 224). Selina clearly wants a different world, but it remains uncertain, undefined, untried.

It is important to note that throughout the novel, Marshall avoids idealizing the mother-daughter relationship.[16] Selina clearly holds a grudging respect for her mother, alternating wanting to be near her but out of her way. As the author delves more deeply into their interactions, she shows that Silla withholds affection from her daughter in order to forge character.[17] However, Silla is so consumed with day-to-day concerns that like the Scylla in Greek mythology, she is metamorphosed into a monster. Silla's multidimensional portrayal also reveals that the mother-daughter conflict really camouflages deep-seated frustrations over the costs to the spirit in a racist, sexist, and materialistic society. Perhaps Marshall best describes Silla's loss when she engages her artistic imagination with the island of Barbados. In the wedding scene referred to earlier, the author briefly introduces an old man who remembers Silla as a young girl back home frolicking in a pasture. Selina tries to imagine her mother back then:

> The world had been when she [Selina] had not. Time stretched behind and beyond her small life. Years ago, on an island that was only a green node in a vast sea, the mother had been a girl who had danced till she had fainted once, and Selina, had been nothing to her. Suddenly she yearned to know the mother then, in her innocence. Above all, she longed to understand the mother, for she knew, obscurely, that she would never really understand anything until she did (p. 145).

Selina begins to seize life much as her mother does. In fact, she might be mistaken for Silla as she devises a coldly calculated scheme to win and abscond with funds netted from the scholarship that the Association has worked hard to accumulate. But she has yet to learn what her mother and the other immigrants have long understood: the difficulty of personal triumph within a white world which refuses to acknowledge black individuality. The notion of invisibility as previously developed by Ralph Ellison is refigured to personalize Selina's devastating confrontation with racism.

Having joined an otherwise all-white modern dance troupe in college, Selina performs a solo part of the group's recital. Significantly, the solo is entitled the "birth-to-death cycle," and in her interpretation, Selina consciously brings to mind the several characters in the novel. It is important, though, that unlike the earlier dance scene at the wedding, no one from Selina's West Indian community is present. Thus, she must face alone the consequences of her deliberate emotional exclusion from her people.[18]

Invited to celebrate her stellar performance at the nearby home of one of the troup's members, Selina is subjected to every conceivable racial and ethnic stereotype by the hostess' mother. Marshall foreshadows this incident through her description of the East-side apartment and the woman's artificial smile. The author is clearly concerned with illustrating the thoughtless cruelty of whites who refuse to acknowledge black individuality. But Marshall equally is interested in describing Selina's feelings of the moment, which culminate in the girl's rushing from the apartment in a blind rage. When Selia collapses in the entranceway of a vacant store, she sees the white woman's imposed image of her reflected in the window. But she also acknowledges that there was a part of her "which had long hated her for blackness and thus begrudged her each small success like the one tonight . . ." (p. 289).

This scene echoes Selina's muffled self-hatred at the beginning of the novel when, as a child, she fantasized about her vulgarity in a holy place. In the present episode, fantasy gives way to self-realization, for Selina understands that she has partially integrated a white illusion. This illusion will not vanish at will. Marshall describes it as "so powerful that it would stalk her down the years, confront her in each mirror and from the safe circle in their eyes, surprise her even in the gleaming surface of a table. It would intrude in every corner of her life, tainting her small triumphs—as it had done tonight—an exulting at her defeats" (p. 291). At last she begins to understand a little more about her mother, who "had not chosen death by water: and the other Bajan women, who had borne daily the brunt of similar humiliations. Selina's identity with a black cultural heritage increases as she painfully realizes that "like her kinsmen, she must somehow prevent illusions from destroying her inside and find a way for her real face to emerge" (p. 291).

Selina seems well on the way toward discovering the differences between realism and illusion. Indicative of this is her address to the audience following the announcement of her scholarship from the Barbadian Homeowners' and Businessmen's Association:

> My trouble was that I wanted everything to be simple—the good clearly separated from the bad—the way a child sees things. But it's not simple or separate and children can't understand it. Now that I'm less of a child I'm beginning to understand . . ." (p. 303).

How much she understands becomes even clearer when Selina tells her mother,

> Everybody used to call me Deighton's Selina but they were wrong. Because you see I'm truly your child. Remember how you used to talk about how you left home and came here alone as a girl of eighteen and was your own woman? I used to love hearing that. And that's what I want." (p. 309).

Appropriately, Silla ends the conversation with a benediction that reaches back in time to her own mother and the African descendants before her: "G'long! You was always too much woman for me anyway, soul. And my own mother did say two-head-bulls can't reign in a flock" (p. 307). The use of the appellation, "soul," connotes both a physical and a spiritual kinship, and Silla's acknowledgment of Selina as a woman suggests she is a worthy opponent. Additionally, the proverb completes in the traditional African style, a succinct summation of mother and daughter personalities.

The novel ends with the architectural imagery which has been so integral to its structure and development. We return with Selina to the brownstones in Brooklyn which no longer are "somnolent." Rather they are now "ravaged." And replacing the calypso rhythms associated with the West Indians are the "staccato beat of the Spanish" and the "frenzied sensuous music" joined with "the warm canorous Negro sounds" (p. 309). As in the beginning of the novel, Marshall describes a neighborhood in transition. In one area, however, the brownstones "had been blasted to make way for a city project," and Selina observes "a solitary wall [standing] perversely amid the rubble, a stoop still [imposing] its massive grandeur, a carved oak staircase [leading] only to the night sky" (p. 309). Selina emerges as the "sole survivor amid the urban wreckage," and as a token of commemoration, she tosses over her shoulder one of the two silver bangles she had worn from childhood. The other bangle she retains as a sign of her acceptance of her West Indian heritage.

A final review of Selina's loved ones brings the novel full circle and bequeaths to our heroine a small but uncertain strength. As she walks down Fulton Street, the "flickering lights" reflect her flickering hope of finding peace and the "things that shaped it: love, a clearer vision, a place . . ." (p. 308). With her arrangement for passage Aboard a ship to the Caribbean, we appreciate more fully the journey Selina must still undertake to firmly establish her cultural identity. Her parents' images of Barbados continue to intrigue, while the American—even the African American perspectives and habits—confuse. But at last she is prepared—indeed, freed—to accept the challenge of defining herself in her own terms within a broader cultural context. With Marshall's subsequent fiction that context becomes expansive enough to include all peoples of the African Diaspora.

---

1 Paule Marshall, "From the Poets in the Kitchen," in *Reena and Other Stories* (Old Westbury, New York: The Feminist Press, 1983), 9.

2 Alexis DeVeaux, "Paule Marshall: In Celebration of Our Triumph," *Essence* 10, No. 1 (May 1978), 98.

3 Ibid., 124.

4 Ibid.

5 Paule Marshall, *Brown Girl, Brownstones* (Chatham, New Jersey: Chatham Bookseller, 1959), 4. The page numbers of subsequent references to the novel are noted parenthetically in the text.

[6] Marshall, "From the Poets in the Kitchen," 6.

[7] Kimberly Benston, "Architectural Imagery and Unity in Paule Marshall's *Brown Girl, Brownstones,*" *Negro American Literature Form* 9 (Fall 1975), 68.

[8] For a discussion of the gang system among women workers during slavery in Barbados refer to Hilary Beckles, *Natural Rebels: A Social History of Enslaved Black Women in Barbados* (New Brunswick, New Jersey: Rutgers University Press, 1989), 29-43.

[9] See Schneider's article "A Search for Selfhood: Paule Marshall's *Brown Girl, Brownstones,"* in *The Afro-American Novel Since 1960,* eds., Peter Bruch and Wolfgang Karrer (Amsterdam: Gruener Publishing Co., 1982), 65.

[10] "Turbulence and Tenderness: Mothers, Daughters, and 'Other Mothers' in Paule Marshall's *Brown Girl, Brownstones,*" *SAGE A Scholarly Journal on Black Women* 1, No. 2 (Fall 1984), 14.

[11] For a discussion of African kinship relations, see John S. Mbiti, *African Religions and Philosophies* (Garden City, New York: Doubleday and Co., Inc., 1970), 267.

[12] Eugenia Collier, "Closing of the Circle: Movement from Division to Wholeness in Paule Marshall's Fiction," in *Black Women Writers (1900-1980): A Critical Evaluation*, ed. Mari Evans (Garden City, New York: Anchor Press, 1983), 302.

[13] Collier, "Closing of the Circle: Movement from Division to Wholeness in Paule Marshall's Fiction," 302.

[14] John P. Davis, ed., *The American Negro Reference Book* (Englewood Cliffs: Prentice-Hall, Inc., 1966), 69; Larry G. Murphy, J. Gordon Melton, and Gary L. Ward, eds., *Encyclopedia of African American Religions* (Hamden, CT.: Garland Publishing, 1993).

[15] Paule Marshall, "Shaping the 'World of My Art,'" *New Letters* (Autumn 1974), 103.

[16] Barbara Christian, "Paule Marshall" in *African-American Writers,* consulting ed., Valerie Smith and general eds., Leah Baechler and A. Walton (New York: Charles Scribners and Sons, 1991), 289-304.

[17] Troester, "Turbulence and Tenderness . . . ," 14.

[18] Collier, "Closing of the Circle . . .," 303.

PART IV

Color and Dominance in Latino History and Literature

Next to African Americans among non-white Americans, Latinos have had a noticeable presence in much of the United States, although their initial concentration was in the Southwestern states. In their essays, Lizabeth Paravisini-Gebert and Frances Aparicio charge that hegemonic forces in the United States have colonized these descendants of Native Americans, Hispanics, and Africans, both inside and outside the forty-eight contiguous states.

In her essay, Aparicio tells us that as Latinos become more politically threatening to interests of the United States, diversity among Latinos is de-emphasized and they are institutionalized in order to offset their influence as agents of cultural transformation that would impact the dominant culture. On the other hand, she asserts that heightened attempts at assimilation through education and English-only-mandates and the "problem" of the darker-hued Latinos make cultural identity by individual groups difficult. Thus, to Aparicio, the idea of multiculturalism has resulted in a superficial appeasement of diverse cultural groups without serious consideration of addressing their social problems and interests.

Puerto Rico, about whose people Paravisini-Gebert writes, became a possession of the United States at the end of the Spanish-American War—the point at which documentation of Puerto Rican migration to the mainland began—and acquired commonwealth status in 1952. These immigrants settled along the East Coast but primarily in New York City and in New Jersey, bringing with them Afro-Latin cultural traditions. By some estimates, there were approximately 2.2 million Puerto Ricans in the United States, a figure somewhat higher than Paravisini-Gebert's.

Paravisini-Gebert employs a historical methodology and literary analysis to argue that from its beginnings in the mid-nineteenth century, Puerto Rican literature became the vehicle for commenting on socio-political problems and for aiming to address issues of foreign dominance—first by Spain and then by the United States. Her thesis holds that the literature of Puerto Rico and of Puerto Rican immigrants to the United States has had the central theme of a dominant, polarizing "other," a phenomenon which is understood in the context of the island's colonized history.

As a member of the marginalized Puerto Rican communities, in the United States and on the island, Paravisini-Gebert takes the position that knowledge derived from the reality of racial and ethnic diversity should be used responsibly to reconceptualize America into a nation of cultural groups, each economically and politically empowered within its own cultural space; such an occurrence, she writes, would create "a true acceptance" of pluralism. More provocatively, she intimates that only insiders of the diverse Latino ethnic groups qualify to interpret their respective historical experiences and cultural traditions.

Andrade's social science approach to analyzing machismo in association with Mexican male-ness brings gendered perspective to the discussion of dominance. By some counts, there were no more than 300,000 Mexicans in the United States before 1900, and many were descendants of residents in Mexican territories ceded to this country in the 1830s and 1840s. From 1900 to 1930, the Mexican population in the southwestern U.S. increased by more than one and a half million. Up to 1910 however, impoverished mestizo and Indian masses—who suffered economic devastation at the hands of the Diaz government—must have been predominant among those who fled across the border in search of economic security. Political disruptions and economic instability followed in the wake of the overthrow of the Diaz dictatorship and ensuing unrest from 1910 to 1920. These conditions caused hundreds of thousands more Mexicans, some more privileged than others, to flee.

With these immigrants came social values that prized respect for elders, family solidarity, and unquestioned authority of the father. Although he refers to it as *machismo*, Andrade discussed its several forms and its positive and negative manifestations. Using the example of the relationship between his Mexican parents, he reminds us that unquestioned-authority-of-the father need not mean misogyny or unrelenting male dominance. Paternal authority may, indeed, translate into a husband's giving deference to his wife in the making of decisions about household and family matters. *Machismo* could have broader social manifestations of a sexist nature. Andrade asserts, in fact, that *machismo* is not a uniquely Mexican trait and that it may take on a racist as well as a sexist quality among Europeans warriors, for example. From his insider's view, Andrade brings a fresh insight into the dynamics of cross-gender relations among our considerable Mexican American populace.

The three essays in this section remind us that despite their being conflated under the Latino label, peoples from the Americas south of the United States are multiethnic off-spring of a variety of classes and cultures. Each ethnic group and its sub-division encounters the United States from the perspective of its historical experiences and contemporary interest. As a result of the varieties of their Latino-historical experiences, Aparicio and Paravisini-Gebert question the likelihood that Latino traditions will survive the onslaught of the European cultural hegemony that predominates in the United States and influences the Western hemisphere. They suggest that pluralism is a centrist movement which marginalizes the masses of workers and benefits white artists/scholars and middle and upper class Latinos. How valid do you think these decidedly pessimistic assertions are? Are these assertions, together with the *machismo* concept, more grounded in stereotype than in actual lived-experience? Our understanding in these regards is facilitated by reading the Paravisini-Gebert and Andrade essays against the backdrop of Aparicio's broadly-pitched discussion of multi-color and multi-culture among Latinos.

American Color(s): U.S. Latinos and Multiculturalism

Frances R. Aparicio
Department of Romance Languages and Literature,
University of Michigan

Willie Colón, the famous Puerto Rican Salsa singer, composer and producer, was nominated last year for the Grammy Award for his song "Color Americano" ("American Color"), in which he described the United States as a cultural space divided by racial tension and cultural dualities. In these lyrics Colon posits himself as a Latino commodity, an exotic Other attractive to the Anglo gaze. He explicitly says, with colorful imagery that he causes a sensation in New York with his coffee-colored skin.

I have begun with this song to illustrate two simultaneous yet contradictory forces that constitute "Latino Culture(s)" in the United States. First, *latinidad* as object—a construct of the Anglo mainstream—a factor referred to above; second, the Latino as cultural subject or agent in the transformations taking place in the Anglo mainstream. This second trend is evident in Willie Colon's song title in which he inverts the traditional racial dichotomy based on skin color. He reinscribes the signifier *America* and stretches it into a more inclusive term, both resisting and subverting its imperialist basis. America's color—the Americas, North, South, Central, and the Caribbean—is coffee, *café con leche*, a *mestizaje* or hybridity of American, European

Reprinted by permission of the author.

and Anglo colors. When considering the Americas as a whole, this discursive repositioning reflects that white Americans become the "other" and, demographically, the minority.

The June 1988 issue of *Time* celebrated the mainstreaming of Latino cultures in the United States. Since then, we have witnessed a double cultural aperture in this country's public arena: Latinos are being tropicalized, while simultaneously they are participating in the tropicalization of the North. The media's celebration of Latinos in the United States implies in a positive way a recognition of our demographic presence and of our future growth into the largest ethnic group by the year 2010. However, this aperture also implies the appropriation of cultural practices and objects by the media, since these are translated into terms and perspectives to be "read" and consumed by others. Caribbean food, Salsa and Latin jazz, Mexican mariachi music, and even Cuban *machismo* already have been appropriated into what I perceive to be inedible versions of *arroz con pollo*, Salsa rhythms in Sting's music, *Canciones a mi Padre* by a Linda Ronstadt overdeterminedly dressed in Mexican folklore, and *Mambo Kings Play Songs of Love* in Oscar Hijuuelos' Pulitzer Prize winning novel.

While many middle and upper middle class Latinos may regard this as a sign of their successful assimilation and acceptance by the larger society, these trends are clear examples of tropicalizations, of *latinidad* as ideological construct. The ideology leads to a series of myths about Latino culture that constitutes a cultural imaginary, allowing us to be named, erased, and contoured by others in accordance with the political and economic interests of U.S. institutions. We cannot afford to forget that while this media hype about Latinos has been developing, economic disenfranchisement, racial segregation, educational exclusions, diminishing health and social services and cultural paternalism constitute the reality of living in the United States for all of our working-class ethnic groups.

As history has illustrated, and as sociologists have documented in the cases of the labor movement, environmentalism—and even feminism—whenever a grassroots movement acquires enough strength to become threatening to the political and economic interests of this country, it becomes institutionalized. In this case, the institutionalization of "ethnicity" has led to the prevailing academic discourse of multiculturalism and diversity. At the same time, I want to reaffirm that

Ethnic Studies, Chicano, Latino and Puerto Rican Studies Programs, like their African American counterpart, did not just appear overnight due to the institutionalizing trend. The history of the Civil Rights movement, coupled with the real, physical, and material struggles of the United Farm Workers, la Raz Unida Party and the Latino student demonstrations across the nation, was such a strong force that universities and educational institutions were mandated to realize that the exclusionary status quo no longer could be maintained.

One finds that this double strand of forces—the radical along with the institutional—explains the presence (albeit small) of Latinos in academia. More than twenty years later, however, the participation of Latinos in academia and in the production of new historical and interdisciplinary scholarship has increased and evolved. Simultaneously, however, the Latin presence in education is less now, in the 1990s, than in the 1970s if it is considered in proportion to the rapid population growth of Latino communities in the United States. The public perception, additionally articulated in the anti-democratic forces and attacks against (so-called) "political correctness," is that there is some kind of ethnic and color invasion in academe. While pioneering criticism of early ethnic scholars clearly impacted the contemporary critique of Western cultural paradigms, I refuse to believe that there are too many Latinos in any one educational institution in this country.

The term *Hispanic* was, as many of you know, coined by the Nixon administration and by the U.S. Census Bureau. This small example reveals the struggle over discourse that has characterized the experience of ethnic groups in the United States. As an integral part of ideological constructs, the term *Hispanic* is a signifier imposed from without, yet many Latinos internalize this colonial/linguistic relationship and further employ it as self-designation. Most self-designated *Hispanos* are usually middle and upper middle class and have accepted this particular label because it reaffirms their need to differentiate themselves from the working-class and darker-skinned sector of Latinos in this country. This example of colonization through language also signals the ways in which the mainstream and the government homogenize ethnic groups, erasing intracultural differences and paternalistically assuming a collective definition for them. Latinos are not *just* Spanish; they represent a number of cultural groups that have merged historically and racially, from Spain, Africa, France, Italy,

Germany, and Russia. Latinos are from Meso America and from the Inca Empire. Some have been born in the Sonoran deserts of the Southwest and in the Caribbean islands surrounded by the seas. Others have been born in the slums of New York and in the urban centers of California. Some came to this country as young adults and speak Spanish; others only speak English, for their parents wanted to protect them from linguistic and racial discrimination that they suffered here in the past.

When considered from the perspective of Luis Valdes,[1] we did not come to the United States; the United States came to us. This is documented in the presence of Mexican Americans in the Southwest and West and in the legacy of Puerto Rican colonialism. Some Latinos are dark whereas some are bronze colored; others are *café con leche*, but some are light-skinned and blonde. These variations are found even among siblings.

Some American Latinos are middle class professionals, but most are employed in labor and the service sector. According to Alejandro Portes, the term *Hispanic* is most pernicious in the context of class. For example, elite universities across the country are recruiting and offering "minority" scholarships to young individuals of Latin American descent (defined as one parent coming from Latin America) who have not been educationally underprivileged or economically marginalized. The concealing and elastic nature of the rubric *Hispanic* has allowed many to include under this category privileged young people who have had access to education because of their social class. Portes, a Cuban professor of immigration at Johns Hopkins University, illustrates this phenomenon with the case of his daughter. Moreover, official government surveys on economic conditions benefit from conflating "all" Hispanics together. Under this label, after twelve years of Republicanism, the solid economic standing of many Cubans and upper class professional Latin Americans dilutes the impoverished conditions of most U.S. Latinos (Mexicans, Central Americans and Puerto Ricans).

Hollywood's obsession with movies about *aliens* either from outer space (*E.T., Mork and Mindy,* or *Close Encounters of a Third Kind*)—or from south of the border (*Red Dawn, Border Patrol*) does not merely reflect a regional emphasis or the development of a particular artistic form such as science fiction. These films articulate a constant national preoccupation in the United States with difference, i. e., via this condition of laterity, the dominant population sector finds a way to cope with the apparent *invasion* of difference. The humor in Cheech Marin's *Born in East L.A.*, with its final scene of a brown invasion of the United States, resides precisely in its subversion of this xenophobia and paranoia concerning invasion (an ironic twist to the historical participation by this country as an imperialist force and invader). Similarly, *The Little Mermaid* proposes that happiness is guaranteed to those who are courageous enough to leave their "sub" cultures and assimilate to the dominant models of being. As these examples illustrate, to Hollywood difference is too painful to be understood, let alone accepted as part of the national self.

Past efforts to maintain cultural identity through educational programs have been under constant attack. Language itself—articulated in the controversies around bilingual education and the English-Only Movements—has become a *locus* of cultural struggles at the national level. In the United States today, to speak in two or more languages is prestigious only when those additional languages are either French or German (And I qualify this, since history has shown that German itself suffered this type of attack and erasure as a result of the political tension created by the Second World War, a destructive effort from which German departments are only now beginning to recover.). To speak both English and Spanish often is seen as symptomatic of the underclass, as a deficiency; Latino students are deemed "alingual" when they speak both languages, alternating them and creating code-switching patterns. Thus, while bilingual education was initiated in this country as a consequence of linguistic resistance on the part of the Chinese-American sector in California, the praxis and its institutionalization have transformed these programs into loci for the erasure of non-English languages. Most U.S. bilingual programs are "transitional," and students move on to an all-English curriculum once they are able to function minimally in their second language.

The English-Only Movement reveals the national ignorance about the linguistic reality of Latinos. While Spanish is retained by many who migrated to the U.S. as adults, most Latinos born or raised here speak English as their first language. If this were not the case, there would be no need for courses in Spanish for Native Speakers, an academic offering which has grown substantially in the last twenty years. In fact, the ability of many U.S. Latinos to express themselves in

Spanish has been unduly hampered by the official duality between "public" and "private" and by the simultaneous repression and undermining of Latin cultures. Recent work by sociolinguists indicates that bilingualism is a functional praxis that changes with age and life stages, with professional and work needs, and with the affective and the cognitive. In other words, bilingualism is not a linear, chronological praxis for an individual, but a circular, concentric one enmeshing the society.[2]

Since the first encounters of Spanish and Portuguese explorers with the Americas, Latin languages and cultures have lived amidst diverse races and cultures. Latino societies have been historically configured by dualities that repel and attract forces between at least two disparate societies, languages and cultures. Latinos have been the conquered and the conqueror, as Joaquin "Corky" Gonzalez announced in *Yo soy Joaquín* more than twenty years ago. Cultural pluralism and multiculturalism have been consistently negotiated throughout our historical past, in the United States and south of the border.

The abuse of terms such as *diversity, multiculturalism*, and *ethnicity* has led to a semantic saturation that has devalued the complexity and the multidimensional histories of each of the particular cultural groups constituting the United States. These terms erase many of the central issues at hand for racialized groups in this country. As E. San Juan Jr. has commented, "ethnicity functions like a floating signifier, a synthesizing figure that can codify all narratives of collective life into something like an updated version of Robert Park's archetype of the 'race relations cycle.'" In fact, he suggests, race and class are relabeled and concealed under the modifier "ethnicity."[3]

Although the media and the New Right capitalize on this national xenophobia and accuse leading institutions of violating free speech, many who champion multiculturalism and diversity in their universities have not made any attempts to address the issues of recruitment of underprivileged constituencies, such as Chicanos and Puerto Ricans, neither do they honestly confront the rhetorized obsession with excellency and academic standards. In other words, let us be multicultural and touch elbows with Latinos, but only with those who come from upper class and upper middle class families. Let us not disturb or lose the academic standards that have made this university such a fine institution. We can assuage our feelings of Anglo-liberal guilt by sprinkling our memos and our speeches with key terms denoting plurality, but let us not engage in many radical changes.

Recruitment of Latino faculty has remained stagnant. For many prestigious universities, opportunities programs have translated into making offers to the same, limited number of privileged Latina and Latino scholars. Untenured Latino scholars face a series of obstacles: their commitment to work with Latino students and to participate in community-oriented events is not only undervalued, but deemed conflictive with scholarly work by faculty peers. Much of their scholarship on ethnic work is not properly evaluated by peers in other fields, and thus it is perceived by many promotion committees as not "serious" or "useful" enough.

Colonized structures have not been dismantled yet. In general, Latino Studies Programs and Ethnic Studies Programs still face condescending attitudes that somehow academic quality in these areas never measured up to other, traditional departments. Joint appointments, while validating interdisciplinary work, also perpetuate the colonized status of ethnic studies. In most universities, Ethnic Studies still hold a "program" status, not a departmental one. While this is also the case with Women's Studies, American Studies and other area programs, I believe that the capacity for decision-making is undermined by the power of traditional departments on which Ethnic Studies Programs depend for faculty recruitment.

Ironically, what many scholars do not seem to remember or acknowledge is that the questioning of Western culture and deconstructive approximations of discourse and texts arose both from the conjuncture of feminist, African American, Chicano, Asian American and Native American scholarship, and European post-structuralist and deconstructive theorizing. Thus, while Chicano or Latino Studies Programs remain colonial in these university structures, colleagues in traditional departments are *now* appropriating (this is exactly the term I want to use) "ethnicity" approaches in order to enhance their own scholarship and, of course, in order to increase their market value (as savvy mainstream academicians know). They think that they are discovering something new, like Christopher Colombus when he "discovered" the Indians. Like Columbus, they are reinventing *us* while they reinvent the wheel. For example, Gloria Anzaldúa's *Borderlands/ La Frontera*[4] still is being quoted by top mainstream scholars ten years after its publication, yet references to it appear as if it is the only avant-garde publication in Chicana feminism or in bicultural theories.

In presentations by mainstream Americanists, the topos of the *border* has become a scholarly metaphor that stands for interdisciplinary and cross-cultural trends in the curriculum of American Studies. However, while this concept is paraphrased, summarized, and developed in professional meetings, Anzaldua and other Chicana/o writers are not being acknowledged as pioneers in border scholarship. While it will be interesting to see the effects of multicultural teaching in a re-canonizing of Latino ethnic literatures and scholarship, many Chicano literary texts will be used without taking into account the dialogue that they have established with other texts within the field. In other words, there is a danger of decontextualizing and of isolating works whose significance and meanings are enhanced by the historical and discursive positions they have assumed within the dialogue of their own cultural group.

At this historical juncture, fields of inquiry into Latino cultural and historical realities have not been demarginalized; yet, they are targeted as objects of consumption by scholars in the center. Those in the center approach the margins and, without de-centering themselves, appropriate marginality. But marginality is not a condition that one borrows, or that one puts on as a costume or a mask. It is a form of life, a way of being that marks one's perspectives. It involves a positioning of the subject (through colonialism, economic oppression, educational exclusion) that allows for critical and new ways of looking, listening and writing. This has allowed for a freedom in scholarship, a newness and vigor that has characterized feminist and ethnic writing. Marginal scholarship does not disavow the values and ethos of everyday life, of manual work, of the person and the family. Well before post-modernism became a catch word in academic circles, Latino and Latina scholars, as well as African American, Asian American and Native American scholars, have been de-centering academic discourse since they were given a space for critical writing, mostly through Ethnic Studies Programs. These scholars consistently thought against the grain, continuously constituting a counterdiscourse, not because it was academic avant-garde, but because it was the only way they could survive psychologically. Many took (and still take) risks in their so-called career paths, and instead of focusing exclusively on their mainstream areas of scholarship (which they are still reminded to do), they invest time and energy and critical thinking that affect (and have affected) them personally: biculturalism, bilingualism, racial and gender exclusions, and trying to understand why their work and words remain unheard, unsung, and invisible to others. The last twenty years have witnessed the growth of small conferences, like NACS and Spanish in the United States, into larger institutionalized events. Our ex-centricity has been dismantled, and now many scholars are part of a system that cannibalized our work, even while it is "defanged" as Martin Espada, a Puerto Rican poet from Massachusetts, describes.

A true acceptance of diversity cannot and must not exclude the roots and the major sector of our cultures, the workers. It must include an anagnorisis of class conflicts and race divisions. It must acknowledge and value the intra-group differences among Latinas and Latinos. True multiculturalism must not remain merely a scholarly paradigm. It must translate into true economic development for the working class. It must allow for empowerment and autonomy in decision-making for Latino and other ethnic scholars. It must not be afraid to establish decolonizing changes in institutional structures.

Multiculturalism from the top down is also essential, but alone it will not be effective. Intradifferences and the historical particularities of each ethnic group must be respected and recognized. We must also recognize that the new knowledge base produced by ethnic scholars in the United States needs to be employed to in(re)form those who now are interested in participating in this historical revolution, from kindergarten to Ph.D. programs. Ethnic scholarship should not remain an "appendage" in revised canons, but it should be regarded as central to the reconcepturalizing of America. We need to recognize the need for scholarly interdependence, coupled with respect for the validity of cultural authority. When those who have been in the center are willing to cede the authority of differential knowledge to others, then the center will expand. It will become a larger circumference of equitable representation at all levels. If not, multiculturalism will only be one more approach within the highest levels of the social and economic pyramid, an object of study uprooted from its vital historical context, from its daily ethos, from its own marginality that gave it strength and voice.

Let us not be afraid of a degree of separatism among the various ethnic and racial groups in the United States.

> Separatism may be one stage of movement toward more egalitarian relationships among groups; it may also indicate polarization between groups or a halt in efforts to work together. . . . Differences may reflect differences in underlying assumptions and goals or simply different strategies to reach similar ends. In addition, processes to bring the groups back together on a more equal footing are needed to prevent fragmentation and particularism. If separation of groups is one part of movement toward multiculturalism, transitional phases and transitional structures (bridge-building) must also become part of the process.[5]

I would argue, then, that every racial and ethnic group needs to be empowered within its own cultural space before it is able to implement the necessary bridge building toward multiculturalism. How can Latinas and Latinos move on to accept renegotiating our own identities with that of others, when we still are struggling in the battle of underrepresentation, colonization, and economic disenfranchisement?

The multicultural paradigm will remain utopic if it is not effectively translated into the world outside academic halls, if it does not influence public policy and political elections; if it fails to ameliorate racial and economic segregation in this country; if it does not transform the attitudes and underlying assumptions of what it means to be an American. As Guillermo Gómez-Peña has clearly articulated:

> Together, we can collaborate in surprising cultural projects but without forgetting that both should retain control of the product, from the planning stages up through the distribution. If this doesn't occur, then intercultural collaboration isn't authentic. We shouldn't confuse true collaboration with political paternalism, cultural vampirism, voyeurism, economic opportunism, and demagogic multiculturalism.[6]

We should clear up this matter once and for all: "We (Latinos in the United States) don't want to be a mere ingredient of the melting pot. What we want is to participate actively in a humanistic pluralistic and political dialogue, continuous and not sporadic. We want this dialogue to occur between equals who enjoy the same power of negotiation."[7]

[1] Luis Valdez, "Introduction to *Aztlán: An Anthology of Mexican American Literature*, eds. Luis Valdez and Stan Steiner. (New York: Vintage Books, 1972), p. xxxiii.

[2] Yolanda Solé, "Hispanic bilingualism in the United States: Stable or Transitional?" Keynote Address, *Tenth National Conference on Spanish in the United States/El Español en los Estadoes Unidos*, Tucson, Arizona, October 6, 1989.

[3] Epiphanio San Juan, Jr., "The Call of ethnicity and the fetish of pluralism" in *Cultural Critique* 18 (Spring 1991: 216-17)

[4] Gloria Anzaldúa, *Borderlands/La Frontera*. (San Francisco: Spinsters/Aunt Lute Books, 1987).

[5] Amy Schultz, "On the road to muticulturalism: A PCMA Seminar Report." Program in Conflict Management Alternatives Working Paper #33, Ann Arbor, MI: University of Michigan, April, 1992, p. 16.

[6] Guillermo Gómez Peña, "Documented/Undocumented," trans. Rubén Martínez. In *Multi-cultural Literacy*, eds, Ricke Simonson and Scott Walker. (St. Paul, MN: Graywolf 1988), 132.

[7] Ibid.

Patterns of Dominance in Puerto Rican Literature: A Historical Overview

Lizabeth Paravisini-Gebert
Department of Hispanic Studies, Vassar College

The response to a dominant "other" is the central theme in Puerto Rican literature. Its importance in our literary tradition can be readily understood through an examination of Puerto Rico's history of colonial relationships and an analysis of the cultural, linguistic, and racial implications of the island's socio-political development within structures where "dominance" has always rested in the hands of a foreign power, an imperial "other." Forced into submissive relationships with the representatives of colonial powers, Puerto Rican intellectuals have responded with a defensive stance against dominance from abroad; this response has been one of the central tenets of our intellectual and literary expression.

Of all the former Spanish possessions in the New World, Puerto Rico was the only one to have entered the twentieth century still a colony. In the roughly four centuries it remained under Spanish control, the island lagged behind other imperial colonies: economically, it languished until the beginning of the nineteenth century, when sugar and coffee production opened links to the worldwide economic system (at the expense, however, of an increased dependence on slave labor and the exploitation of the free labor force). Politically, it suffered from the

Reprinted by permission of the author.

repressive backlash prompted by the Latin American wars of independence, which awakened Spain to the need for repressive measures in order to hold on to what remained of its crumbling empire. Culturally, it suffered from lack of educational opportunities for the majority of the population, dependence on foreign cultural models, and deplorable internal communications. On the eve of the 1898 American invasion, after over four hundred years under Spanish control, roughly ninety three percent of the population was illiterate, only fifteen percent of Puerto Rican families owned land, medical care was unavailable to an overwhelming percentage of the population, and travel from the interior of the island to the capital could take days of laborious effort.

The 1898 U.S. invasion had a considerable impact on material conditions in the island, for it brought better educational opportunities for the masses, improved health care and communications, and a democratic system of political participation with extensive but not universal franchise. It did not, however, change the structures within which political development took place, and the island's social and economic problems were exacerbated. One immediate result of the American takeover was the collapse of the island's coffee industry (already ailing in the 1890s and rapidly moving towards foreign control) and its replacement with large, highly technological sugar mills controlled by foreign consortia. The development of a system of agricultural monoculture in absentee hands was accompanied by the amassing of large extensions of fertile lands under American corporate control, precluding the continuing growth of most local capital investments and leading to the bankruptcy of a large number of Puerto Rican planters and businessmen. The collapse of the local economy intensified the formation of an impoverished proletariat subsisting on low wages, and plunged the island into a vicious cycle of dependence on foreign capital, with the concomitant result of profits being drained out of the island.

Economic control was accompanied by attempts at imposing American cultural values on the Puerto Rican population, beginning with English being made compulsory in island schools in 1905 (an imposition that lasted into the late 1940s and that succeeded in making the Spanish language the centerpiece of anti-American resistance). Conscious efforts were made to stifle all important cultural manifestations in the belief that only the adoption of American values would make loyal American citizens of the Puerto Rican population. These efforts included a virtual invasion of the island by Protestant missionaries in an attempt to eradicate Catholicism, the virtual elimination of the teaching of Puerto Rican history and literature in local schools, the discouragement of traditional cultural practices and their replacement of these with American rituals that had no roots in Puerto Rican culture.[1]

As the Puerto Rican example shows, the most damaging result of colonial relationships lies in the subordination of local cultural, political, and socio-economic development to the colonizer's interests, precluding internal development and resulting in the discouragement or interdiction of everything that is deemed threatening to continuing control over the colonized territory. The essence of colonial relationships is precisely the defining of everything belonging to the dominant culture as superior and everything belonging to the dominated culture as inferior. Relations thus defined, it becomes the self-imposed "duty" of the dominant group to use its power to impose its values onto the colonized country as the means of forestalling any effort at gaining independence.

After almost a century under American domination, the issue of Puerto Rico's political status continues to thwart and obscure all other local political concerns. Throughout the twentieth century, political debate on the island has centered around the question of sovereignty, with any consideration of national autonomy placed in abeyance until it can be determined whether the island will become a state of the United States or an independent nation. The Commonwealth option—called in Spanish "Estado Libre Asociado" or "Free Associated State"—resolving nothing, left the country in a political limbo that perpetuated colonial irresolution. In the meantime, Puerto Rico's political life remained in a state of arrested development, and democratic growth was static and inapplicable to other issues and concerns.

Not surprisingly, the problems posed by the island's unresolved political situation became the central topics of Puerto Rican literature. Thus, the recurring themes in our literary history converged on the following issues: the island's unresolved political status and its resulting unresolved sense of national selfhood; alienation from the self arising from the subordination of a predominantly mulatto population to a white and fundamentally racist colonial power; the concomitant struggle to preserve local traditions in the face of the onslaught from the powerful American media and its cultural message; the conflict between American values and traditional Puerto Rican mores; and the struggle to uphold the Spanish language as the vehicle of national communication and identity. As a consequence, language became synonymous with nationality for Puerto Ricans.

Literature began to be written and published in Puerto Rico in the mid-nineteenth century, a crucial time in the development of our national identity. The emergence of Puerto Rican literature coincided with the Creole planter class's attempts to consolidate its economic strength in the struggle against Spanish expatriates who controlled commerce and banking on the island. Because it is so closely linked to the articulation of the Creole upper-class ideology as it defined itself in opposition to foreign (i.e. colonial) interests and concerns, Puerto Rican literature was identified with factors related to our search for a national identity: regionalism, the struggle against colonial rule and extraneous cultural influences, the Puerto Rican vernacular, and the affirmation of the culture's profound roots in the land. Literature quickly became (for the literate middle and upper-middle classes at least) the vehicle to illustrate the socio-political problems of the island and to counteract foreign dominance.

By some accounts, the signal publication in the emergence of Puerto Rican literature was Manuel Alonso's *El gíbaro*, an 1849 collection of vignettes about peasant customs and traditions in the Puerto Rican countryside. *El gíbaro* was a seminal work in that it attempted to define Puerto Rican culture in its own terms, separating it from the traditions and customs of the Spanish metropolis. It showed Puerto Rican literature as attempting, from its very inception, to delineate the essence of Puerto Rican nationality and character against that of the colonizer. As with any other attempt to catch the essence of something as elusive as identity or nationality, *El gíbaro* embodied a concept of *Puerto Rican-ness* that was limited by Alonso's planter-class ideology. Politically, *El gíbaro* was not a revolutionary book in as much as it did not call for a rejection of the colonizing power. Socially, it rooted national identity in the customs and traditions of the idealized, light-skinned, mountain-based peasant of Spanish descent, ignoring the culture and contributions of the large coastal-based population of African descent. These limitations aside, Alonso's stance was "progressive" in that he brought "the spirit of the island to a literary work" that he recreated from the "nonofficial language." He, therefore, gave "literary status to the marginalized," and he exposed and revealed "the country's [ambiguous] reality."[2] Thus, with Alonso's *El gíbaro*, our literary tradition opened with a question that would dominate it throughout the first century of development: *How can Puerto Rico, without independence, define itself against domination from the outside?*

Puerto Rico's *engagée* literary tradition spawned an analogous critical discourse wherein rewards and "punishments" were correlated to the writer's degree of commitment to the evolution of the national identity movement. The towering figures of Puerto Rican literature in the latter half of the nineteenth century—Eugenio María de Hostos, Alejandro Tapia y Rivera, Salvador Brau, José de Diego, Lola Rodríguez de Tió, and others—articulated the vision of an island in a ceaseless struggle to assert itself culturally and politically. This tradition, in its zeal, frequently lost sight of other literary causes—protofeminism, aestheticism, Africanism. These causes were not directly bound with the nation-building agenda of the island's intellectual elite, therefore, they were relegated to the margins of our cultural history. The publication of two major works in 1895, a key year in Puerto Rico's struggle for political autonomy from Spain, is a case in point. Carmela Eulate Sanjurjo's realistic masterpiece, *La muñeca*, the story of a selfish young woman whose greed ruins and destroys her husband, quickly faded into an oblivion. It was not rescued until almost one hundred years later, despite an enthusiastic endorsement by Sanjurjo's fellow writer Manuel Zeno Gandía. Meanwhile Zeno Gandía's own *La charca*, an analysis of Puerto Rico as a nation undermined by disease and powerlessness, was immediately heralded as a Puerto Rican classic.

La charca, a naturalistic novel modeled on the works of Emile Zola, chronicles life in of a small village in the interior of the island, showing peasants overcome by disease, hunger, violence, illiteracy, and miscegenation. The author intended that work to be the first in a series of chronicles depicting the ills of colonization that left Puerto Rico a morally weakened and aimless society. Through disease, the central metaphor of *La charca*, Zeno Gandía portrayed his country "as a great organism beset by innumerable ills."[3]

In subsequent volumes of the series, Zeno Gandía's message, one typical of the liberal-progressive intellectuals of early twentieth-century

Puerto Rico, was that "U.S. racism and contempt shackled the Island's spirit and culture."[4] In his 1922 novel *El negocio*, he focused on the sale of the country to foreign businesses and monopolies, and chastised Puerto Ricans for the greed that had led them into connivance with the enemy. His analysis of colonial exploitation prompted him to conclude that Puerto Rico was "a nation of hostages."[5]

Zeno Gandía's conclusions were supported by his younger colleague Antonio S. Pedreira, author of *Insularismo*. Published in 1934, influential islanders considered this work to have articulated the official frame of reference for any evaluation of Puerto Rican culture. In his analysis of the island's cultural development, Pedreira echoed Gandía's pessimistic outlook on Puerto Rico's prospects for cultural autonomy in a colonial situation. Referring to imperial dominance as "one of the most repressive signs of our culture . . . and the factor that explains our carbonized personality," Pedreira concluded:

> Puerto Rico has lived a fictitious historical life, foreign to its ethnic nature, having to react by reflex action to stimuli and events not born in the depths of our collective conscience. . . . The constant disciplinary watch over us has conditioned our identifying character, . . . and we have had to focus our sights on ourselves, completely abandoning the contemplation of the peoples surrounding us. . . . Puerto Rico's history has developed in a defensive attitude, unfolding upon itself, looking only within in order to avoid strategic surprises. . . . The duty of Puerto Rico's youth is to break the walls of this isolation, to be able to look around us.[6]

Pedreira's analysis of Puerto Rican culture was prompted by his desire to outline the defining characteristics of Puerto Rican identity and lay to rest the notion that the American cultural onslaught had been successful in destroying the island's national character. His conclusions, therefore, pointed to the need to bring an end to the colonial relationships threatening Puerto Rican culture and sense of self. Only the end of colonial dominance, he reminded readers, could prevent the dissolution of the national character.

For all their efforts at depicting the ills of colonialism and the need to oppose the submissive stance that colonial relationships forced on Puerto Rico, both Pedreira and Zeno Gandía seem to have internalized colonial racial attitudes. Zeno Gandía blamed what he saw as the country's lack of determination to revolt against miscegenation.

Racial mixture, he argued, had weakened the population, diluted the moral and physical strength characteristic of the white race, "contaminating" it with the black race's propensity to ethical and biological decay. Pedreira presented a similar argument, working from a notion of biological determinism or the assignment of specific moral characteristics to specific races. Pedreira declared that racial "fusion" was responsible for Puerto Rico's "con-fusion."[7] Their views on race can be likened to a phenomenon explored in detail by Frantz Fanon in *The Wretched of the Earth* and *Black Skins, White Masks:*

> The Antilleans have no inherent values of their own; they are always contingent on the presence of The Other.[8] The question is always whether he is less intelligent than I, blacker than I, less respectable than I. Every position of one's own, every effort at security, is based on relations of dependence, with the diminution of The Other. It is the wreckage of what surrounds me that provides the foundation of my virility. . . . The Antillean is characterized by his desire to dominate The Other. . . . Therefore, in any given group, . . . one finds the man on top, the court that surrounds him—the in-betweens (who are waiting for something better)—and the losers. The last are slaughtered without mercy. One can imagine the temperature that prevails in the jungle. There is no way out of it.[9]

This theme of domination prevailed in Pedro Juan Soto's *Usmaíl*, a Fanonian exploration of the Puerto Rican as "an oppressed person whose permanent dream is to become the persecutor."[10] Usmaíl, the main character, is named after the U.S. Mail system in a poignant illustration of colonial misunderstanding. He is the mulatto son of a black woman and the colonial official who seduced and abandoned her; he is a character straddling two worlds, alienated from both. Victim of an alienation so intense that he cannot readily identify himself in a mirror, Usmaíl surrenders to the cycles of oppression that are characteristic of colonial society, where everyone is in a constant struggle to master somebody, anybody. Built on the concept of "trickle-down" oppression, relationships between the characters in *Usmaíl* cannot escape the patterns of personal violence and abuse that are intrinsic to a dominant/submissive colonial relationship.[11] Always on the lookout for someone to dominate because s/he is dominated from above, the colonized one is doomed to reproduce the patterns of oppression that characterized his society. Usmaíl's final act—the murder of a U.S.

Marine that follows his sudden awakening from his deep alienation—is futile in that it becomes a self-destructive, individual act incapable of changing the established colonial patterns.

A different perspective on the effects of colonization was offered by René Marqués, whom critics described as "a militant nostalgia."[12] Actually he is remembered as Puerto Rico's most distinguished twentieth-century dramatist and leader of a generation of writers whose work came to full fruition in the fifties and early sixties. In his work, Marqués, repudiates the rapid process of industrialization that took place on the island after the collapse of the sugar industry in the 1940s, arguing in turn for a return to the old nineteenth-century patriarchal agrarian society he idealizes in his plays, short stories, and one novel. He insisted on the need to reestablish the benevolent patriarchy of the *hacienda* if Puerto Rican culture was to be saved from the Anglo-Saxon matriarchy threatening it. In his famous essay "The Docile Puerto Rican," Marqués pointed to the influence of U.S.-styled "Anglo-Saxon matriarchal patterns" as a principal cause of the island's cultural disintegration. He also saw those matriarchal influences as being an obstacle to the masculine energy necessary for salvaging the "existential integrity" of the Puerto Rican nationality.[13] Marqués' ideas come to life in a story titled "En la popa hay un cuerpo reclinado," translating in English to "there is a body leaning against the stern." It was at the stern that the protagonist saw himself as a victim of a domineering mother, a materialistic wife, and a host of other women in positions of power granted by the American system. The protagonist found a solution to his plight by poisoning his wife and castrating himself in front of her dead body. The symbolic act, as in *Usmail,* is that of a self-destructive one who symbolizes the dire effects of colonial castration and the destruction of traditional Puerto Rican *machismo.*

Although he denounced American imperialism in its political and cultural aspects, Marqués embraced the Hispano-Christian heritage. That led him to an idealization of the nineteenth-century *hacienda* system with its patriarchal and racist attitudes, class rigidity, and dependence on slave labor or the poor rural proletariat. Marques' lot was to be nostalgic for an idyllic world that never truly existed, that could only be idealized if seen from the masters' position, that was economically and socially untenable positions in its rejection of the need for industrialization, and that was classist, racist, and sexist. His works offered the paradigm against which a new generation of writers would react.

The salient symbols of the Puerto Rican national identity were taken from literature written prior to the 1960s; it was an essentially conservative articulation that intended to conserve and/or restore values of the Spanish, planter-bourgeois pastoral past. Until the mid to late fifties, to the degree that Puerto Rican literature reflected other experiences or themes, those of women, the proletariat, the urban population, the mulatto, and the African were relegated to the margins of literary discourse. That marginality was coordinate with the social marginality of these groups.

The island-brand of 1960s and 1970s social upheavals brought to the center topics and issues that previously were considered marginal to intellectual discourse in Puerto Rico. The 1950s had set the backdrop against which these upheavals would be played out, for in that earlier decade, the island had rapidly industrialized under the force of Operation Bootstrap, a program designed to attract light manufacturing industries. Industrialization forced the transformation of Puerto Rico from a plantation-based economy to one dominated by technological production. This process naturally affected traditional values and institutions associated with the patriarchal, agrarian society of the past. Combined with an expansion in the educational system, it also opened new employment possibilities for both men and women and contributed to the growing urbanization of Puerto Rican society. These socioeconomic shifts were reflected in Puerto Rican literature.

The publication in 1966 of Luis Rafael Sánchez' pioneering work—*En cuerpo de camisa* (*In Shirtsleeve*, a collection of short stories)—ushered in an era of literary criticism that even Sanchez referred to as "an oppressive paradigm." The characteristic elements of the new Puerto Rican literature were the literary agency that previously marginalized groups acquired and the reinterpretation of colonial dominance from the perspectives of the newly emerging literati, leading to the rewriting and re-interpreting of Puerto Rican history. It was protest literature that targeted what the writers perceived to be a decaying patriarchal, middle and upper classes. It lauded the feministic, anti-patriarchal brand of social protest, and identified with the language and experiences of the Puerto Rican proletariat, and infused the protest literature with a Puerto Rican reality that was manifest in the Antillean and Latin-American context.

These new writers were products of Puerto Rican disillusionment with the ideologies and programs generated by the Commonwealth status that the United States Congress had granted the island in 1952. These writers exorcised their disillusionment with the U.S. experiment that had intended to transform Puerto Rico into the showcase society which Latin American and Caribbean nations would seek to emulate. Observing that the experiment had failed, the new breed of writers launched into a profound re-evaluation of Puerto Rico's cultural and political values, drawing upon the feministic, socio-linguistic, Marxist ideologies for their discourse, considerably broadening the themes and perspectives in their literary works.

The short stories of Rosario Ferré, collected in the 1976 volume *Papeles de Pandora*, exemplify this literary school. Ferré channeled the rage provoked by colonial and patriarchal limitations into "eclosions of fury" which destroyed her heroines but also brought the established order crashing down. A member of one of Puerto Rico's wealthiest families and daughter of a former pro-statehood governor, Ferré paradoxically mirrored in her fictional world that of René Marqués, offering the horrifying exploitative side of Marqués' idealized agrarian society. Her fictional goal is the unmasking and destruction of the very class she belonged to but came to view as having connived with the colonizers in order to maintain its power and privileges.

Ferré's works shifted the balance of the dominant/submissive dichotomy towards the class and gender struggles of Puerto Rican society. They brought to the issue of political status the added responsibility of dealing with gender problems that have been exacerbated by colonial domination. In her work, feminism becomes a colonial issue, and solutions to the status question must deal with the position of women. Nowhere were these themes and intent clearer than in her short story, "Pico Rico Mandorico," a work based on Christina Rosetti's *Goblin Market.*[14] "Pico Rico Mandorico" responds to Marqués' view of Puerto Rican docility through the retelling of the story of the two sisters in Rosetti's tale. The sisters live in a Puerto Rican town of zombie-like workers driven to a desire for constant physical labor by the poisoned fruit fed to them by an evil sugar planter. When one of the sisters is tricked into eating the fruit, the other goes to her rescue, cutting the evil planter's nose—a symbolic castration that unveils his true identity to the town's people and unmasks his true intentions. The castration of the evil planter makes it possible for the working masses to shed their "masochistic passivity."

A similar response to the theme of dominance was found in Edgardo Rodríguez Juliá's 1976 novel—*La renuncia del héroe Baltasar.* The novel is the fictional account of a bloody rebellion by Blacks in eighteenth-century Puerto Rico. The rebels were motivated by the arrest and imprisonment of Baltasar Montañez, a fictional character in which Rodríguez Juliá merges two legendary figures—Miguel Henríquez, an eighteenth-century mulatto of enormous wealth and prestige, and Baltasar Montañez, a young man believed (mistakenly) to have miraculously survived a riding accident in 1753. Baltasar's imprisonment by the authorities unleashes a ferocious massacre that Juliá described in excruciatingly graphic detail, never losing sight, nonetheless, of the social and racial injustices that serve as justification for the mob's uncontrollable rage. The novel presents a vivid picture of Black revenge and murder against the white planter class in a Fanonian attempt to return society to a *tabula rasa* upon which a new society can be built. In this work, Rodríguez Juliá rewrites eighteenth-century Puerto Rican history, making it as it would have been if colonial rule had given way to the rebellious passions of a Black and mulatto population tired of colonial racial policies. His history, responding to a Fanonian insistence on the annihilation of the colonial past, tries to bring us closer to an understanding of the historical processes through which revolution and renewal are accomplished.

If Ferré and Rodríguez Juliá appear to respond to Marqués' concept of Puerto Rican docility and his idealization of the planter class, Luis Rafael Sánchez seems to react to Zeno Gandía's presentation of a weakened and alienated peasantry in his comic depiction of a media-obsessed urban proletariat in his 1976 novel—*La guaracha del Macho Camacho.* This novel is a disk jockey's hilariously long-winded introduction to Macho Camacho's phenomenal hit song, "Life is a Phenomenal Thing." Alternating with the voices of characters caught in a horrendous traffic jam of the sort that plague San Juan, the snarled traffic becomes a metaphor for the effects of colonialism on Puerto Rican society. Sanchez comments:

> Here in Puerto Rico, the successive colony of two empires and an island in the archipelago of the Antilles, . . . today Wednesday five post meridian, . . . Senator Vicente Reinosa . . . is tied up, held up, caught up in a traffic jam as phenomenal as life Made in Puerto Rico. The jam is an active example of the Creole capacity for getting bogged down.[15]

In *La guaracha del Macho Camacho*, Sánchez has re-created Puerto Rico's social reality through its multiplicity of languages: the language of the disk jockey, that of advertisements, the language of the media-besieged slum dwellers, the language of radio, television, film and comic strips, the language of conspicuous consumerism, the language of popular magazines, that of the Americanized bourgeoisie, and the language of political groups. The resulting linguistic melange appears to negate the paralysis implicit in the traffic jam that frames the novel. It is a language full of rhythm, whose pulsating qualities match the beat of the "guaracha":

> It was said by a respectable man: the country doesn't work, the country doesn't work, the country doesn't work; repeated to the point of provocation, repeated like the zéjel at the end of a guaracha; facing a red light that was black because the traffic signal wasn't working, the respectable man indignant, his stomach contracted with indignation, his jaw rigid: the country doesn't work. The passengers signed up in two opposing parties: one a minority of timorous citizens in agreement, and the other a vociferous majority who proceeded to intone with a zest usually reserved for national anthems Macho Camacho's irrepressible guaracha, "Life is a Phenomenal Thing."[16]

And indeed the country portrayed by Sánchez "doesn't work." There is nothing at all phenomenal about Puerto Rico as portrayed in the novel. It is a contradictory, paradoxical, absurd, erratic, mercurial society where injustice, abuse, and lack of communication prevail, so that nothing is resolved in a conciliatory synthesis, but in the violent confrontation of opposite forces.[17] It is a society of separations and difference where the disparity and isolation of the characters are taken to grotesque extremes. Thus the text allows no communication between the characters, except for the link provided by their listening to the same radio station. Their isolation in space emphasizes their social isolation: that of the senator's mistress, impatiently awaiting her delayed *laboris fornicatio,* fearful that she may miss her idol Iris Chacón's TV show once again; that of Benny, apologizing to his car because Puerto Rico "hasn't got the autostrada that was built for the smooth flow of Ferraris by the immortal Benito Mussolini";[18] that of Graciela Alcántara de Montefrío, "most ladylike lady" perusing a life-style-of-the rich-and-famous magazine that reminds her of her youthful flight to a Swiss finishing school to escape the insular vulgarity "which it was, is, and will be a Christian duty to flee."[19] The language privileged by Sánchez in the novel, the language of the people, is the Rabelaisian language of the marketplace—that of unofficial culture, the language of the have-nots. Although parodied (sometimes mercilessly) by the narrator, this language offers, in its subversion of official Spanish and textbook English, an example of the Puerto Rican people's capacity to carnivalize official culture and the foreign models it imposes. It is characterized chiefly by its protean quality, its capacity for constant renewal, its ability to continuously parody itself. It is a language with an unrealized potential to be an agent of change, unrealized here because it is at the service of an alienating mass-media message that the novel counsels to reject.

The language of the upper classes, on the other hand, is founded on the principle of an immovable and unchanging hierarchy in which the higher and the lower never merge. These upper classes reject the guaracha, its language and its proletarian perspective. The senator, catching himself in the act of singing its refrain, feels the guaracha on him like a taint: "Macho Camacho's guaracha, its vulgar furor, has tainted him, contaminated him, laid him waste: high or low, a little or a lot, the guaracha: a tiara of vulgarity, a headdress of trash, a banner of the rabble, has alighted on his lips."[20]

This linguistic polarization in the novel is used by Sánchez to emphasize the economic and social polarization of the world of the novel and is linked to patterns of class exploitation addressed in the novel through the labyrinthine aspects of Puerto Rican sexual mores. The characters' very sense of being seems bound up in their erotic personas. The senator is overly concerned with his "established credentials as a tempestuous lover and (his) widespread fame as a meticulous wooer."[21] His mistress draws her assurance from having "more than enough studs who want to mount me for myself and five other women,"[22] while his wife Graciela is not "the kind of lady who considers *that* important," pronouncing the pronoun with moral repugnance, tying it up with "knots of sacred disgust."[23] These highly stereotypical characterizations of the Latin lover, the tempestuous mulatto woman, and the frigid white wife are used by Sánchez to explore the forces that have led the poor to regard their sexuality as one of their few marketable commodities.

Colonialism, the patriarchy, the media's sex-obsessed messages, all coalesce into a singular stage where traditional and revolutionary sexual mores wage a battle for supremacy. In the carnivalesque twists of sexual exploitation in the novel, it is no longer clear who exploits whom since, while the senator seems bound to obsolete notions of macho performance, his mistress appears secure in the infinite marketability of her charms: "Sucking the juice out of his pocket is what I love. Plucking him like chicken is what I love. Hypnotizing him in the wallet is what I love. . . . Sucking out his last penny is what I love. . . . That's it, that's it: make something out of her dirty work: dollars, dollars, dollars: hot coals in her eyes: dollars, dollars, dollars: malefic and hair-raising: dollars, dollars, dollars. . . ."[24] Sánchez allows the senator's mistress a carnivalesque sexual freedom in her erotic liaisons (particularly with her three cousins Hugo, Paco, and Luis—named after the Spanish renditions of the names of Donald Duck's nephew)—all of whom seem paralyzed by Puerto Rico's stultifying gender roles. As the representative of the people's perspective in the text, her erotic openness mirrors the openness of the people's language, stressing the people's role in challenging obsolete and class-bound cultural patterns. By turning the erotic tables, and thus implying a carnivalesque reversal of the officially-accepted patterns of sexual behavior, the mistress joins the parodic spirit at the heart of the Puerto Rican people's carnivalization of official language to reveal the glimmer of the possibility of transforming Puerto Rico into a country that works.

Perhaps the most telling evidence that "the country doesn't work" is offered by the devastating by-product of Puerto Rico's economic dependence: the massive exportation of workers to the United States, an exportation that served through the nineteen fifties and sixties as a safety-valve to forestall political unrest in the island. Puerto Rico exported an average of fifty-five thousand of its people a year during the fifties and sixties, and an estimated half million Puerto Ricans (about thirty-five percent of the total Puerto Rican population) now live in the United States.

The impact of this massive migration was explored for the first time by Pedro Juan Soto (the author of *Usmaíl*) in a collection of short stories titled *Spiks*, published in the early 1950s. *Spiks* offers a bleak assessment of Puerto Rican life in Spanish Harlem in short narratives, some of them vignettes, of characters facing discrimination, poverty, disillusionment, drugs, and death. It portrays lives shattered by alienation from their natural surroundings, of people finding the gates to their American dream blocked by racial discrimination, lack of marketable skills, and the violence of the urban American ghetto. In Soto's short stories, the ghetto is seen as recreating the destructive aspects of colonial life while exacerbating its impact by the sheer uprootedness of a population forced to emigrate to survive. The traits that give Soto's stories their impact—brutality, privation, death, disaffection—form the core of the literature written by Puerto Ricans in New York. It is a literature about people displaced in an environment of cultural and racial discrimination and economic exploitation—a literature written by authors living in the midst of the dominant "other."

Piri Thomas' *Down These Mean Streets*, published almost a decade after *Spiks*, brings that thematic legacy to full fruition. A classic of Latino anguish and despair, it is the first in a tradition of heart-wrenching memoirs depicting the destruction of Puerto Rican souls in the American ghetto. The aspects of Nuyorican (or Neorican) life that Thomas dissects in harsh detail—pointing to the drug-peddling culture, the horrors of heroin addiction, the brutality of prison life, the loss of the saving power of faith and family, the constant struggle against the diminishing value of life—are the very factors that have contributed to the many crises the Puerto Rican community in the United States has faced. The crises are evident in the deplorable statistics that stand as representative of the Nuyorican experience, i.e., the high incidence of drug addiction, teenage pregnancy, welfare dependence, child and spousal abuse, crime and incarceration, suicide, low scoring on standardized tests, and dropping out of school. The exploration of the despair of Puerto Rican life in New York in the fifties and sixties gave Nuyorican literature its early themes, creating a "tradition" as *engaged* with socio-political reality as that of the island and Black-American literatures that served as its models. Thomas' *Down These Mean Streets*,

Miguel Piñero's brilliantly-bleak play *Short Eyes*, and Pedro Pietri's *Puerto Rican Obituary* form the core of a literary tradition growing out of a need to portray the infinite complexity of the relationships of dominance and submission emerging out of the encounter between a racist America and the essential mulatto-ness of the Puerto Rican people.

The literature that emerged from the bleak experiences of the fifties and sixties also grappled with the role of language in the dominance/submission dichotomy emerging from the colonizer/colonized encounter in a new and more violent environment. Every Puerto Rican writer in the United States must first of all face the barrier of language, since the choice of a language as the vehicle of literary expression—be it Spanish or English—comes laden with enormous cultural and political significance. Do they write in Spanish and attempt to fit their work into the Puerto Rican literary tradition despite the marked differences in themes and experiences between island and mainland Puerto Ricans? Do they write in English and become minority voices, footnotes in mainstream American literature? Can they write in English and still remain Puerto Rican writers? For all its importance, it is a choice not always open to the writer, especially to second and third generation Puerto Ricans in the United States whose only language is English. Miguel Algarín, a Puerto Rican-born poet raised in the United States, has made language one of the central themes in his poetry.[25]

For Puerto Rican authors writing in English, whether labeled Neoricans or Nuyoricans, relationships of dominance have become more complex. They find themselves exiled from two worlds: that of the dominant culture which labels their work substandard and irrelevant to the mainstream American literary tradition, and that of their own cultural background, where they are often denied their right to belong because their language and themes are not those of the tradition. This theme is explored by Pedro Juan Soto in *Hot Land, Cold Season*. His is a tale of a young man returning to the island after many years in New York to face distrust and discrimination from island Puerto Ricans. As a result of this rejection, and because their work stems from the same oppression, Neorican authors tend to identify their literature with that of other minority groups in the United States—African-Americans, Chicanos, Native Americans, the American "third world."[26] Neorican works share most of their essential characteristics with the literatures of these groups: a similar use of the spoken language, a similar exploration of the impact of racial and cultural discrimination, and the need to recreate a primeval, utopic world where the roots of their literature and culture can be found.[27]

Puerto Rican literature in the United States, nonetheless, shares a common basis with the literature written in the island: that of responding to the dominance inherent in American power structures. But Nuyorican authors add a new level to that response, since they write from within the world of the American dispossessed classes and speak particularly to them. Their direct daily contact with America—a contact most island Puerto Ricans do not experience—makes more patently clear the negative definitions of themselves they confront at every turn. Julio Marzán's poem "Nutshell" offers a subtle expression of this reality.[28] In Puerto Rican poetry written in English, we find an urgency imposed on the text by the immediate presence of the dominant culture and by the consciousness of the destructive elements that surround the poet, aspects of dominance not often experienced by the island writer. Miguel Piñero's "A Lower East Side Poem" reveals the immediacy of that dominance.[29]

Nuyorican writing of the seventies and eighties is more complex and harder to categorize, since it has partly transcended the sociopolitical commitment of works like Piñero's "A Lower East Side Poem" to embrace a multiplicity of themes and approaches. Ed Vega's work is representative of recent Nuyorican writing; his fiction, parodic and highly satirical, incorporates multiple linguistic registers and many popular genres such as police procedurals and science fiction, political thrillers, fantasy literature and folklore. Vega is a Puerto Rican-born novelist and short-story writer who has lived for many years in New York City's El Barrio. He has published two volumes of short stories, *Mendoza's Dreams* (1987) and *Casualty Report* (1992), and a novel—*The Comeback* (1985).

In *The Comeback*, Vega chisels out a hybrid of the dominant popular narrative forms of his times in his quest for a suitable novelistic form that draws as much on traditional Puerto Rican culture and literature (and on their Spanish models) as on American cultural and ethnic experiences. The result is a Latino picaresque tale with a very unlikely hero, a Puerto Rican hockey player and economics professor seeking integration into the American system who believes himself to be part-Eskimo. Through his politically committed Puerto Rican girlfriend, this character gets involved with a pro-independence revolutionary group which attempts a daring para-military rescue mission, at which time our character suffers a nervous breakdown and is given over to the care of a loony psychiatric establishment. The tale is a zany melange of the strange adventures told with a broad satiric eye, but its focus remains always clearly on the character's confused identity and on his attempts at finding his true self through activities which always end up being political, whether he wants them to be or not.

Vega explores, in *The Comeback*, the foundations of personal identity in ethnic identification and cultural symbols. However, he counsels against an identity that is solely ethnically and politically driven, finding in such a narrow sense of self a denial of the potential richness of human experience. The possible extremes are represented by Frank Garboil, the hero, and his girlfriend, Maritza Soto. Whereas Frank is floundering in a sea of confusion about his true self, needing to explore aspects of his personality which appear to have been buried under his "nondescript, anonymous, turned-off, white intellectual" life, Maritza is too dependent on her identity as a "Puerto Rican through and through," suffering from "too much identity," acting "like a walking Puerto Rican day parade 365 days out of the year." The juxtaposition of these two extremes in a couple that wants to remain together allows Vega to explore the foundations of identity and to seek a compromise that makes possible an ethnic identity that is enriching rather than limiting.

Thus, the end of *The Comeback* finds our now avowedly Puerto Rican hero and heroine caught in the trap of politically-driven ethnicity, seeking from the author a re-write that, while not denying their ethnicity and political goals, broadens their possibilities of personal fulfillment in an American society in which they must find a niche since a return to Puerto Rico is not feasible. A character identified as the author/narrator appears at the end of the text as a *deux ex machina* that can resolve a seemingly unresolvable situation. Counseling against total absorption in island politics, he advocates a focus on strengthening the economic basis of the mainland Puerto Rican community as the best weapon in the protracted war against oppression. He advises Maritza to forget the romantic notion of an armed struggle against the United States for Puerto Rican independence and to go to law school instead, since independence will more likely be achieved through a legal battle. The character, named Vega like the author, finds that: "Even little skirmishes and bombings in order to draw attention to our plight and raise the consciousness of the people are a waste of human resources and part of the martyr mentality and very romantic. Except it's outmoded.[30]

Vega's *The Comeback* offers a complex assessment of the political options open to the mainland Puerto Rican. Rejecting a commitment to the armed struggle for Puerto Rican independence as a viable option, and repudiating total assimilation and its concomitant cultural suicide as well, this novel promotes instead something akin to a cultural guerrilla movement, an "underground," surreptitious struggle from within the system. A Vega character says: "The better the cover you create, the more invisible you become. Study what this country is about and then beat its brains out at its own game."[31]

Vega's admonition is based on his belief that the only viable route to achieving Puerto Rican independence is a political route. Since the struggle for independence must be fought within the context of world opinion, Vega urges Puerto Rican leaders to play-down color and ethnic-specificity so the notable issues can be heard and impact peoples around the world. He cautions, moreover, that leaders will have to put their egos aside in order to effectively think and fight that which keeps Puerto Ricans from being free.[32] This encouragement of covert war is consistent with Vega's description of his novel as a "mickey" to slip onto the unsuspecting reader. The novel argues that successful, politically-conscious Latinos, like cultural and political "mickeys," can undermine the system's foundations from within, appropriating and transforming them to make the system more responsive to the needs of the masses.

Puerto Rican critic Efraín Barradas calls the Nuyorican literature writings of transition, attempting to bridge the gap between an island literature written in Spanish and a mainland literature written in English. They are literatures which differ in many ways: one working within a century-long tradition, the other trying to carve a tradition within the country into which they migrated. Both have developed around the need to respond to the dominance imposed by history. Both share an ethnic experience and a cultural background which transcend language differences and which demand a militant definition of self in the face of the dominant "other." Puerto Rican literature, whether written in Puerto Rico or the United States and whether written in English or Spanish, continues to respond to the concerns articulated by Manuel Alonso in 1849: How can Puerto Ricans—colonials in the island and oppressed minority in the mainland—most effectively define themselves amidst colonial dominance?

---

[1] A case in point was the gradual replacement of the traditional exchange of Christmas-season presents on January 6th, the Feast of the Epiphany (known popularly as Three Kings' Day) by the American custom of exchanging gifts delivered by Santa Claus on Christmas Day. The process was accomplished primarily through clever promotional campaigns by American-owned department store chains promoting the "convenience" of the earlier date, which allowed children a longer period of vacation days to play with presents before returning to school.

[2] Iris M. Zavala, "Introduction," *The Intellectual Roots of Independence: An Anthology of Puerto Rican Political Essays,* ed. Iris M. Zavala and Rafael Rodríguez (New York: Monthly Review Press, 1980), 15.

[3] Zavala and Rodriguez, eds., *The Intellectual Roots of Independence: An Anthology of Puerto Rican Political Essays,* 29.

[4] Ibid.

[5] Manuel Zeno Gandía, "What Are We? How Are We?" in *The Intellectual Roots of Independence: An Anthology of Puerto Rican Political Essays,* 160.

[6] Antonio S. Pedreira, *Insularismo* (Río Piedras: Editorial Edil, 1973), 115-117. All translations are mine.

[7] Ibid., 27.

[8] Frantz Fanon's analysis of the impact of colonialism on the individual and social psyche, built on a model combining Muslim, African, and French-Antillean elements, is not universally applicable to the Puerto Rican situation, where different forces are at work. His evaluation of the "trickling-down" effect of the patterns of dominance in colonial societies, however, offers useful insights for the understanding of power structures in Puerto Rico.

[9] Frantz Fanon, *Black Skins, White Masks* (London: Paladin, 1970), 144-151.

[10] Frantz Fanon, *The Wretched of the Earth* (London: Penguin, 1969), 41.

[11] These patterns of violence have been linked to the high incidence of wife- and child-abuse in Puerto Rico. Domestic violence is said to have reached epidemic proportions in Puerto Rico.

[12] José Luis González, *El país de cuatro pisos* (Río Piedras: Huracán, 1982), 90.

[13] See Margarite Fernández Olmos' "Repuestas antipatriarcales en la narrativa puertorriqueña contemporánea" for a detailed critique of Marqués' position. The article is included in her *La narrativa puertorriqueña de aquí y de allá: aproximaciones feministas* (Santo Domingo: Taller, 1991).

[14] Refer to Fernández Olmos for a detailed discussion on the themes in Marques' works.

[15] Luis Rafael Sánchez, *La guaracha del Macho Camacho* (Buenos Aires: Editorial de la Flor, 1976), 5, 6, 17 (my translation). Except when noted, passages quoted in English are from Gregory Rabassa's translation, published as *Macho Camacho's Beat* (New York: Avon, 1980).

[16] Sánchez, *La guaracha del Macho Camacho*, 21; Based translation by the author.

[17] María Teresa Gozo, "Algunos aspectos de la carnavalización en *La guaracha del Macho Camacho* de Luis Rafael Sánchez." *Revista Iberoamericana* 26 (1985), 125.

[18] Ibid., 106.

[19] Ibid., 35.

[20] Ibid., 122.

[21] Ibid., 18.

[22] Ibid., 8.

[23] Ibid., 137.

[24] Ibid., 64-65.

[25] "Inside Control: My Tongue," *Nuyo-rican Poetry*, 58.

[26] Efraín Barradas, "Introducción," in *Herejes y mitificadores: muestra de poesía puertorriqueña en Estados Unidos*, ed. Efraín Barradas and Rafael Rodríguez (Río Piedras: Huracán, 1980), 15.

[27] Ibid., 15.

[28] Ibid., 94.

[29] Piñero, an accomplished poet and playwright whose triumphs included *Short Eyes* and many of the powerful scripts of the first seasons of *Miami Vice*, died recently of AIDS. He was one of the many victims of a disease that has taken a particularly deadly toll among island and mainland Puerto Ricans.

[30] On Vega's *Comeback*, see Barradas and Rodríguez, ed., *Herejes y mitificadores: muestra de poesía puertorriqueña en Estados Unidos*, 98.

[31] Ibid., 475-476.

[32] Ibid., 473-474.]

Machismo: Meanings in the Mexican/ Mexican American Experience

A. Rolando Andrade
Ethnic Studies Department, Bowling Green State University

Ever since I can remember my father was a significant and powerful figure in my life. To me he seemed a wise person who in concert with my mother knew what was good for the family and acted in such a way as to provide all we needed. He was a faithful husband, as far as we know, without any other female liaisons. He was always alongside the family, never the supreme master nor the servant, never the oppressor nor the oppressed and never the ruthless dictator I have been told all Mexican males are. He would get up early in the morning to read, write, fix breakfast and, finally, call us out of bed. He was a most warm human being who played with us, hugged, kissed and loved all of us. And yet, my father was a Mexican, born in Mexico City, deeply proud of his cultural birthright and deeply committed to his Mexican heritage.

There is something different and, for those who believe in stereotypes, wrong about this picture of my father. He just does not fit the popular American image of the Mexican or the *machismo* they are accused of. Most American literature on the topic suggests the Mexican *machos* are monster womanizers and debased individuals who prefer to destroy rather than to build. In this literature the *macho,* almost always

Reprinted by permission of the author.

synonymous with Mexican and Mexican American, is a hopeless individual who abuses women and seeks to destroy all male competition. In the article "*Machismo*: A Universal Malady," it has been suggested that *machismo* is a historical and worldwide problem. Further, it suggests that all historical periods and most of the cultures analyzed include an expressed *machismo* in one or several of its forms.[1] To somehow suggest this malady is a purely Mexican phenomenon is to close our eyes to some strong proof which clearly indicates otherwise. However, it must be admitted that *machismo* has existed and continues to exist in the Mexican and Mexican American cultures. The expressions of this *machismo* in Mexican culture is what we seek to demonstrate.

Any person who studies *machismo* and the Mexican culture can find examples of its reality. The ugliness and ruthlessness of it can be seen and heard in Mexican streets, in school bathrooms, bars and countless other locales. The Mexican homes often are centers for its dissemination and in many ways the church has promulgated and given its blessing to it. In the article already mentioned, four types of machismo are discussed and these same divisions will be used in this study: the conqueror macho, the playboy macho, the masked macho, and the authentic macho.

Raúl Bejar Navarro, in *El Mexicano: aspectos culturales psicosociales* (1979), defines *machos* as those individuals who seek to conquer. He suggests these *machos* sees themselves as invincible in all areas of human endeavor and as individuals who can never fail. These individuals see themselves as persons who show excessive valor, as they willingly flirt with death, use reckless methods to solve problems, and, individually think they can conquer whatever comes their way.[2] Marvin Goldwert, in his book, *History as Neurosis,* brings together the Latino male and Freud's psychological and philosophical views. Through this marriage, the author suggests *machismo* reacts through the psychological human needs to accomplish the conqueror's ends.[3] The conqueror macho, then, is a man with a especial fondness for aggressive behavior and a need to show extravagant courage, demonstrate virility, strength, intransigence and stubbornness.[4] Anything that makes the individual feel like a winner, like "number 1" is acceptable and a part of the conqueror mentality.

To the Mexican, the Spanish conquerors of the sixteenth century represent this *machismo*. These men's bravado, desire for adventure, aggressive behavior fit the image of machismo. Hernán Cortés and Pedro de Alvarado especially fit this mold. Cortés and about five hundred men moved across the *Sierra Madre* from Veracruz to Tenochtitlan, confronted and warred against and destroyed Tlaxcaltecans and Cholulans, then faced one of the most aggressive civilizations on the continent, the Aztecs, and after a momentary failure, the conquistadores crushed this great empire. These men never admitted failure, they moved forward against all odds, against overwhelming challenges and conquered them through all means available to them.

Pedro de Alvarado, perhaps even more so than Cortés, represents the most vocal, most aggressive, most zestful and destructive spirit of the conqueror. He participated in so many significant enterprises that it is hard to believe one man alone could have done so much. As a captain in Cortés's army, he was deeply involved in the destruction of the Aztec Empire. Later, he and Cortés prepared extensive plans to explore the South Seas. In 1532 he made a contract for the exploration of vast areas in the Pacific but instead he followed the Peruvian "gold rush." By 1538 he planned to explore either China, the Spice Islands, or the lands north of New Spain. Historians Herbert E. Bolton and Thomas N. Marshall report that in 1539, Alvarado "left Spain with equipment for a fleet, which he transported across Honduras and Guatemala on the backs of Natives."[5] That same year he rushed back to Mexico to participate in the Coronado expedition, but before he could get immersed in that project he was ordered to the west coast of Mexico where he became entangled in the Mixton War. At a battle, in which the Indians appeared to be winning, he spurred his horse forward ready to attack. He tried to rally the soldiers, and—as a man of courage, a *macho* among the best—he stood and fought to his death.[6]

Some historians consider Alvarado to have been among the most wicked of the *conquistadores*. It is believed he developed the "*Proceso de Alvarado,*" i.e., the use of ferocious dogs to control and attack the indigenes.[7] Thus, he became the infamous director of a sadistic terrorism that is referred to in history as the Massacre of the *Templo Mayor.*[8] These are significant examples of this *macho's* temerity. About his death it is said, in a bit of understatement: "Thus ended the charmed life of Pedro de Alvarado, one of the most brilliant members of a brilliant breed—and, unfortunately, one of the most inflexible."[9]

Super heroes, whether they thought themselves as such or not, have also existed in the history of Mexico. Among them: Antonio López de Santa Anna, the eternal general, the perennial president of Mexico and a gnat fly who considered himself essential, and even though he never won a war or a battle, he thought himself a great Mexican hero; Hermenegildo Galeana who, during the Mexican War of Independence, allegedly roped an enemy cannon and using his faithful steed pulled it to the insurgents side; Pancho Villa and Emiliano Zapata, of the Mexican Revolution, stood against all odds and against superior armies, whether the Mexican federal army which they defeated or the American army which Villa sent on a wild goose chase through the Mexican deserts. At the Battle of Celaya Pancho Villa sent his troops forward to cannon and withering machine gun fire seeking a triumph that did not come; he was a giant to himself. The legends of these men have made them super heroes and their image should be considered one of conquering *machos.*

Latino gang members in California and other areas appear to have taken the qualities of conquering *machos.* Whether the gang members have a psychological need or have experienced a socialization problem in American society is beyond the scope of this paper, but the expressions, the activities, and the membership of these groups clearly point at conquering *machismo.* The use of guns, intimidation and warfare is too clear to call it something else. These young people are in fact *pistoleros* (men who love to use guns and to whom the gun is essential to express their being). These are individuals who strut, who brag about their accomplishments and forgive nobody, for entering their territory.

In the movie "Treasure of Sierra Madre," Mexican bandits reach the hiding place of the three Americans, Howard, Dobbs and Curtin, who have been mining the hills. During the conversation between the bandits and the Americans the Mexicans seek to convince them that they are not thieves but the police. When the Americans demand proof, saying: "Show us your badges!" The irate Mexican responds: "What badges, we have no filthy badges, we don't need badges!" Here is the macho insulted by the petition of an insignificant item that only those below his estate need. A macho does not need a badge or any other proof of his righteousness and prerogative.

Mexican popular music presents an interesting perspective as in a significant number of songs the image of Mexican *macho* is glorified.

Nationalist songs have a tendency of becoming expressions of the conquering *macho*. An example of this may be Manuel Esperón's song, "*Yo soy Mexicano.*" The first few lines establish the meaning: "*Yo soy Mexicano mi tierra es bravia. Palabra de macho que no hay otra tierra más linda y más brava que la tierra mia. . . .*" and "*Yo soy Mexicano, y orgullo lo tengo, nací despreciando la vida y la muerte. . . .*" ("I am Mexican my country is brave. As a macho I give you my word that there is no other land more beautiful and brave than my own land. . . . I am Mexican and that gives me pride I was born to disdain both life and death. . . .") There is nothing wrong, of course, with having pride in being Mexican, but here there is something wrong when we need *machismo* to make the point that Mexico is beautiful and courageous. In this case the protagonist uses *machismo* and a dose of fatalism to express the significance of being a Mexican. Neither is needed, being a Mexican by itself should give the individual pride to express the beauty of the nation. In the song "*La feria de las flores*" ("The flower's fair"), the lyrics underline the male's desire to control and dictate. "*Aqui vine porque vine a la feria de las flores, no hay cerro que se me empine, ni cuaco que se me atore.*" ("I have come here because I have come here, to the flower's fair, there is no hill I cannot cross nor horse that can refuse to take me.") The song goes on to suggest there is a flower (a woman) whom the troubadour is fond of and wants it for himself. "*Y aunque otro 'querá' cortarla yo la 'devisé' primero. . . . Yo la he de ver transplantada en el huerto de mi casa y si sale el jardinero pos a ver . . . a ver que pasa.*" ("And even if another wants to cut my flower, I saw it first... and I will transplant it to the orchard of my home and if the gardener comes out . . . well . . . let's see what will happen.") It is obvious that he believes nothing can stand between him and his obtaining the flower and, if the gardener comes out, well—that would just be too bad. Here is the *macho* threatening the gardener, the keeper of the flower for doing his/her job. These are clear examples of conqueror machismo. Both of these songs, as well as an infinite number of others, suggest man controls, whether with a gun, with threats or with the magnetic personality, but he controls. The man, in many of the songs, makes himself to be seen as the King, the master, the owner, the *gran chingón.* These men command, dictate, demand, manipulate and, of course, get what they want.

Conqueror *machismo* is a reality among Mexicans and Mexican Americans and it has affected the culture and history in a never ending fashion. Whether we are willing to see machismo in Cortés or Santa Anna or in any of the others may be secondary because machismo was and continues to be there. Further, in the myths, legends, literature and music, Conqueror *machismo* is present and often glorified.

Playboy is the second type of machismo to be discussed.

> This *macho* is the male who considers himself superior to women. [Playboy *machismo*] frees this individual to act in sexually suggestive manners and, under some circumstances, to become the raper, the abusive male who feels he can rip open the female to abuse and demean her whether in the sexual act or in any other physical, mental, or psychological process. This sense of superiority is the same passion that makes possible for the male to commit adultery, claim to be a good drinker, a great lover, and believe himself to be totally capable of "chasing women."[10]

Above all the playboy macho seeks his own pleasure wherever he may find it. Playing games and using women as pawns, toys, and pleasure is his ultimate goal.

Mexican and Mexican American culture has never been successful in avoiding this type of *machismo*. Walking any street of Mexico at any hour of the day or of the night would quickly demonstrate this point. Any group of men, sitting or standing together, become their own reference group and individually or as a group react with statements containing sexual overtones at the passing of a female. These statements are called *piropos* and are common on such moments. A *piropo* is, then, any statement uttered by men with either prurient or sexually suggestive connotations. Some of these statements can be very sophisticated, poetic, or even beautiful but they are all undesired and repugnant to most women. In translation, and in the process of writing them, something is lost. Without the sound of the voice and the intonation given to the words the impact of these sentences appear dull and dim witted. Still, the *piropos* sound like this: "*Este es el día en que Dios se sonrio y te mando a darme vida.*" ("This must be the day God smiled at me, sending someone like you to give me life!"); "*Ay mamacita linda, con una mujer como tu mi vida estaria completa*" ("Oh beautiful mother, with a woman like you my life would be fulfilled."), and "*Ay, que cosas tan bonitas, todo mi cuerpo esta tieso*" ("Oh, what beautiful things, all my body has become hard."). Individuals using such statements, at times, get very close to the girl while others in the group use wolf whistles.

To the playboy *macho* the women's only assets are her physical characteristics, her beautiful face, her beautiful eyes, her sex and, of course, "the well built body." The reality is that the playboy *macho* believes he is the answer to all the needs women have, especially sexual needs. The young woman is prey waiting to be caught. In some cases beauty is not a significant issue because what is really important is that she is a female.[11] Like Don Juan Tenorio, the female is the target and if she happens to be a virgin, that much the better, because he believes she wants to give him her virginity as a special gift.

Even though playboy *macho* songs are difficult to find, some carry the message of love freely given or desired at any cost, in some cases, love has been taken in significant numbers. The *corrido* (ballad), "Juan Charrasqueado," strongly suggests playboy *machismo.* The song's words are: "*la triste historia de un ranchero enamorado, que fue borracho, parrandero, y jugador.*" ("The sad story of a farm boy who was a drunk, a philanderer, and a gambler.") "*era valiente y arriesgado en el amor, a las mujeres más bonitas se llevaba, de aquellos campos no dejaba ni una flor.*" (He was courageous and daring in his love. . . . He would take away the most beautiful women and in those regions he left not a single flower.") The imagery of the song is obvious when the *macho* man gets drunk and seeks the most beautiful women to use and not a single one could avoid him. Or Ernesto Cortazar's song, "*La numero cien*" "(The Number 100"). This song suggests the male is reproaching the woman who left him waiting and says: "*Perdono tus ofensas porque sé lo que eres: la mujer que en mi vida fue la número cien.*" ("I forgive your offense because I know what you are: the woman who in my life was the number one hundred.") Playboy machismo? Of course.

Playboy machismo is a highly individualistic attitude. It is a case of one man seeking to abuse all the women of the world. This view is strongly seen in what has been called *Jorgenegretismo*, coined from the name of Mexican singer-actor Jorge Negrete and meaning the swaggering, hypermasculine hero, the virile, powerful stud who struts his stuff as the women "go wild in his presence."[12] Fernando Peñalosa's 1968 study of the Mexican and Mexican American family looks at their male/female relations and finds them based on strongly held beliefs in the superiority (biological, intellectual, and social) of the male. The female is "clearly valued less, despite the various circumstances in which she is placed on a pedestal by males."[13] This ambivalent generalization has been widely accepted even though it is supposed to merely suggest areas of study.

There may not be a *Playboy Magazine,* per se, in Mexico but you can buy the American magazine which is published for international consumption and hawked from many of the magazine shops all over the nation. You can also purchase posters and pictures that make the playboy *macho* grin and feel satisfied. Other pornographic magazines are available with pictures, stories and articles demeaning women. To suggest there is no playboy *machismo* in Mexico is ridiculous but to suggest all Mexicans suffer this malady is just as wrong.

A less commonly used definition of *machismo* is the man who hides behind a mask all his *macho* tendencies and his desire to rule over women. Orrin E. Klapp, in his articles, "Mexican Social Types" and "The Clever Hero," makes a case for this form of *machismo* without giving it a name. Here is the man who hides his interests, abilities and concerns but when the time comes they explode in any of the different aspects of *machismo.*[14] These people can lie, be thieves, a Robin Hood, or live with a Machiavellian philosophy that sees them through all kinds of crises.

There are significant elements in Machiavellian philosophy that match this macho style. This self-centered manipulative philosophy suggests the individual can approach and solve any problem or challenge without a preconceived notion, set aside conventional wisdom and morality and look at the issue with practical reason and virtual autonomy.[15] Through these means the end result will be totally satisfactory to the enhancement of one's own goal without the loss of conscience and prestige.

Richard Christie, in *Studies of Machiavellianism* first chapter, "Why Machiavelli," suggests there are four characteristics to the Machiavellian manipulation:

1. *A relative lack of affection in interpersonal relationships.* Here, success in getting others to do what one wishes them to do would be enhanced by viewing them as objects to be manipulated, assuming no moral view of their interaction with others.

2. *A lack of concern with conventional morality* carries the implicit premise that those who manipulate have utilitarian rather than a moral view of their interaction with others.
3. *A lack of gross psychopathology* suggests that the manipulator was hypothesized as taking an instrumentalist or rational point of view of others. And
4. *Low ideological commitment* holds that the essence of successful manipulation is a focus on getting things done rather than a focus upon long-range ideological goals.[16]

In the book *Profile of Man and Culture in Mexico,* Samuel Ramos discusses the Mexican *pelado.* This individual is introduced as a person who has lost all hope, all incentives to life; to this person life is meaningless, worthless and, above all, an empty chasm that brings no joy, no hope and no real tomorrow. The only meaning and the only thing this person can relate to and understand is where they find pleasure. Sex and all those prurient expressions of it bring them pleasure.[17] The *pelado*, then, must become Machiavellian to create and bring about all types of sexual experiences whether real or imaginary. The talk among these individuals will be saturated with sexual innuendos and connotations. Such terms as *cabrón, chingar, pinche*—Mexican curse words with sexual connotations, as well as hand gestures, whistles, and other expressions come out of that subculture as these individuals seek meaning and expression of their own hopelessness. This is a form of masked *machismo* because these individuals are not primarily seeking sexual pleasure; they will take it if it comes, but they are really using this motive to express their own hopelessness, their own inadequacies, their own escapism.

The Mexican *Zona de Tolerancia* (Red district) gives hidden, masked machos an opportunity to express themselves. Here they get their thrills, their stories, their innuendoes to go back out into the streets and brag about their empty, hollow triumphs. They realize, as José Alfredo Jiménez clearly suggests in his song, "*La que se fue*," "*Puedo comprar mil mujeres y darme una vida de gran placer. Pero, el cariño comprado ni sabe querernos ni sabe ser fiel.*'" (I can buy a thousand women and give me a life of great pleasure. But, purchased love neither does it know how to care nor how to really give pleasure.) But, to the masked *macho* this is meaningless; what is important is to get his pleasure and move on, to prove, even momentarily, that he is *muy hombre*, very virile; he can have sex with anyone, even though he has to purchase that love.

The danger in this man is manifested when he is cornered and forced to show proof or to prove to those he respects that what he is talking about is, in fact, the truth. The danger comes in his effort to show proof. This is a cornered tiger, a cornered animal who has to defend the last vestige of respect and honor, though it is shallow and really non-existent, to him it is all important. This person will come out in a desperate posture and acting out of desperation, he might rape, or commit mayhem, and murder is very possible. It may be better to allow this innocent, yet disturbed, immature person to keep his veneer of lies, half truths, warped views, than to corner him and create a fire we cannot extinguish.

It would appear that masked *machos* can be considered as nuisance or as purely innocent elements of society. Their immaturity, their shallowness, can be seen as temporary elements which humans tend to experience. "Boys will be boys" may be the answer that we get when concern is expressed. But their guile, shrewdness, slyness and other abilities to trick and deceive their fellow humans, at times, may become destructive; beyond what can be repaired. Masked macho cannot be recognized as a proper form of social behavior.

As individuals study Mexican *machismo* in an objective and thorough manner, they come to realize that the ancient meaning of the concept has changed and has come to mean all the negative attitudes we have discussed. However, the traditional meaning and the original concept of *machismo* can still be found and can still be meaningful. The authentic *macho* is the honest man who seeks to carry out his family responsibilities to the best of his ability and the man who loves and tries to take care of his wife and family in all social, cultural and, above all, economic matters. John Gillin, in his article "Ethos components in Modern Latin American culture," asserts that "a 'real *macho*' is one who is sure of himself, *cognizant of his own inner worth, and willing to bet everything on such self confidence.*"[18] Also, Alfredo Mirandé in his article, "The Chicano Family: A Reanalysis of Conflicting Views," suggests that "*machismo* is not a pathological force or a tool for protecting male prerogatives but a mechanism for upholding family pride and honor."[19]

Machismo in its responsible mode and within the family life is best expressed in the following examples: "My mother *mandaba en la casa* (My mother was the boss in the house), but decisions were made by both her and my father. If my father wanted to sell all the *maiz* (corn) or a cow, he first consulted with my mother." In this case the man is not judged to be superior but, at best, an equal and the home, which happened to be in Texas, was enriched by the shared authority. Or, again, "*Yo nunca sufrí en la casa de mis padres* (I never suffered at my parents' home); . . . my father never gave my mother any *disgustos* (sorrow), never got drunk, only worked hard for all of us."[20] These are outstanding examples of responsible traditional machismo.

In different parts of Mexico including sections of Yucatán, Oaxaca, Veracruz and others, women are seen both as the head of the family and as community leaders. In some cases even the regional dance suggests that matters are in the hands of the woman.[21] An example that suggests common sharing of authority across gender lines took place in the city of San Luis Potosí. During an evening, a guest in the Martinez family realized that the husband had been a major contributor in preparing the meal, that he helped the children with homework, and that his authority was not total but shared with his wife. At the after dinner conversation it became obvious that this family had no understanding of the popular misconception in defining *machismo.* The family shared responsibilities, tasks, authority, and helped each other achieve their goals.

It is quite difficult to find outstanding examples of responsible *machismo.* There may be many reasons for this. Television gets attention for promulgating popular perspectives, therefore it is full of stereotypical *machos.* It is difficult to sell that which is not flamboyant and glaring. News and popular programs are not there because of goodness and morality. Faithfulness to one wife, honesty, responsibility toward your children, going to work and going home are not elements of an exciting life and are not worth receiving publicity. It is, then, difficult to cite such examples. And yet, the streets, parks, and public places of Mexico and where Mexican Americans live are full of examples of caring, responsible men who live and die with their families. These individuals are not seeking thrills, extramarital liaisons, but are contented with their families.

Cultural elements are also difficult to pinpoint. What words or images can be used for faithfulness, responsibility? Two songs which appear to represent the ideals of the authentic macho are "*Amor de mis amores*" ("Love of my loves") and "*Solamente una vez*" ("Only once," but we know this song in English as "You belong to my heart"). Both of these songs were composed by Agustín Lara to represent the authentic macho concept. The lyrics of "Amor de mis amores" clearly point out that the woman is his only love, that she represents and is all he breathes. There is no sign here of other loves, of authority over the female, or of any form of control over the woman. In "Solamente una vez," the suggestion is that the individual can truly love only once. That only once in life the person really gives the soul to the beloved and at that time there are bells that ring and sing within the heart. These words speak about and express the ideas of the responsible *macho,* for this man can only give his heart once and he will not go seeking other loves and other liaisons to keep him entertained.

It is realistic to say that our world and within it the Mexican culture has had, and continues to have, a significant number of all types of *machos.* The conquerors, the playboys, the masked of the world are present, destructive, and demeaning. The victimization of women and the abuse of the weak and unfortunate victims have been consequences of man's feelings and desires to be superior to others or to compensate for feelings of inadequacy.

We have looked at Mexican *machismo* from four different perspectives and find that three of them have destroyed much and have extremely negative attributes we believe to be unacceptable. The conqueror destroys life, property, values and gives back misery and pain. The playboy seeks recognition and pleasure at an awesome cost to women who are seen as worthless and become victims of womanizing processes. The masked *macho* represents the negative characteristics of the small, weak, and troubled males who manage to get ahead through trickery, cunning, and shrewd methods that bypass the law and moral social standards. Finally, we have the positive aspect of *machos* but, in reality, we could merely call that being a responsible person and leave the silly idea of *macho* completely out.

I return to my father whom I always considered a real *macho.* His salary was small but he worked hard to give us pride, self respect, and reverence for all. He suffered quietly, shared his love with mother and us and pushed us toward a healthy fulfillment.

---

[1] A. Rolando Andrade, "Machismo: A Universal Malady." *Journal of American Culture*, 15 (Winter, 1992), 33-41.

[2] Raúl Bejar Navarro, *El Mexicano: aspectos culturales psichosociales* (México: Universidad Autónoma de México, 1979), 62.

[3] Marvin Goldwert. *History as Neurosis: Paternalism and Machismo in Spanish America* (Lahnam, MD): University Press of America, 1980), x.

[4] Evelyn Stevens, "Mexican Machismo: Politics and Value Orientation." *The Western Political Quarterly*, 18(Dec., 1965), 849; Salvador Reyes Navares, "El Machismo en México," *Mundo Nuevo*, 46(Abril, 1970), 15.

[5] Herbert E. Bolton and Thomas M. Marshall, *The Colonization of North America, 1492-1783.* (New York: The Macmillan Co., 1920), 47.

[6] Arthur S. Aiton, *Antonio de Mendoza: The First Viceroy of New Spain,* (Durham: Duke University Press, 1927), 150.

[7] Ibid., 69.

[8] Miguel León Portilla, *The Broken Spears: The Aztec Account of the Conquest of Mexico* (Boston: Beacon Press, 1962), 71-75, 134.

[9] Ibid., 11-26.

[10] Andrade, "Machismo: A Universal Malady," *Journal of American Culture,* 35.

[11] Reyes Navares, "Machismo en México," *Mundo Nuevo,* 14.

[12] Ibid., 36.

[13] Fernando Peñalosa, "Mexican American Family Roles," In *Journal of Marriage and the Family* 28(Nov., 1968), 684.

[14] Orrin E. Klapp. "Mexican Social Types," *American Journal of Sociology,* 69 (Jan., 1964), 405-406 and Orrin E. Klapp, "The Clever Hero," *Journal of American Folklore* 67(June-March, 1954.

[15] Eugene Carver, *Machiavelli and the History of Prudence* (Madison: University of Wisconsin Press, 1973), 3-4.

[16] Richard Christie and Florence L. Geis, *Studies in Machiavellianism* (New York: Academic Press, 1973), 1, 3-4.

[17] Samuel Ramos, *Profile of Man and Culture in Mexico* (Austin: University of Texas Press, 1962), 57-63.

[18] John Gillin. "Ethos Components in Modern Latin American Culture," *American Anthropologist*, 57(June, 1955), 493.

[19] Alfredo Mirandé. "The Chicano Family: A Reanalysis of Conflicting Views," *Journal of Marriage and the Family* 39 (Nov., 1977), 750.

[20] Douglas E. Foley, et. al., *From Peones to Politicos: Ethnic Relations in a South Texas Town, 1900-1977* (Austin: University of Texas Press, 1977), 55-56.

[21] Alberto Escalona Ramos, "El hombre en México," *Filosofía y Letras*, 21 (Enero-junio, 1953), 34-35.

PART V

CULTURE AND ECONOMICS IN TWO ASIAN AMERICAN COMMUNITIES

Although more noticeable numbers of Asians began to migrate to the United States in recent decades, Asians were in this country early in the nineteenth century. Chinese have had a notable presence here since the days of the gold rush, and by 1882 when Congress passed the Chinese Exclusion Act, they numbered around 300,000. While they have been less populous on the U.S. mainland until recently, Koreans migrated to Hawaii to work in sugar cane in the late nineteenth century and after 1900, a number of them migrated to the United States to work as laborers on commercial farms and in railroad construction industries. Following the Korean War, larger numbers migrated here, and in the 1960s and 1970s, immigrants from Indochina joined them. Concentrated primarily in California and other western states, their entrepreneurial successes and strong family orientations made them targets of hostility and subjects of wonderment.

From her insider's perspective, Cynthia Wong reminds us that cultural diversity was a reality in Chinese social history and that it continued to be a factor in immigrant social relations. The diversity surfaces as she treats the question of the legitimacy of Maxine Hong Kingston's *The Woman Warrior* as Chinese American autobiography. Wong reacts to Kingston's critics who allege that *The Woman Warrior* is less an authentic autobiography than a contrivance designed to make fiction appealing to white American readers. Wong inspires us to ponder questions about the nature of autobiography in general and Chinese autobiography in particular: *To what extent, she asks, should accurate cultural representation and reader perceptions be standards determining the literary value of Chinese (-American) autobiography?*

Pyong Gap Min is the author of several works on Korean economic enterprise. In the second article in this section, he enumerates the components which contribute to and sustain the effectiveness of this ethnic community's business ventures. His essay is particularly insightful in that he examines the factors of Korean cultural homogeneity, ethnic solidarity, the Korean church, and the Korean small business-orientation in Korean economic successes in the United States. Min simultaneously offers an Asian American perspective on the cultural conflict between Korean merchants and African American consumers and on how European American suppliers and wholesalers discriminate against Korean merchants. What factors other than those Min discussed would you cite as probable contributors to the relative economic successes of Korean Americans?

How these Chinese and Korean immigrants' respective lifestyles in the United States were informed by their rich Asian heritages amidst American individualism and capitalistic competition long has been a point of speculation by other Americans. These essays provide us windows through which to view the impact of internal social values and pressures and external cultural forces on the respective Chinese and Korean communities.

Autobiography as Guided Chinatown Tour? Maxine Hong Kingston's *The Woman Warrior* and the Chinese-American Autobiographical Controversy

Sau-ling Cynthia Wong
Department of Ethnic Studies—Asian Studies, University of California-Berkeley

Maxine Hong Kingston's autobiography, *The Woman Warrior*, may be the best-known contemporary work of Asian-American literature. Winner of the National Book Critics Circle Award for the best book of nonfiction published in 1976, *The Woman Warrior* remains healthily in print and on the reading lists of numerous college courses; excerpts from it are routinely featured in anthologies with a multicultural slant. It is safe to say that many readers who otherwise do not concern themselves with Asian-American literature have read Kingston's book.

In spite—or maybe, as we shall see, because—of its general popularity, however, *The Woman Warrior* has by no means been received with unqualified enthusiasm by Kingston's fellow Chinese Americans. A number of Chinese-American critics have repeatedly denounced *The Woman Warrior*, questioning its autobiographic status, its authenticity, its representativeness, and thereby Kingston's personal integrity. Though often couched in the emotionally charged, at times openly accusatory, language characteristic of what the Chinese call "pen wars," the critical issues raised in this debate are not merely of passing interest.

From *Multicultural Autobiographies*, edited by James Payne. Reprinted by permission of University of Tennessee Press.

Rather, they lie at the heart of any theoretical discussion of ethnic American autobiography in particular and ethnic American literature in general. It would therefore be instructive to set out the terms of the controversy and explore their theoretical ramifications, with a view to understanding the nature of Kingston's narrative enterprise in *The Woman Warrior.*

The most fundamental objection to *The Woman Warrior* concerns its generic status: its being billed as autobiography rather than fiction, when so much of the book departs from the popular definition of autobiography as an unadorned factual account of a person's own life. Responding to a favorable review of the book by Diane Johnson in the *New York Review of Books,* Jeffery Chan notes how "a white reading public will rave over ethnic biography while ignoring a Chinese American's literary art" and attacks Knopf, "a white publishing house," for "distributing an obvious fiction for fact" (6). The thrust of Chan's message is that the autobiographical label is a marketing ploy in which the author, to her discredit, has acquiesced. Chan's stricture is echoed by Benjamin Tong, who finds *The Woman Warrior* "obviously contrived," a work of "fiction passing for autobiography" ("Critic of Admirer" 6). By way of contrast, while the unusual generic status of *The Woman Warrior* is also widely noted by non-Chinese-American critics, it is seldom cited as either a weakness or a matter of personal, as opposed to artistic, purpose.[1]

How far is Kingston personally responsible for the nonfiction label on the covers of *The Woman Warrior*? According to her, very little:

> The only correspondence I had with the publisher concerning the classification of my books was that he said that Non-fiction would be the most accurate category; Non-fiction is such a catch-all that even "poetry is considered non-fiction."

And poetry is something in whose company she would be "flattered to see her books."[2] The entire matter might have rested here—but for some theoretical issues raised by the controversy which command an interest beyond the topical.

Although Kingston's detractors do not use the term, at the heart of the controversy is the question of fictionalization: to what extent "fictional" features are admissible in a work that purports to be an autobiography. The Chinese-American critics of *The Woman Warrior* focus their attention on the social effects of admitting fictionalization into an autobiographical work. Their concern, variously worded, is summed up most concisely, if baldly, by Katheryn Fong:

> I read your references to mythical and feudal China as fiction. . . Your fantasy stories are embellished versions of your mother's embellished versions of stories. As fiction, these stories are creatively written with graphic imagery and emotion. The problem is that non-Chinese are reading your fiction as true accounts of Chinese and Chinese American history. (67)

Thus stated, the *Woman Warrior* "problem" is seen to rest ultimately on the readers, not the author; the basis for denouncing *The Woman Warrior* is pragmatic, response-contingent, and reader-specific. Why, then, has Kingston been implicated at all in the misreadings of her audience? It is possible to reject the very question as irrelevant, in that authors have little control over how their published works will be read. On the other hand, when critics like Chan, Tong, or Fong hold Kingston responsible for her readers' failings, they do so from a set of assumptions about ethnic literature that are grounded in a keen awareness of the sociopolitical context of minority literary creation. Such an awareness is precisely what is missing in many white reviewers' remarks on *The Woman Warrior*; moreover, the autobiographical genre, with its promise (perceived or real) of "truthfulness," by nature encourages preoccupation with a work's sociopolitical context. Thus the charge of unwarranted fictionalization must be addressed.

The Woman Warrior can be considered fictionalized in a number of ways. On the most obvious formal level, it violates the popular perception of autobiography as an ordered shaping of life events anchored in the so-called external world. It aims at creating what James Olney calls "a realm of order where events bear to one another a relationship of significance rather than of chronology" ("Some Versions" 247). According to an early student of the genre, autobiographies must contain, "in some measure, the germ of a description of the manners of their times" (Pascal 8-9). Although recent scholars have found the referential grounding of autobiography much more problematic and its defining essence much more elusive (e.g., Olney, "Autobiography and the Cultural Moment" 3; Bruss 2; Eakin 5), the term *autobiography* usually does evoke, at least among general readers, a chronologically sequenced account with verifiable references to places, people, and events. As one critic puts it, in more abstruse language: "Texts bound by the real insist upon an epistemological status different from works of the imagination in which the real is more nearly hypothetical" (Krupat 25). But what if the "real" that an autobiography is bound by is the "imagination" of the protagonist?[3] This is the thorny problem of generic differentiation posed by *The Woman Warrior.*

By an outwardly oriented definition of autobiography, *The Woman Warrior* is at best only nominally autobiographical: to borrow a phrase from Pascal, it is a work "so engrossed with the inner life that the outer world becomes blurred" (Pascal 9), told by a narrator who, as a child, regularly sees "free movies" on "blank walls" and "[t]alks to people that aren't real inside [her] mind" (221). The prose slips from the subjunctive to the declarative with but the slightest warning: the No Name Woman story begins with *perhaps's* and *could have been's* (7) but soon dispenses with these reminders of conjecture. Likewise, while the Fa Mu Lan segment in "White Tigers" initially marked as an enumeration of the possible and desirable—"The call *would* come from a bird. . . . The bird *would* cross the sun. . . . I *would* be a little girl of seven. . . ." (24-25; my italics)—the bulk of the narration is in the simple past tense, recounting completed events in the actual world. Two divergent accounts are given of Brave Orchid's encounter with the Sitting Ghost (81-84, 85-86), neither of which could have been definitive since the event (or alleged event) predates the birth of the daughter/narrator. "At the Western Palace," presented as a deceptively conventional, self-contained short story, is revealed in the next chapter to be a third-hand fiction (189-90). In short, the referential grounding of *The Woman Warrior* is tenuous and presented in a potentially misleading manner. A few public places and events in the "outer" world are recognizable from what we know about author Kingston's life; all else is recollection, speculation, reflection, mediation, imagination. Verifi-ability is virtually out of the question in a work so self-reflexive. Presumably, then, readers who do not pay sufficient attention to the narrative intricacies of *The Woman Warrior,* especially white readers with biased expectations, will mistake fiction for fact.

The critics of *The Woman Warrior* also detect fictionalization—in the sense of "making things up"—in the way Kingston has chosen to translate certain Chinese terms. A central example is the word *ghost,* based on Cantonese *kuei* or *gwai,* a key term in the book appearing in the subtitle as well as several important episodes.[4] Kingston renders *kuei* as *ghost.* Chan and Tong ["Critic of Admirer" 6), while conceding that the character can indeed mean "ghost" (as in "spirit of the dead"), insist that it be translated as *demon* (or *devil* or *asshole*). They object to the connotations of insubstantiality or neutrality in Kingston's translation, finding it unsanctioned by community usage and lacking in the hostility toward whites indispensable to true works of Chinese-American literature.[5]

Tong further elevates the rendition of *kuei* as *ghost* into a "purposeful" act of pandering to white tastes and adds another example of "mistranslation" ("Critic of Admirer" 6): referring to "frogs" as "heavenly chickens" (77), which should have been "field chickens" in Cantonese. (*Tien,* "sky" or "heaven," and *tien,* "field" or "meadow," differ only in tone, which is phonemic in Chinese dialects.) Tong suggests that Kingston must have knowingly selected the wrong term, the one with the "familiar exotic touristy flavor" relished by "whites checking out Chinese America" ("Critic of Admirer" 6).

A more serious charge of fictionalization concerns the way Kingston handles not just single Chinese terms but Chinese folklore and legends. The story of Fa Mu Lan,[6] the woman warrior invoked as the young protagonist's patron saint, is recognizable only in bare outline to a reader conversant with traditional Chinese culture. The section on the girl's period of training in the mountains draws extensively on popular martial arts "novels" or "romances" (*wuxia xiaoshuo*) as well as from traditional fantasy lore on *shenxian* ("immortals").[7] As for the way Kingston makes use of the traditional Fa Mu Lan story, at least the version fixed in the popular "Mulan Shi" or "Ballad of Mulan,"[8] deviations from it in *The Woman Warrior* are so numerous that only a few major ones can be noted here. The tattooing of the woman warrior is based on the well-known tale of Yue Fei, whose mother carved four characters (not entire passages) onto his back, exhorting him to be loyal to his country. Also, the spirit-marriage to the waiting childhood sweetheart, a wish-fulfilling inversion of the No Name Woman's fate (7), is utterly unlikely in ancient China, considering the lowly place of women. The traditional Fa Mu Lan is never described as having been pregnant and giving birth to a child while in male disguise. The episode of the wicked baron is fabricated. The Fa Mu Lan of "Mulan Shi" is a defender of the establishment, her spirit patriarchal as well as patriotic, a far cry from a peasant rebel in the vein of the heroes of *Outlaws of the Marsh.*[9]

Because of these and other liberties Kingston has taken with her raw material, *The Woman Warrior* has been criticized by a number of Chinese Americans varying in their knowledge of traditional Chinese culture. Chinese-born scholar Joseph S. M. Lau dismisses the book as a kind of mishmash, a retelling of old tales that would not impress those having access to the originals (Lau 65-66). Writer Frank Chin, who is fifth-generation, attacks Kingston for her "distortions" of traditional Chinese culture. In a parody of *The Woman Warrior* filled with inversions and travesties, Chin creates a piece entitled "The Unmanly Warrior," about a little French girl growing up in Canton and drawing inspiration from "her imagined French ancestor Joan of Arc."

> [Her] picture of Joan of Arc . . . was so inaccurate as to demonstrate that the woman has gone mad, the French people of Frenchtown on the edge of the port city said. The French girl is writing not history, but art, the Chinese who loved the book said, and continued: She is writing a work of imagination authenticated by her personal experience. ("Most Popular Book" 7)

Clearly, the personal authority of an autobiographer is not easy to challenge. Perhaps sensing this, some of Kingston's critics concede it but blend the charge of fictionalization with that of atypicality. Again, the projected reactions of the white audience are kept constantly in sight. Speaking of the protagonist's account of not knowing her father's name, Chan calls this experience "unique" and expresses fears that Kingston "may mislead naive white readers" by not giving any background on the system of naming unique to Chinese Americans. Fong complains: "Your story is a *very personal* description of growing up in Chinese America. It is *one* story from one Chinese American woman of one out of seven generations of Chinese Americans" (67; italics in original). Like Chan, she feels that a narrative as personal as Kingston's must be made safe for white consumption by means of a sobering dose of Chinese-American history; the historical information to be incorporated should emphasize the "causes" behind the "pains, secrets, and bitterness" portrayed in *The Woman Warrior* (67).[10] Fong lists various excerpts that she finds especially dangerous and glosses each with a summary of experiences considered canonical to an ideologically correct version of Chinese-American history. Without such a corrective, she suggests, Kingston will reinforce the white readers' stereotype of Chinese Americans as eternally unassimilable aliens, "silent, mysterious, and devious" (67). Tong feels that Kingston's upbringing in the one-street Chinatown of Stockton, an agricultural town in California's Central Valley (instead of in a bigger, geographically more distinct and presumably more "typical" Chinatown) disqualifies her from attaining "historical and cultural insight" about Chinese America ("Chinatown Popular Culture" 233).

According to Kingston's critics, the most pernicious of the stereotypes that might be supported by *The Woman Warrior* is that of Chinese-American men as sexist. Some Chinese-American women readers think highly of *The Woman Warrior* because it confirms their personal experiences with sexism (e.g., Suzie Wong, Nellie Wong). Others find Kingston's account of growing up amidst shouts of "Maggot!" overstated, yet can cite little to support the charge besides *their* own personal authority."[11] Contrasting *The Woman Warrior*'s commercial success with the relatively scant attention received by books like Louis Chu's *Eat a Bowl of Tea* and Laurence Yep's *Dragonwings,* both of which present less negative father images, Fong implies that Kingston's auto-biography earns its reputation by "over-exaggerat[ing]" the ills of Chinese-American male chauvinism (68). She is willing to grant that a more understanding response from white readers might have given Kingston more creative license but finds the existing body of Chinese-American literature small enough to justify a more stringent demand on the Chinese-American writer, especially the woman writer.

If Chinese-American women disagree about the accuracy of Kingston's portrayal of patriarchal culture, it is hardly surprising to find male Chinese-American critics condemning it in harsh terms. Chan attributes the popularity of *The Woman Warrior* to its depiction of "female anger," which bolsters white feminists' "hallucination" of a universal female condition; and Tong calls the book a "fashionably feminist work written with white acceptance in mind" ("Critic of Admirer" 6). If Chinese-American literature is, according to the editors of

Aiiieeeee!, distinguished by emasculation (Chin et al. xxx-xxxi), then Chinese-American writers cannot afford to wash the culture's dirty linen in public. Frank Chin declares that personal pain—merely a matter of "expression of ego" and "psychological attitudinizing"—must be subordinated to political purpose ("This Is Not an Autobiography" 112).

For Chin, the very form of autobiography is suspect because of its association with the Christian tradition of confession. Although *The Woman Warrior* does not deal with Christianity, Chin places it in a tradition of Christianized Chinese-American autobiographies from Yung Wing's *My Life in China and America* through Pardee Lowe's *Father and Glorious Descendant* to Jade Snow Wong's *Fifth Chinese Daughter.* His rationale is that all autobiography, like religious confessions and conversion testimonials, demonstrates "admission of guilt, submission of my self for judgment," for "approval by outsiders." "[A] Chinaman can't write an autobiography without selling out." In fact, claims Chin, the autobiography is not even a native Chinese form, and Chinese-American writers have no business adopting it. Unfortunately, however, "[t]he Christian Chinese American autobiography is the only Chinese American literary tradition" ("This Is Not an Autobiography" 122-24).

Some of the generalizations made by Kingston's critics, such as the exclusively Western and Christian origin of autobiography, may be called into question by existing scholarship. According to one student of the genre, a complex autobiographical tradition does exist in Chinese literature, its origins traceable to the first century A.D., in the Han Dynasty (Larson; esp. chap. 11). Moreover, the confessional mode attributed by Chin solely to a guilt-obsessed Christianity can also be found in traditional Chinese writing (Wu). This does not invalidate Georges Gusdorf's important insight on the cultural specificity of the modern Western autobiography: the point is not to claim that the modern Western autobiography as we know it was practiced in ancient China (It was not.) but merely to point out the oversimplification in many of the statements that have been made about *The Woman Warrior.* When Chin links the genre with Christian self-accusation, he overlooks the possibility that the late medieval *breakdown* of Christian dogma might have been responsible for the emergence of autobiography as an autonomous literary tradition (Gusdorf 34). Furthermore, emphasis on the confessional element represents only one school of autobiographical scholarship, the Anglo-American; there are others (Eakin 202). Even if autobiography were an entirely Western phenomenon, according to Chin's own pronouncements on the unique, non-derivative nature of Asian American literature (especially on its separateness from Asian literature), Chinese-American writers have a right to appropriate a genre not indigenous to the Chinese In China but indigenous to the Chinese in America. As Chin and his *Aiiieeeee!* co-editors put it in their prefatory manifesto on Chinese and Japanese-American literature, an "American-born Asian, writing from the world as Asian-American," should not be expected to "reverberate to gongs struck hundreds of years ago" (Chin et al. xxiv).

Other more or less self-contained disputes on isolated assertions by Kingston's critics could be explored. On the whole, however, one may say that the entire Chinese-American autobiographical debate touches on articles of ideology so jealously held that the existence of a variety of opinions, scholarly or otherwise, may itself be seen as a problem rather than as a possible source of solutions. Given the peremptory tone in which much of the criticism of *The Woman Warrior* has been conducted, it is important that the tacit assumptions of the critics be articulated.

The theoretical underpinnings of the hostile criticism may be summarized as a series of interlocking propositions, some concerning the nature of autobiography as a genre "regardless of the author's background), others generalizable to autobiography by all American ethnic writers, still others peculiar to Chinese-American autobiography.

First of all, autobiography is seen to be self-evidently distinguishable from fiction. If the two genres blur at all at the edges, the interaction merely takes the form of fiction providing "techniques" to render the mundane material of autobiography more attractive; the epistemological status of the narrated material is not affected. In the same way that language is considered a sort of sugarcoating on dry nuggets of fact, the autobiographer's subjectivity is seen as having little or no constitutive power; rather, it is a Newtonian body moving about in a world of discrete, verifiable—and hence incontrovertible—facts, its power being limited to the choice between faithfully recording or willfully distorting this external reality. In principle, therefore, autobiography is biography which just happens to be written by one's self. It claims no special privilege, poses no special problems.[12] Finally, the *graphe* part of *autobiography*, the act of writing, the transformation of life into text, as seen by Kingston's critics as a mechanical conveyance of facts from the autobiographer's mind to the reader's via a medium in the physical world, the process pleasant or not depending on the author's literary talents. In the case of the *Woman Warrior* debate, correspondence between word and thing is deemed so perfect that a Chinese term, *kuei*, is supposed to be translatable by only one English equivalent, with all other overtones outlawed. The arbiter here is to be the individual critic backed by the authority of "the Chinese American community" (as if Kingston herself were not a member of this community).

Recognition of a preexisting external reality, however, imposes a special obligation on the ethnic American autobiographer: to provide a positive portrayal of the ethnic community through one's self-portrayal. At the very least, the autobiographer's work should be innocent of material that might be seized upon by unsympathetic outsiders to illustrate prevalent stereotypes of the ethnic group; the author should stress the diversity of experience within the group and the uniqueness and self-definition of the individual. Ideally, an ethnic autobiography should also be a history in microcosm of the community, especially of its sufferings, struggles, and triumphs over racism. In other words, an ethnic autobiographer should be an exemplar and spokesperson whose life will inspire the writer's own people as well as enlighten the ignorant about social truths.

The collective history of the ethnic community—one does not speak of a history in this theoretical framework—provides the ultimate reference point for the ethnic autobiographer. Here is where the Newtonian analogy begins to break down, for the self proves, after all, to be subjective in the everyday sense of "biased" or "unreliable." Handicapped by its interiority, it cannot be the equal of other "bodies" which can be summed up as a bundle of externally ascertainable properties. The self is epistemologically underprivileged, not privileged; to discover the validity of its private truths, it must appeal to the arbitration of the community (however defined). The history of the collectivity is ballast for the ethnic autobiographer, subjectivity; it is a yardstick against which the author can measure how representative or how idiosyncratic his or her life is, how worthy of preservation in writing. Should individual experience fail to be homologous to collective history, personal authority must yield to ideological imperatives, and the details of the narrative must be manipulated to present an improved picture. According to this logic, the ethnic woman autobiographer victimized by sexism must be ready to suppress potentially damaging (to the men, that is) material; to do less is to jeopardize the united front and prostitute one's integrity for the sake of white approval. *Bios* is of little worth unless it is "representative"—averaged out to become sociologically informative as well as edifying.

A series of mutually incompatible demands on ethnic autobiography follows from the tenets outlined above. Initially, ethnic autobiography is thought useful because its focus on the uniqueness of the individual establishes a minority's right to self-definition; a sufficient number of autobiographies will disabuse white readers of their oversimplified preconceptions. Autobiography's allegedly pure factuality is also prized for its educational value: unlike fiction, it can be counted on to "tell it like it is" and resist charges of artistic license made by doubting readers. Nonetheless, autobiography cannot, by definition, be more than *one* person's life story, thus it cannot be fully trusted. What if the single individual's life happens to confirm or even endorse white perceptions instead of challenging them? Hence the insistence that ethnic autobiography be "representative." The requirement would have been easily fulfilled if the autobiographer happened—that vexatious word again!—to have already been "representative," in the sense of conforming to a view of the group agreed upon by the members making that determination. Short of that, the "representativeness" will have to be formed out of recalcitrant material, through an editorial process true to the spirit but not necessarily the letter of the "ethnic experience."

The minute this is done, however, the attempt to make absolute the generic distinctions between autobiography and fiction ends up dissolving the boundaries altogether: autobiography loses its putative authority in fact and turns into fiction. Language loses its innocuous transmitting function and assumes the unruly power of transmutation. The individual loses his or her uniqueness and becomes a sociological category. From the effort to counter homogenization by offering depictions of diversity, a new uniformity emerges: one set of stereotypes is replaced by another. In the final analysis, the main reason the critics attack *The Woman Warrior* is not that it is insufficiently factual but that it is insufficiently fictional: that the author did not tamper more freely with her own life story. And ironically—given the critics' claimed championship of self-definition and literary autonomy—the kind of fiction they would like Kingston to have written is closely dictated by the responses of white readers.

Only when safeguards against misreadings are supplied may the autobiographical label once more be affixed with confidence, the benefits of the genre now purged of the inconvenient admixture of potential harm. The ignorance of white readers seems to be taken for granted as immutable by Kingston's critics. The possibility that the less unregenerate readers may learn to read the allusions in *The Woman Warrior*, just as generations of minority readers have learned to read the Eurocentric canon, is never once raised; nor is the possibility that a Chinese-American writer may by right expect, and by duty promote, such learning in his or her audience.

These issues naturally have their counterparts in other ethnic American literatures. The differing versions of Frederick Douglass's early life found in his autobiographies provide a classic example of how a black autobiographer might feel compelled to edit "factual" details in the interest of anticipated social effect (e.g., Gates 98-124). It is worth noting that, while critic Henry Louis Gates, Jr., justifies the crafting or making [of a 'fictive self'] by design," citing the urgent need to establish the black man's right to speak for himself, he also finds a certain flatness of aesthetic effect when Douglass begins to substitute "one ideal essence for another." "Almost never does Douglass allow us to see him as a human individual in all of his complexity" (103, 119, 109).

Though the dilemma is shared by other ethnic American autobiographies, the conflicting claims of typicality and uniqueness take a particularly acute form in Chinese-American autobiography: at stake is not only the existence of the minority writer's voice but the possible perversion of that voice to satisfy the white reader's appetite for exoticism. Indeed, it is only within the context of the Chinese-American autobiographical tradition that both the vehemence of Kingston's critics and the novelty of the narrative undertaking in *The Woman Warrior* can be understood.

To borrow a phrase applied to early African-American writers, Chinese-American writers "entered into the house of literature through the door of autobiography" (Olney, "Autobiography and the Cultural Moment" 15). Autobiographies predominate in Chinese-American writing in English.[13] Some autobiographies are by Chinese-born writers who grew up in China (Lee, Yung, Kuo, Su-ling Wong, Wei); others are by writers born and brought up in the United States (Lowe, Jade Snow Wong, Goo, Kingston). An autobiography from the former group typically focuses on the protagonist's early experiences in China, often ending very abruptly upon his or her arrival in the United States. The author tends to believe the life depicted as representing Chinese life of a certain period or social milieu, and of interest to the Western reader chiefly for this reason rather than for its uniqueness; such a conviction may easily degenerate into the accommodating mentality of a friendly guide to an exotic culture.[14] The autobiographies in the second group, those by American-born writers, are primarily set in the United States.[14] Given the distressing tendency of white readers to confuse Chinese Americans with Chinese in China, and to attribute a kind of a historical, almost genetic, Chinese essence to all persons of Chinese ancestry regardless of their upbringing, the pressure on American-born writers to likewise "represent Chinese culture" is strong. Removed from Chinese culture in China by their ancestors' emigration, American-born autobiographers may still capitalize on white curiosity by conducting the literary equivalent of a guided Chinatown tour: by providing explanations on the manners and mores of the Chinese-American community from the vantage point of a "native." This stance has indeed been adopted by some, and, in a sort of involuntary intertextuality, even those works that do not share it will most likely be read as anthropological guidebooks. The curse is potent enough to extend at times to nonautobiographical literature; for a book like *The Woman Warrior*, then, it would be all but impossible to prevent some readers from taking the auto-biographical label as a license to overgeneralize.

A few examples will characterize the stance of the cultural guide found among both Chinese-born and American-born autobiographers. In Lee Yan Phou's *When I Was a Boy in China*, personal narrative slows at every turn to make room for background material; seven of the twelve chapter titles—"The House and Household," "Chinese Cookery," "Games and Pastimes," "Schools and School Life," "Religions," "Chinese Holidays," "Stories and Story-Tellers"—could have come out of a general survey of Chinese society. The individual's life serves the function of conveying anthropological information; the freight, in fact, frequently outweighs the vehicle. Lee directly addresses white American readers as "you" throughout the book and consciously assumes the persona of a tour guide: "The servants were . . sent out to market to buy the materials for breakfast. Let us follow them"; "Now, let me take you into the school where I struggled with the Chinese written language for three years" (27, 57). In Helena Kuo's tellingly titled *I've Come a Long Way*, the tour guide role seems to have become second nature to the author. Like Lee, Kuo addresses her audience as "you" and constantly takes into account their likely reactions. Her descriptions of place are filtered through the eyes of her white readers (e.g., 27); the similes she favors are pure *chinoiserie* (e.g., 23). In the midst of a narrative about her journalistic career, Kuo solicitously inserts a mini-disquisition on traditional Chinese painting, to ensure that her charges will not be lost in the future when she is no longer around (171).[15]

It is perhaps no accident that a good number of the autobiographies by Chinese-born writers are rather abruptly cut off soon after the author's arrival in the United States, in apparent contrast to the structure of immigrant autobiography described in William Boelhower's typology (*Immigrant Autobiography* 25-52). Unlike the European works cited by Boelhower, these do not chronicle the author's experience of encountering and coming to terms with American culture. While only further study can elucidate this observed difference, one might venture a guess on its cause: the Chinese authors may have sensed how far American interest in their life writings is based on the image of otherness, on exotic scenery and alien cultural practices. As the autobiographers become Americanized, the fascination they hold for the reader would fade; hence the sketchy coverage of their experience in the United Stares.[16]

Some American-born Chinese autobiographers also seem to have adopted the narrative stance of a cultural guide, though the presence of the audience is more implicit in their works than in Lee's or Kuo's. *Father and Glorious Descendant*, by Pardee Lowe (a contemporary and friend of Kuo's), abounds in descriptions of Chinatown customs and rituals, such as tong banquets, Chinese New Year festivities, celebration of the father's "Great Birthday," preparation of unusual (by Western standards) foods, and funeral practices. The name of the Lowes' ancestral village in China, Sahn Kay Gawk, is periodically rendered by the quaint circumlocution "The-Corner-of-the-Mountain-Where-the-Water-Falls," although that etymological information has been given on the first page of the book. Two chapters are devoted to a series of letters between Father and his cousin, written in a comically florid, heavily literal prose purporting to be a translation of classical Chinese (249-58). Lowe's handling of the English language betrays a habitual awareness of the white audience's need to be surprised and amused by the mystifying ways of the Chinese. Jade Snow Wong's autobiography, *Fifth Chinese Daughter,* shares with Lowe's an emphasis on Chinatown customs and rituals; with Lee's and Kuo's, a tendency to intersperse the narrative of her life with discursive segments of information on Chinese culture. A description of a dinner party for her American friends includes a step-by-step record of how egg foo young and tomato beef are cooked; an account of a visit to a Chinatown herbalist for her cough is interrupted by a clarification of the Chinese medical theory of humors (160-62, 224).[17]

Although there is much else in Lowe's and Wong's books besides these gestures of consideration for the sensibilities of white readers, it is undeniable that both of these authors, like their Chinese-born counterparts, are conscious of their role as cultural interpreters who can obtain a measure of recognition from whites for the insider's insight they can offer. The title of a chapter in Wong's book, "Rediscovering Chinatown," aptly epitomizes one way American-born Chinese may make peace with their cultural background in the face of intense assimilative pressures: to return to one's ethnic heritage with selective enthusiasm, reassessing once-familiar land, once-despised sights and sounds according to their acceptability to white tastes.

As a form characterized by simultaneous subjectivity and objectivity, simultaneous expression and documentation (e.g., Stone 10-11; Sands 57), autobiography easily creates in its readers expectations of "privileged access" (Olney, "Autobiography and the Cultural Moment" 13) to the experience and vision of an entire people. From an intraethnic point of view, the writing of autobiography may be valued as a means of preserving memories of a vanishing way of life, and hence of celebrating cultural continuity and identity; in an interethnic perspective, however, the element of *display,* whether intentional or not, is unavoidable. Many "outsiders" will thus approach ethnic autobiographies with the misguided conviction that the authors necessarily speak for "their people." The practice of reading autobiography for "cultural authenticity" may be a particularly serious danger for Chinese-American autobiography given the group's unique situation in

United States society. The ancestral land of Chinese Americans due to its long history, sophisticated civilization and complex encounters with American imperialism in recent history, casts an inordinately strong spell on the white imagination. Moreover Chinese Americans who have been subjected to genocidal immigration policies[19] are placed in the situation of permanent guests who must earn their keep by adding the spice of variety to American life—by selectively maintaining aspects of traditional Chinese culture and language fascinating to whites. In the terminology of Werner Sollors, if the essence of the American experience is the formation of a society based on "consent" rather than "descent," Chinese Americans have clearly been (and still are) excluded from participation in "consent" by the dominant group's insistence on the primacy of their "descent." The irony is that many readers from within the ethnic group itself have, like the detractors of *The Woman Warrior*, inadvertently contributed to this simplified and often condescending view by likewise positing a direct pipeline of cultural authenticity between the collectivity and the individual. The idea of overdetermination by "descent" is thus left unchallenged. Demanding "representativeness," the Chinese-American critics of Kingston differ from the white literary tourists only in the version of cultural authenticity subscribed to.

This tension between "consent" and "descent" is reminiscent of W. E. B. Du Bois's well-known concept of "double consciousness."[20] The writers are aware of themselves as "insiders" with unique experiences that cannot be fully captured by ethnic categories alone. On the other hand they cannot but sense the "outsiders'" constant gaze upon their skin color, their physiognomy, their "difference." Their American right of "consent"—here taking the form of the freedom to create literature true to their felt lives—is perpetually called into question or qualified by reader expectations based on "descent." Some Chinese-American autobiographers have, indeed, sought distinction in their exotic "descent," allowing the dominant group's perceptions to define their identity. However, it is important to recognize that Kingston has taken an altogether different path in *The Woman Warrior*. The protagonist has eschewed the facile authority which self-appointment as guide and spokesperson could confer on her. The discursive space occupied by *The Woman Warrior* is between the two poles of the "double consciousness"; the audience the narrator addresses in the second person is composed of fellow Chinese Americans sharing the protagonist's need to establish a new Chinese-American selfhood:

> Chinese-Americans, when you try to understand what things in you are Chinese, how do you separate what is peculiar to childhood, to poverty, insanities, one family, your mother who marked your growing with stories, from what is Chinese? What is Chinese tradition and what is the movies? (6)

Boelhower writes:

> In the mixed genre of autobiography, . . . the question of identity involves matching the narrator's own self-perception with the self that is recognized by others, so as to establish a continuity between the two (self and world), to give a design of self-in- the-world. ("Brave New World" 12)

If the "others" are the potential "misreaders" among her white audience, Kingston is in truth far less obsessed than her critics with "the self that is recognized by others." There are, of course, other "others" in the protagonist's lonely struggle: her Chinese family, relatives, fellow "villagers," whose perceptions of her do not match her self-perceptions either. "Descent" notwithstanding, connection to them has to be forged, which can take place only after an initial recognition of difference. Neither American nor Chinese culture, as given, offers a resting place; the protagonist of *The Woman Warrior* has to discover that there is "[n]o higher listener. No higher listener but myself" (237). Her project is to reach "an avowal of values and a recognition of the self by the self—a choice carried out at the level of essential being—not a revelation of a reality given in advance but a corollary of an active intelligence" (Gusdorf 44). This project is so bold, so unfamiliar, that even her fellow Chinese Americans sometimes mistake it for the accommodationism of earlier autobiographers. For resemblances can indeed be found between *The Woman Warrior* and its predecessors—like Lee, Kingston retells Chinese tales heard in childhood; like Kuo, she makes general remarks on Chinese culture; like Lowe, she speaks of unusual Chinese foods; like Wong, she recounts experiences of sexist oppression. The crucial question is whether these resemblances are merely superficial or whether they bespeak a basic commonality in autobiographical stance. Only a careless reader, I submit, would be able to conclude that Kingston's stance in *The Woman Warrior* is that of the trustworthy cultural guide.

For the "native" in this case, having been born and raised in "ghost country" without benefit of explicit parental instruction in cultural practices, is barely more enlightened than an "outsider" would be: "From the configuration of food my mother set out, we kids had to infer the holidays" (215). Quite unlike the generalizations about Chinese culture in *I've Come a Long Way* or *Father and Glorious Descendant*, which are meant to be encapsulations of superior knowledge, those in *The Woman Warrior* bespeak a tentative groping toward understanding. From fragmentary and haphazard evidence the protagonist has to piece together a coherent picture of the culture she is enjoined to preserve against American influence. The effort is so frustrating that she exclaims in exasperation: "I don't see how they kept up a continuous culture for five thousand years. Maybe they didn't; maybe everyone makes it up as they go along" (216). But the point, of course, is that the Chinese who remain in Chinese-dominant communities would have no trouble at all transmitting culture through osmosis. It is the protagonist's American-born generation who must "make it up as they go along." The emigrant parents' expectation of a "continuous culture" is, if entirely human, ahistorical and therefore doomed. (So, one might add, is the critics' similar demand for cultural authenticity. Purity is best preserved by death; history adulterates.)

Given *The Warrior Woman's* situation in the broader cultural timescape of Chinese America, then, the so-called distortions of traditional Chinese culture found in the text are simply indications of how far removed from it the protagonist has become. As Deborah Woo rightly observes, "where culture is problematic as a source of identity, cultural ignorance itself is part of what is authentic about the experience" (186). Thus the substitution of "heavenly chicken" for "field chicken" is not exoticization but an example of how a young Chinese child in an English-dominant society may misunderstand a tonal language. The protagonist's cosmological speculations on the omnipresent number six (91), involving a misinterpretation of *dai luk* (which in Cantonese pronunciation can be "the big six," a nonexistent collocation, or "the big continent/the mainland"), betray her "craving for coherence" in the face of a bewildering mass of unexplained cultural data (Hsu 434). It is not an actual Chinese fortune-teller who confuses the homophones, which might have justified the charge of willful distortion on Kingston's part; the phrase "the Big Six" is framed by the young girl's meditation on her mother's life, the fortune-teller a fictive one whom she imagines her mother consulting.

It is, in fact, essential to recognize that the entire *Woman Warrior* is a sort of meditation on what it means to be Chinese American. To this end, the protagonist appropriates whatever is at hand, testing one generalization after another until a satisfactory degree of applicability to her own life is found. As she says of the differing versions of the No Name Woman's story: "Unless I see her life branching into mine, she gives me no ancestral help" (10). The aphoristic statements about Chinese ways interspersed in the narrative—"Women in the old China did not choose" (7); "Chinese communication was loud, public" (13); "Among the very poor and the wealthy, brothers married their adopted sisters, like doves" 114)—are not offered for the benefit of readers hungry for tidbits of anthropological information. Rather, they are threads in a larger tapestry of inferences, some sturdy, some thin, which the protagonist weaves for her own use. Rejecting the theory that the aunt is a "wild woman" (9) or a passive rape victim, the narrator decides on a version relevant to her life in an immigrant family; a story of assertion of "private life" (14) against the harsh demands of group survival.

Even with material that tempts with its air of certainty, the protagonist finds it necessary to tailor-make meanings from altered details. Thus she spurns the simplistic lesson of the traditional Fa Mu Lan tale, creating instead a potentially subversive woman warrior to whom even traditions yield. While the heroine of "Mulan Shi" sees herself merely as a second-best substitute for an aged father (there being no elder son to take his place), the little girl in "White Tigers" is a *chosen* one, destined to be called away by "immortals." Martial artists typically pass on their skills to sons or male disciples; the old couple in the mountains, in contrast, devote years exclusively to her training. For the traditional Mulan, the campaigns are but a detour; at the end of the poem, the erstwhile general puts on makeup, ready to resume her interrupted feminine life. Kingston's Fa Mu Lan chooses wifehood and motherhood in the midst of battle. Her fellow villagers know of her identity before her triumphant return from battle (43); their relinquishment of their precious sons to her army is thus an affirmation of faith in her female power. Of course, the very necessity of male disguise means that the narrator's fantasized challenge to patriarchy can never be complete; in the last analysis, she would like to be remembered for "perfect filiality" (54). Yet even Fa Mu Lan's return to her parents' house has an element of active choice. All in all, working within the constraints of internalized values, the protagonist has done her best to make of unpromising material an inspiring, if not entirely radical, tale.

The treatment of the T'sai Yen story (241-31 follows much the same pattern of sifting out details to arrive at a relevant meaning. Kingston's retelling omits a crucial scene in the original "Eighteen Stanzas for a Barbarian Reed Pipe":[21] T'sai Yen's painful leave-taking from her half-barbarian sons. Though by now attached to her captor and heartsick at the prospect of never seeing her children again, T'sai Yen nevertheless chooses Han lands as her real home, negating the twelve years spent in the steppes as a mere unfortunate interlude. Herself a half-barbarian to her China-obsessed parents ("Whenever my parents said 'home,' they suspended America" [161]), the narrator might have found such a detail too close for comfort, and too contrary in spirit to her own undertaking of forming a Chinese-American self. Thus we find a shift of emphasis: the last pages of *The Woman Warrior* celebrate not return from the remote peripheries to a waiting home but the creation of a new center through art. Singing a song that transcends cultural boundaries, T'sai Yen can now leave "her tent to sit by the winter campfires, ringed by barbarians" (243).

As with the "Eighteen Stanzas," the moral that the protagonist draws from the assorted Chinese ghost stories diverges from the one intended by the source. No automatic authority on Chinese culture simply by virtue of "descent," the protagonist must resort to public, written texts in her quest for meanings not forthcoming in her mother's private oral tradition. Contrary to one critic's judgment that the Mandarin transliteration of some names in *The Woman Warrior* betrays how Kingston passes library research for her Cantonese musher's bedtime stories,[22] Kingston does not attempt to cover her trails, as any self-respecting cultural guide would. She provides dates with the Mandarin names and identifies the source, "the research against ghost fear published by the Chinese Academy of Science" (Zhongguo Kexueyuan Wenxueyanjiusuo 104). The lesson she constructs to make sense of her experiences in a frugal immigrant family?—"Big eaters win" (105)—

bears little relation to the political allegory of the Communist-compiled anthology. But what matters is not the fit (for which Procrustean beds are notorious). The most useful lesson the protagonist can learn from her research is that a passive staking of her life on some pre-established reality, like looking up *Ho Chi Kuei* (237-38) in a dictionary filled with decontextualized definitions, will always prove fruitless.

The narrator's methodology of self-redemption is thus remarkably consistent. Over and over, we find her forgoing the security of ready-made cultural meanings, opting instead to painstakingly mold a new set suited to her condition as a Chinese-American woman. The many questions about "facts" plaguing the narrator—Were there an Oldest Daughter and Oldest Son who died in China (120)? Did Brave Orchid cut her frenum (190)? Did the hulk exist or was he made up (239)?—function much like a series of Zen *koan* frustrating because impossible to answer by appeal to an external authority [mother, in this case). In the end, realization of their very impossibility frees her to explore the fecund uncertainties of her Chinese-American existence.

The readers who fault *The Woman Warrior* for not being more responsible toward "facts" would do well to meditate on their own *koan.* To read departures from traditional material found in *The Woman Warrior* as Kingston's cynical manipulations of naive white readers, as her critics have done, is not only to fly in the face of textual evidence but to belittle the difficulty and urgency of the imaginative enterprise so necessary to the American-born generation: to make sense of Chinese and American culture from its own viewpoint (however hybrid and laughable to "outsiders!" to articulate its own reality, and to strengthen its precarious purchase on the task of self-fashioning. The Fa Mu Lan story itself, which many of Kingston's critics take to be a fixed and sacred given, actually exists in a multitude of Chinese texts differing from each other in purpose as well as detail.[23]

Kingston's critics have been measuring *The Woman Warrior* "against some extra-textual order of fact," not realizing that this order is "based in its turn on other texts (dignified as documents)" (Eakin 23): an ideologically uplifting version of Chinese-American history revising earlier racist texts, a version of the Fa Mu Lan legend sufficiently hoary to be considered "historical." The critics' concern is understandable in view of widespread ignorance about the sociopolitical context of Chinese-American literary creation, the inherent duality of the autobiographical genre (which encourages reading for "cultural authenticity"), the existence of autobiographies by both Chinese- and American-born writers promising privileged glimpses into the group's secret life and the apparent similarities between them and Kingston's work. These issues are, indeed, vital ones generalizable to other ethnic American auto-biographies, even to all ethnic American literatures. Nevertheless, intent on liberating Chinese-American writers from one set of constraints, Kingston's detractors have imposed another, in the meantime failing to take note of the most fundamental freedom of all that *The Woman Warrior* has wrested from *a priori* generic categories and cultural prescriptions: the freedom to create in literature a *sui generis* Chinese-American reality.

I am grateful to King-Kok Cheung, Samuel Cheung, Maxine Hong Kingston, Kathy L. Stephen Sumida, Shelley Wong, Deborah Woo, and Yiheng Zhao for their assistance in the writing of this essay, and to James Payne for his many valuable suggestions on revision. I am solely responsible for its content.

---

1 For example, both Juhasz and Rabine relate the unconventional narrative structure *of The Woman Warrior* to the feminist act of creating identity, although their interpretations differ.

2 Personal communication to the author from Kingston, 21 May 1988; quoted with her permission.

3 On the "real" and the "imaginary," Kingston writes: "My Idea [in *The Woman Warrior* and *China Men*] was to invent a new form for telling my stories and thoughts. I needed a form in which I could have real, true human beings who have very imaginative minds tell their lives and dreams. My real characters have artful minds, the minds of fiction writers and storytellers." Personal communication to the author, 21 May 1988; quoted with Kingston's permission.

4 For example, Brave Orchid's encounter with the "Sitting Ghost"; the Chinese stories of big eaters who devour ghosts and other monsters (104-6); the protagonist's girlhood interactions with many types of "ghosts" [113-16]; and Moon Orchid's reunion with her husband, troth now having entered the "land of ghosts" (178).

5 For a reading of the multilayered significance of the term *ghost,* see Sato, who demonstrates how Kingston's rendering of *kuei* focuses many aspects of Chinese-American life and is hardly a "white-washed" usage.

6 This version of the name appears to be a composite of Cantonese and Mandarin transliterations, *Fa Muk Lan* and *Hua Mu Lan*—another "impurity?"

7 The prolonged training in still "stances" and feats of balance (like sleeping on a rope), the copying of animal movements, and the gaining of control over normally involuntary bodily functions are standard fare in *wuxia xiaoshuo.* The "calling" of a chosen one for spiritual discipline, the hermit's retreat on misty mountains, the magic water gourd, and the cultivation of immortality are images from *shenxian* stories, which have passed fully into the Chinese popular mind. These and other features from folk traditions found in *The Woman Warrior* would be familiar to children growing up in a Chinese community.

8 A translation of "The Ballad of Mulan" may be found in Liu and Lo 77-80 (cited in Chua).

9 *Outlaws of the Marsh*, a classic in Chinese literature, is based on oral tales depicting peasant heroes who form "righteous armies" to defy the corrupt imperial government. The earliest extant written version dates from the sixteenth century. The English title of Shapiro's recent translation, rather than the older *Water Margin,* is used here.

10 Note that in her next book, *China Men,* Kingston has included a list of discriminatory legislation against Chinese Americans "The reviews of my first book made it clear that people didn't know the history—or that they thought I didn't. While I was writing about China Men, I just couldn't take that tension any more" (Pfaff 26; cited in Kim xvii).

11 Fong cites her relationship with a "warm, generous and loving father" (68-69) to support her complaint against *The Woman Warrior.*

12 The critics of *The Woman Warrior* supply almost a textbook example of the assumptions about autobiography, common prior to the recent shifting of critical focus from *bios* to *autos*, described by Olney, "Autobiography and the Cultural Moment" 20.

13 Chinese-American literature has a large Chinese-language component, the exclusive domain of immigrant writers, which is only beginning to be studied and translated. This component falls outside the scope of this essay, but one should note that it contains very few autobiographies.

A partial list (in chronological order) of works explicitly presented as autobiography, of varying literary interest and popularity, include Lee Yan Phou's *When I Was a Boy in China* (1887), Yung Wing's My *Life in China and America* (1909), Helena Kuo's *I've Come a Long Way* (1942), Pardee Lowe's *Father and Glorious Descendant* (1943), Jade Snow Wong's *Fifth Chinese Daughter* (1945), Su-ling Wung (pseud.) and Earl Herbert Cressy's *Daughter of Confucius: A Personal History* (1952), Jade Snow Wong's *No Chinese Stranger* (1975), Thomas York-Tong Goo's *Before the Gods* (1976), Maxine Hong Kingston's *The Woman Warrior* (1976), and Katherine Wei and Terry Quinn's *Second Daughter: Growing Up in China, 1930-1949* (1984).

14 See Kim's discussion of "ambassadors of goodwill" in her chapter on early Asian immigrant writers 124-291.

15 Goo, who undergoes assimilation into Chinese culture in China, is an exception to this pattern.

[16] A passage in Korean American Younghill Kang's fictionalized autobiography, *East Goes West* (1937), provides an interesting gloss on the practice of "cultural guiding," which is apparently generalizable from Chinese to other Asian-American autobiographies. Kim, an older Korean exile, advises the protagonist Chungpa Han to retain his classical Oriental learning: "You have to eat. And to eat, you must enter into the economic life of Americans. . . . In making a living, Oriental scholarship may help you more than your American education. . . . [I]n such a field, you would have the advantage. There would be less competition. . . . *You must be now like a Western man approaching Asia.* . . . As a transplanted scholar, this is the only road I could point to, for your happy surviving" (277-78; my italics). Despite his rhetoric of cultural catholicity, what Kim s suggesting is really a kind of self-Orientalization

[17] This possibility is further explored in my "Immigrant Autobiography: Some Questions of Definition and Approach."

[18] Recipes are again included in the sequel to *Fifth Chinese Daughter, No Chinese Stranger* (e.g., 187-88). In the latter, Wong and her husband lead tours to the Far East, thus making cultural interpretation their trade.

[19] The Chinese Exclusion Act, passed in 1882 to keep out Chinese laborers, as well as subsequent anti-Chinese measures (including antimiscegenation laws and laws prohibiting laborers' wives from entering), created a "bachelor society" unable to reproduce itself. The situation did not begin to change until the Exclusion Act was repealed in 1943.

[20] This concept has been related by more than one scholar (e.g., Rubin 75; Rampersad 13) to the duality of autobiography.

[21] Rorex and Fong provide a complete translation of the poem as well as color illustrations from a traditional scroll. Kingston's use of the T'sai Yen material is discussed in greater detail in my forthcoming "Kingston's Handling of Traditional Chinese Sources."

[22] Statement delivered by Marlon Hom at the roundtable discussion, "Asian American Literature: State of the Art and Criticism," Fifth National Conference of the Association for Asian American Studies, 26 Mar. 1988, Washington State University, Pullman.

[23] According to Zhao 77-79, since the Tang dynasty (618-907) there have been many versions of the Fa Mu Lan story, some poetic, others operatic or novelistic. One Qing dynasty (1644-1911) version features a sister; another adds a cowardly cousin. During the Anti-Japanese War (1937-45), the Fa Mu Lan story was frequently staged as plays, with the moral modified to emphasize nationalism (even though the "original" heroine was not Han but a member of a northern tribe.) I have seen a film version from the 1960s sung in *huangmeidiao*, a variety of popular Chinese opera, available in videotape rental outlets serving Chinese-American communities. This version includes statements on the equality of the sexes reflecting modern, Westernized ideas.

Works Cited

Boelhower, William. "The Brave New World of Immigrant Autobiography." *MELUS 9*, no. 2 (1982): 5-23.

———. *Immigrant Autobiography in the United States.* Verona: Essedue, 1982.

Bruss, Elizabeth. *Autobiographical Acts: The Changing Situation of a Literary Genre.* Baltimore: Johns Hopkins UP, 1976.

Chan, Jeffery Paul. "Jeff Chan, Chairman of SF State Asian American Studies, Attacks Review." *San Francisco Journal*, 4 May 1977, 6.

Chang, *Diana. Frontiers of Love.* New York: Random House, 1956.

Chin, Frank. "The Most Popular Book in China." *Quilt* 4 (1984): 6-12.

———. "This Is Not an Autobiography." *Genre* 18, no. 2 (1985): 109-30.

Chin, Frank, Jeffery Paul Chan, Lawson Fusao Inada, and Shawn Wong, eds. *Aiiieeeee! An Anthology of Asian-American Writers.* 1974. Rpt. Washington, DC: Howard UP, 1983.

Chu, Louis. *Eat a Bowl of Tea.* Seattle: U of Washington P, 1961.

Chua, Cheng Lok. "Golden Mountain: Chinese Versions of the American Dream in Lin Yutang, Louis Chu, and Maxine Hong Kingston." *Ethnic Groups* 4 (1982): 57.

Chuang Hua (pseud.) *Crossings.* New York: Dial, 1968.

Eakin, John Paul. *Fictions in Autobiography: Studies in the Art of Self-Invention.* Princeton: Princeton UP, 1985.

Fong, Katheryn M. "To Maxine Hong Kingston: A Letter." *Bulletin for Concerned Asian Scholars* 9, no. 4 (1977): 67-69.

Gates, Henry Louis, Jr. *Figures in Black: Words, Signs, and the "Racial" Self.* New York: Oxford UP, 1987.

Goo, Thomas York-Tong. *Before the Gods.* New York: Helios, 1976.

Gusdorf, Georges. "Conditions and Limits of Autobiography." Trans. James Olney. In Olney, *Autobiography*, 28-48.

Hsu, Vivian. "Maxine Hong Kingston as Psycho-Autobiographer and Ethnographer." *International Journal of Women's Studies* 6, no. 5 (1983): 429-42.

Johnson, Diane. "Ghosts." Rev. of *The Woman Warrior*, by Maxine Hong Kingston. *New York Review of Books*, 3 Feb. 1977, 19+.

Juhasz, Suzanne. "Maxine Hong Kingston: Narrative Technique and Female Identity." In Rainwater and Scheik 173-89.

Kang, Younghill. *East Goes West: The Making of an Oriental Yankee.*

Chicago: Follett, 1937.

Kim, Elaine H. *Asian American Literature: An Introduction to the Writings and Their Social Context.* Philadelphia: Temple UP, 1982.

Kingston, Maxine Hong. *China Men.* New York: Knopf, 1980.

———. *The Woman Warrior: Memoirs of a Girlhood among Ghosts.* 1976. New York: Random [House?], 1977.

Krupat, Arnold. "The Indian Autobiography: Origins, Type, and Function." *American Literature* 53, no. 1 (1981): 22-42.

Kuo, Helena. *I've Come a Long Way.* New York: Appleton, 1942.

Larson, Wendy Ann. "Autobiographies of Chinese Writers in the Early Twentieth Century." Diss. U of California, Berkeley. 1984.

Lau, Joseph S.M. [Liu Shaoming]. "Tangrenjie de xiaoshuo shijie" ["The Fictional World of Chinatown"]. *Ming Pao Monthly* 173 (1980): 65-66.

Lee, Yan Phou. *When I Was a Boy in China.* Boston: Lothrop, 1887.

Lim, Genny, ed. *The Chinese American Experience: Papers from the Second National Conference on Chinese American Studies (1980)).* San Francisco: Chinese Historical Society of America and Chinese Culture Foundation, 1980.

Liu, Wu-Chi, and Irving Yucheng Lo, trans. *Sunflower Splendor: Three Thousand Years of Chinese Poetry.* Bloomington: Indiana UP, 1975.

Lowe, Pardee. *Father and Glorious Descendant.* Boston: Little, 1943.

Olney, James. "Autobiography and the Cultural Moment: A Thematic, Historical, and Bibliographical Introduction." In Olney, *Autobiography* 3-27.

———, ed. *Autobiography: Essays Theoretical and Critical* Princeton: Princeton UP, 1980.

———. "Some Versions of Memory/Some Versions of Bios: The Ontology of Autobiography." In Olney *Autobiography* 236-237.

Pascal, Roy. *Design and Truth in Autobiography.* Cambridge: Harvard UP, 1960.

Pfaff, Timothy. "Talk with Mrs. Kingston." *New York Times Book Review,* 18 June 1980.

Rabine, Leslie W. "No Lost Paradise: Social Gender and Symbolic Gender in the Writings of Maxine Hong Kingston." *Signs: Journal of Women in Culture and Society* 12, no. 3 (1987): 471-92.

Rainwater, Catherine, and William J. Scheik, eds. *Contemporary American Women Writers: Narrative Strategies.* Lexington: UP of Kentucky, 1985.

Rampersad, Arnold. "Biography, Autobiography, and Afro-American Culture." *Yale Review* 73, no. 1 (1983): 1-16.

Rorex, Robert A., and Wen Fong. *Eighteen Songs of a Nomad Flute: The Story of Lady Wen-Chi.* New York: Metropolitan Museum of Art, 1974.

Rubin, Steven J. "Ethnic Autobiography: A Comparative Approach." *Journal of Ethnic Studies*, 9 no. 1 (1981): 75-79.

Sands, Kathleen Mullen. "American Indian Autobiography." In *Studies in American Indian literature: Essays and Course Designs*, ed. Paula Gunn Allen. New York: MLA, 1983. 55-65.

Sato, Gayle K. Fujita. "Ghosts as Chinese-American Constructs in Maxine Hong Kingston's *The Woman Warrior.*" In *Haunting the House of Fiction: Feminist Perspectives on Ghost Stories by American Women*, ed. Lynette Carpenter and Wendy K. Kolmar. Knoxville: U of Tennessee P, 1991. 193-214

Shapiro, Sidney, trans. *Outlaws of the Marsh.* Beijing: Foreign Language Press, 1980.

Sollors, Werner. *Beyond Ethnicity: Consent and Descent in American Culture.* New York: Oxford UP, 1986.

Stone, Albert. "Autobiography in American Culture: Looking Back at the Seventies." *American Studies International* 19, no. 3-4 (1981): 3-14.

Tong, Benjamin R. "Chinatown Popular Culture: Notes toward a Critical Psychological Anthropology." In Lim 233-41.

———. "Critic of Admirer Sees Dumb Racist." *San Francisco Journal*, 11 May 1977, 6.

Wei, Katherine, and Terry Quinn. *Second Daughter: Growing Up in China, 1930-1949.* New York: Holt:, 1984.

Wong, Jade Snow. *Fifth Chinese Daughter.* 1945. Rev. ed. New York: Harper, 1950.

———. *No Chinese Stranger.* New York: Harper, 1975.

Wong, Nellie. Review of *The Woman Warrior. Bridge* 6, no. 4 (1978-79): 46-48.

Wong, Sau-ling C. "Immigrant Autobiography: Some Questions of Definition and Approach." In *American Autrbiography: Retrospect and Prospect,* ed. Paul John Eakin. Madison: U of Wisconsin P, 1991. 142-70.

———. "Kingston's Handling of Traditional Chinese Sources." *Approaches to Teaching Kingston's The Woman Warrior,* ed. Shirley Geok-lin Lim. New York: MLA, 1991.

Wong, Shawn. *Homebase.* New York: I. Reed, 1979.

Wong, Su-ling (pseud.), and Earl Herbert Cressy. *Daughter of Confucius: A Personal History.* New York: Farrar, 1952.

Wong, Suzi. Review of *The Woman Warrior. Amerasia Journal* 4, no. 1 (1977): 165-67.

Woo, Deborah. "Maxine Hong Kingston: The Ethnic Writer and the Burden of Dual Authenticity." *Amerasia Journal* 16, no. 1 (1990: 173-200.

Wu, Pei-Yi. "Self-Examination and Confession of Sins in Traditional China." *Harvard Journal of Asiatic Studies* 39, no. 1 (1979): 5-38.

Yep, Laurence. *Dragonwings.* New York: Harper, 1975.

Yung, Wing. *My Life in China and America.* New York: Holt, 1909.

Zhao, Jingshen. *Minzu wenxue xiaoshi [A Brief History of National Literature].* N.p.: Shijie Shaju, 1940.

Zhongguo Kexueyuan Wenxueyanjiusuo [Chinese Academy of Science, Institute of Literary Studies]. *Bupagui de gushi [Stories of Those Who Are Not Afraid of Ghosts].* Hong Kong: San Lian, 1961.

Cultural and Economic Boundaries of Korean Ethnicity: A Comparative Analysis

Pyong Gap Min
Department of Sociology,
City University of New York-Queens College

The extent to which members of an ethnic/immigrant group maintain their native cultural tradition and social interactions with co-ethnic members is referred to as "ethnic attachment" or "ethnicity."[1] Korean immigrants in the United States maintain a high level of ethnicity. That is, the vast majority of Korean immigrants speak the Korean language, eat mainly Korean food, and practice Korean customs most of the time. Most Korean immigrants are affiliated with at least one ethnic organization and involved in active informal ethnic networks. For example, Hurh and Kim (1988) report that 90 percent of Korean immigrants in Chicago mainly speak the Korean language at home and that 82 percent are affiliated with one or more ethnic organizations. A comparative study of three Asian ethnic groups—Korean, Chinese, and Filipino—indicates that a much larger proportion of Korean Americans (75 percent) than Filipino (50 percent) or Chinese Americans (19 percent) have joined one or more ethnic associations.[2]

Theorists of ethnicity have emphasized two major factors as bases of ethnicity. First, commonalities in culture and historical experiences that members of a group share provide an important basis of ethnicity.[3]

From *Ethnic and Racial Studies*, Vol. 14, April 1991, pp. 225-241. Reprinted by permission of Routledge.

A minority group that has a common language, a common religion, and/or other cultural and historical commonalities is likely to maintain higher levels of ethnic identity and ethnic subculture than other minority groups. Second, productive activities, particularly associated with job-market concentration, also contributed to ethnic solidarity and ethnic identity.[4] Minority/immigrant groups usually concentrate in certain occupations, and the occupational concentration puts them in conflict and competition with the majority population or other minority groups over economic interests. Inter-group conflicts for economic survival enhance also in-group solidarity.

When cultural boundaries coincide with boundaries defined by productive activities, "ethnic solidarity is doubly reinforced."[5] Korean immigrants in the United States maintain a high level of ethnicity exactly because of this coincidence of cultural and economic boundaries. That is, Korean immigrants are a culturally homogeneous group, and at the same time they are occupationally concentrated in a limited range of small businesses. This article intends to explain Korean immigrants' strong ethnic attachment, focusing on their cultural homogeneity and occupational concentration. The extent to which Korean immigrants are culturally homogeneous or economically segregated can be effectively assessed in comparison with other immigrant/ethnic groups. Thus, this article will very often compare Korean immigrants with other minority/immigrant groups in the Untied States, particularly with other Asian ethnic groups, in order to explain Korean ethnicity.

The 1970 US census estimated that the Korean-American population was less than 70,000. It increased to more than 350,000 in 1980 and has probably reached one million in 1990.[6] This suggests that the predominant majority of Korean Americans are the post-1965 immigrants from South Korea. South Korea is a small and culturally homogeneous country, and Korean immigrants sustain a high level of ethnicity partly because of their strong cultural and historical ties.

The cultural homogeneity of Korean immigrants becomes clearer when they are compared with other immigrants groups in the United States. It is a well-known fact the Filipino immigrants consist of a number of subgroups based on language and place of origin. The absence of a common native language and regional differences partly contribute to factionalism and disunity characterizing Filipino-Americans' community organization.[7] Asian-Indian immigrants, like Filipino immigrants, consist of many linguistic-regional subethnic groups. Thus, close friends and visiting patterns among Indian immigrants usually involve people from the same region or the same language group.[8] Moreover, Indian immigrants consist of religiously heterogeneous subgroups, which is one major source of internal conflicts.[9]

Researchers have described earlier Chinese immigrants as having maintained strong in-group ties.[10] This generalization is, however, no longer applicable to recent Chinese immigrants, who are composed of several nationality groups: Chinese immigrants from Taiwan, Hong Kong, Singapore, Vietnam, and mainland China. Immigrants from Taiwan and mainland China differ significantly in political ideology, socioeconomic background, and other characteristics.[11] Even immigrants from mainland China consist of several linguistic-regional subgroups and thus are not a culturally homogeneous group. Another national-origin immigrant group that has significant subgroup differences is the Iranian. The Iranian immigrant group contains four ethnic-religious subgroups: Armenians, Baha'is, Jews and Muslims. Each Iranian ethnic-religious subgroup has its own economy, which is only weakly tied to an encompassing Iranian ethnic economy.[12] By contrast, Korean immigrants have only one native language and regional differences are insignificant in their ethnic identity. South Korea is a small country, smaller than the state of Georgia. More than half of recent Korean immigrants have come from Seoul, the capital of South Korea, and more than three-quarters of them have come from the five largest cities.[13] The vast majority of them have received high-school and/or college education in Seoul and other large metropolitan cities. Thus, alumni associations, which play an important role in maintaining Koreans' friendship networks, can include most Korean immigrants. Schools in the homeland may well be an important basis for ethnic organizations for Chinese, Indian, and Filipino immigrants as well. Yet, since the source country of each of these other Asian immigrant-groups is so large, alumni associations can tie only a small proportion of immigrants.

Koreans in the US, with the exception of Koreatown in Los Angeles, do not maintain a territorial community. Widely scattered in the whole metropolitan area, they maintain a non-territorial community. Ethnic media play the central role in integrating geographically dispersed Korean immigrants. Ethnic media seem to be more effective in enhancing ethnicity for Korean immigrants, especially since Koreans have only one native language. Almost all Korean immigrants can read Korean-language newspapers and understand Korean-language television programmes. Native-language media, however, can serve only a small proportion of Indian or Filipino immigrants, who consist of several language groups.

The vast majority of Korean immigrants are affiliated with Korean immigrant churches, which also facilitates Koreans' ethnic attachment. Christianity is a minority religion in Korea, with approximately 16 percent of Koreans affiliated with Protestant churches and another 5 percent with Catholic churches.[14] However, Christians are overrepresented among Korean immigrants. In a pre-departure survey conducted in Seoul, 54 percent of the 1986 Korean immigrants to the US reported that they were affiliated with a Christian church in Korea.[15] Korean immigrants have largely come from the urban, middle-class segment of the Korean population in which the Christian religion is very strong. This is one of the major reasons why Christians are overrepresented among Korean immigrants. Many Christians fled from North to South Korea before and during the Korean War, and North Korean refugees, who have no strong family ties in South Korea, have immigrated to the US in a greater proportion than the general population in South Korea. This is another reason for the overrepresentation of Christians among Korean immigrants. Finally, Korean Christians are more likely to choose immigration to the US than are Buddhists or Confucianists, which has also contributed to the disproportionate Christian background of Korean immigrants.

Many Korean immigrants, who were not Christians in Korea, probably attend the Korean ethnic church for practical purposes. Thus, an overwhelming majority of Korean immigrants are involved in ethnic churches. In a survey conducted in Los Angeles in 1986, 66.8 percent of the Korean respondents were found to attend the Korean ethnic church at least every two weeks. The 1988-89 Korean Churches Directory of New York shows what there were 165 Korean churches in five boroughs of New York City. Assuming that the Korean population of New York City in 1988 was 72,000, there was one Korean church for every 436 Koreans in New York City.

Korean immigrant churches serve several practical functions for Korean immigrants, which are indispensable to Koreans' adjustment in the United States.[16] Two of these practical functions contribute to Korean ethnicity. Many Korean immigrants attend ethnic church for the purpose of fellowship. In this connection, it is useful to note the finding from the 1986 Chicago study of Korean immigrants.[17] In the study 23.6 percent of the church-going respondents indicated fellowship or meeting friends as the primary motive for attending church. After Sunday service all Korean immigrant churches have a fellowship hour, which usually lasts half an hour to one hour. During the fellowship hour, church members exchange greetings and enjoy informal talks with fellow church-members. All Korean churches serve refreshments during the fellowship hour, and a significant proportion of them serve a Korean-style full lunch.[18]

Korean immigrant churches are usually small. A survey of Korean churches in New York City indicates that the median number of members is eighty-two. The small congregations of Korean immigrant churches can be explained by the need of Korean immigrants for small-group, primary social interactions. As I. Kim rightly points out the ethnic church plays the role of "a pseudo-extended family" for many Korean immigrants.[19] Korean immigrants attending a small church enjoy intimate friendship networks with church members not only inside the church but also outside it. A significant proportion of Korean immigrants seem largely to establish informal friendship networks with other members of their church by inviting them to dinner or to go picnicking, by playing sports with them or by taking trips together. In this connection, it is important to note that 45 percent of those Korean immigrants in Chicago with one or more intimate Korean friends in the same city first made friends with them in the ethnic church.[20]

Whereas a large Korean church provides more formal programmes for church members, it is less effective than a small church when it comes to providing Korean immigrants with an intimate social environment. However, even large Korean immigrant churches have made adjustments in such a way that they meet the needs of Korean immigrants for fellowship and belongingness. Korean immigrant churches usually divide church members into several groups by area of residence, and help each group to hold regular district meetings called

Kuyok Yebae. It has been found that nearly 80 percent of Korean churches in New York City have district groups, and that they hold district meetings once or more a month.[21] A district meeting combines a religious service and a dinner party at a member's private home, thus providing members with ample opportunity for informal social interactions. Church members who belong to the same district rotate hosting the meeting, usually offering a prepared dinner.

The other practical function of Korean immigrant churches that contributes to Korean ethnicity is maintenance of the Korean cultural tradition. Korean churches help to preserve Korean culture in several different ways. First, they contribute to the maintenance of Korean culture partly because the Korean language and customs are more strictly observed inside the Korean ethnic church than outside it. Korean pastors give sermons in Korean for almost all adult services of worship. Even for children's services, they use the Korean language more often than English. A survey reveals that only 20 percent of the New York City Korean churches provide services for children in English alone, and the others use either Korean (24 percent) or a bilingual mix (55 percent).[22] Moreover, a large proportion of Korean immigrant churches provide a Korean-language programme for children, which is central to language retention for the Korean American community.

Exposure to Korean culture in the Korean immigrant church is not limited to the Korean language. All Korean immigrant churches celebrate religious and Korean traditional holidays such as Easter, Thanksgiving, and New Year's Day by serving a variety of traditional Korean food. Many Korean church participants wear traditional Korean dress on important Korean holidays. Korean churches also teach children traditional Korean values, such as filial piety, in a number of ways. For example, the youth programme in some Korean immigrant churches teaches children to prepare breakfast for parents on Mothers' Day. Almost all Korean churches organize an end-of-year party at a member's private home on New Year's Eve, when church members usually play a traditional Korean game called *yoot.*

Of course, ethnic churches contribute to maintaining ethnicity for other immigrant groups. However, they seem to be far more effective immigrant groups, since Koreans have a much higher level of affiliation with ethnic churches than do other groups. Although more than 80 percent of Filipino immigrants are Catholics, most of them seem to attend American Catholic churches.[23] A survey shows that only 17 percent of Filipino immigrants are affiliated with their ethnic churches.[24] A much smaller proportion of Chinese immigrants than Korean immigrants have a Christian background.[25] As previously noted, Asian-Indian immigrants consist of religiously heterogeneous groups such as Hindus, Sikhs, Muslims, and Jains. Although Judaism is considered to have played a significant role in uniting Jewish Americans, less than 50 percent of Jewish Americans are affiliated with synagogues. A survey conducted in Boston, for example, shows that only 38 percent of Jewish Americans are affiliated with synagogues.[26]

The Christian religion is not an indigenous Korean religion, whereas Judaism is a Jewish religion. Some readers may wonder how Korean immigrants can revive Korean ethnicity through a religion adopted from the West. Participation in an ethnic church in itself enhances Korean ethnicity regardless of religious dogmas and rituals, because it helps Korean immigrants to get together for fellowship. Moreover, Korean immigrants have modified the Christian religion in such a way that it is supportive of Korean ethnicity. Of course, part of the reason why the Christian religion has gained such popularity in Korea is because it has embraced some of Korea's indigenous principles, particularly Confucian ethics and shamanism.[27] In their efforts to preserve Korean culture and Korean identity through ethnic churches, Korean immigrants have further Koreanized the Christian religion. In spite of the great influence of Korean indigenous thought on the Korean Christian religion, Christians in Korea are on average less Korean than other Koreans. By contrast, Korean immigrants affiliated with ethnic churches are more Korean than those not so affiliated. This nationalization of the Christian religion is not unique to Korean immigrants. Different Catholic groups in the United States—French, Irish, Italian, and Polish—have modified the Catholic religion in such a way that its religious way of life fits into their ethnic subculture. This is why Greeley argued that "the various nationality groups were, at least to some extent, quasi-denominations within American Catholicism."[28]

Korean immigrants concentrate heavily in a limited range of small businesses, and their economic segregation also enhances ethnic attachment and ethnic solidarity. The 1980 Census shows that Korean immigrants had the highest self-employment rate, with 12 percent among seventeen recent immigrant groups.[29] The Census reports greatly undercounted the self-employment rate of Korean immigrants as well as those of other groups. Moreover, the self-employment rate of Korean immigrants has substantially increased since 1980. Thus, more recent case-studies show Koreans' exceptionally high levels of small-business concentration and economic segregation. For example, a survey conducted in 1986 shows that 45 percent of Korean workers in Los Angeles are self-employed and that another 30 percent are employed in Korean firms.[30] The New York Korean community is even more entrepreneurial than the Los Angeles Korean community. A 1988 study revealed that 61 percent of married male and 49 percent of married female Korean workers in New York City were engaged in their own businesses and that only 14 percent of the Korean labour force was in the general labour market.[31]

Whereas Korean immigrants' family and group ties facilitate their entrepreneurial activities, their involvement in small businesses further strengthens ethnic ties. Korean immigrants' occupational concentration in small businesses enhances ethnic attachment in three different ways. First, it contributes to Korean ethnicity by bonding Koreans together. Korean proprietors depend mainly upon family members and other co-ethnic employees for their operation of businesses. Korean workers employed in Korean firms in Los Angeles are found to have an average of 93 percent of Korean workers, in comparison to 22 percent of those Koreans employed in non-Korean firms.[32] Thus, only a small proportion of adult Korean immigrants maintain social interactions with Americans at the workplace, since most Koreans are segregated in the ethnic subeconomy. Korean immigrants, both proprietors and ethnic employees working for Korean stores, speak the Korean language, eat Korean lunch, and practice Korean customs during most of the working hours. Of course, Korean businesses largely serve non-Korean customers and thus need to speak English for business transactions. However, their English is limited to basic conversation and to the names of merchandise items.

Moreover, Koreans segregated in the ethnic market extend frequent social interactions with fellow Koreans to off-duty hours. In the 1986 Los Angeles survey, 47 percent of Koreans in the ethnic market reported that they met other Koreans for dinner or picnics at least once a week, whereas only 23 percent of Koreans employed in the general labour market said that they did.[33] The same survey indicated that

Koreans in the ethnic market exhibited a higher level of ethnicity than those in the general labour market in terms of the frequency of speaking Korean at home, the frequency of watching Korean television programs, and the number of subscriptions to Korean newspapers and magazines.

No comparative study has examined the differentials in the proportion of workers in the ethnic market among different Asian immigrant-groups. Nevertheless, the vast majority of Filipino and Indian immigrants are believed to work for American firms, since their self-employment rates are much lower than those of Korean immigrants.[34] This suggests that most Filipino and Indian immigrants speak English and observe American customs at least at the workplace, whereas a marked majority of Korean immigrants remain faithful to the Korean cultural tradition both at home and at the workplace.

Second, Korean ethnic business strengthens ethnic solidarity partly because Korean immigrants in each Korean community concentrate in a few types of business. When a minority-immigrants group specializes in small business, it is usually in a few or several business lines, for instance, Chinese restaurants and garment-manufacturing for Chinese Americans.[35] Koreans in Los Angeles concentrate in the grocery/liquor trade, dry-cleaning service, and Korean-imported items such as wigs, handbags, clothing, and jewelry.[36] Koreans in New York City concentrate heavily in the greengrocery business.[37] Korean grocers in Los Angeles feel a strong sense of group solidarity because their class and ethnic interests overlap. That is, Korean grocers in Los Angeles as a *petite-bourgeois* maintain a higher level of class unity than white grocers in Los Angeles because they share brotherhood associated with the same nationality. Few Korean immigrants in Los Angeles would be interested in white-dominant trade-associations or labour-unions. Yet, most Korean grocers in Southern California are affiliated with the Korean Grocers' Association and active in protecting their group interests.

Third, Korean immigrant entrepreneurship enhances ethnic solidarity because the operation of small businesses involves conflicts with out-group members. The fact that minority/immigrant groups are segregated in certain business specialities may not be a sufficient condition for stimulating ethnic solidarity. The clustering of ethnic businesses can increase internal solidarity because minority/immigrant proprietors engaged in the same line or similar lines of business face conflicts with outside interest groups for economic survival. Middleman-minority theory posits that middleman groups specializing in small businesses receive a high level of hostility from the host society, which in turn strengthens ethnic solidarity.[38] Korean immigrant proprietors have come into conflict with several interest groups:

1. minority customers,
2. white suppliers,
3. white landlords,
4. local residents,
5. white labour unions, and
6. government agencies such as the State Labor Department.

The most serious intergroup conflicts have arisen between Korean ghetto merchants and black customers. A large proportion of Korean immigrant businesses are located in low-income black areas.[39] Korean immigrant merchants in black ghettos take the role of middleman minorities in that they distribute merchandise produced by big corporations to low-income black customers.[40] Korean store-owners operating businesses in black areas, like middleman minorities in other societies, have faced a high level of hostility and violent reaction from black customers. Blacks have indicted Korean merchants for treating black customers disrespectfully, for failing to contribute money to the black community, and for not hiring black employees.[41] For these and other reasons, blacks in New York, Baltimore, Philadelphia, Los Angeles, and other Korean centres have reacted against Korean ghetto-merchants by resort to murder, arson, boycott, demonstration, and mass-media attack.

Korean/black intergroup conflicts have probably been more serious in New York than in any other city. Several large-scale black boycott movements against Korean merchants have occurred in New York City. The boycotting of two Korean-owned greengrocery stores on Flatbush Avenue, Brooklyn, New York is probably the most serious one. The boycott started in January 1990 after a scuffle between a black female customer, who allegedly tried to steal merchandise from a Korean greengrocery store, and Korean employees, who allegedly beat up the customer. The boycott, led by Mr. Sonny Carson, the president of the December Twelfth Movement, has received wide coverage by the national media. The New York City government, the Federal Bureau of Investigation, and the Department of Justice have all intervened to stop the boycott, but have so far not produced any fruitful results.

A series of conflicts with blacks has made Korean store-owners aware of the potential collective threat in this country from black ethnics and has thus contributed to the fostering of Korean ethnic solidarity. In many Korean communities various business associations have been established mainly to deal with intergroup conflicts associated with Koreans' involvement in black-ghetto businesses. Korean community leaders and ethnic newspapers identify attacks on Korean merchants with attacks on the Korean community as a whole. Thus, problems related to Korean ghetto-businesses have led not only business proprietors but also other Koreans to be concerned about their common fate and marginal status in the USA.

The positive effects of business-related conflicts with blacks on Korean ethnic solidarity are clearly exemplified in the current boycott of the two Korean greengrocery stores in Brooklyn New York. The sales volume for each store has been reduced to almost nothing since the boycott started in January 1990. However, both stores have been able to stay open for approximately five months largely because of the contributions made by various Korean organizations and individuals. The Korean Green Grocers' Association of New York has raised a fund of more than $50,000, mostly from its members, to help the two Korean greengrocery stores in trouble.[42] In addition, the boycott has led to the establishment of the Civil Rights Committee under the Korean Association of Greater New York to deal with intergroup relations effectively. The committee consists of fifty well-known Korean community leaders in the New York metropolitan area—lawyers, university teachers, journalists, educational leaders, pastors, social workers, and business tycoons. No other Korean ethnic organization in New York includes so many experts in different fields as this organization.

Korean immigrants' concentration in small businesses has also led to intergroup conflicts with white wholesalers, and this, too, has strengthened ethnic solidarity. Korean retailers in all lines of business, with the exception of those who sell Korean-imported items, find themselves in conflict with white wholesalers. They have encountered discrimination by white wholesalers in the quality, prices, and speed of delivery, of merchandise, in parking allocations, and in other aspects of service to customers. As a large number of Korean retailers in each major Korean centre concentrate in a few business lines, they have resources to make collective responses to discriminatory practices by white wholesalers.

One can document a number of cases in which Korean retailers have taken collective action against white wholesalers to protect their common interests. For example, in 1977 approximately a hundred Korean greengrocers in New York staged a demonstration against a Jewish wholesale store at the Hunts Point Market to protest about an ethnic slur made by an employee of the store.[43] In 1988 Korean fish-retailers in New York boycotted a large fish-wholesaler, Slain and Sons, Inc., to protest against "selling rotten fish," "cheating in scaling", and "unkind treatments."[44] The boycott lasted five months, until the wholesaler, who had experienced a significant reduction in sales, sent a written apology to the Korean Fish Retailers' Association. Also, the Korean Grocers' Association in Atlanta was established in 1983 to take concerted action against "monopolistic prices" by white wholesalers.[45] Korean grocers through their organization have negotiated with white wholesalers over prices of some grocery items and they have been moderately successful in protecting their common interests.

Korean entrepreneurs also clash with white landlords over economic interests, and this conflict, too, has contributed to fostering in-group ties. Many Korean immigrants buy a failing business or open a new one and then within a few years make it thrive.[46] As Korean-owned businesses become more successful, so white landlords raise rents by significant margins over a short period. This escalating-rent problem is most serious in the New York Korean community. A large number of Korean immigrants operate general-merchandise shops and greengrocery stores in Manhattan. Most of these Korean merchants have experienced rent increases by white landlords, especially by Jewish landlords, two or even three times over a period of between three and five years. Many Korean store-owners in Manhattan have to stay open twenty-four hours to cover the high rents.[47] Korean business-owners in New York have held demonstrations several times, asking the city government to legislate on the regulation of rents. In 1988 a group of Korean leaders representing the Korean American Association and other Korean business associations in New York joined the New York Small Business Coalition for Regulation of Commercial Rents and was active in lobbying the city council to pass a law regulating commercial rents.[48] In the 1989 mayoral election, Korean business owners endorsed Mr. David Dinkins, the current black mayor, mainly because he promised to take some measures, if elected, to regulate commercial rents.

The effects of Koreans' small-business operations on their ethnic solidarity become evident when the Korean group is compared with other Asian immigrant-groups. Other non-entrepreneurial Asian immigrant-groups also specialize in certain occupational categories. For example, 15.1 percent of Asian-Indian immigrants work as medical professionals.[49] Indian medical professionals in the New York metropolitan area maintain a higher level of class unity than white medical professionals in the city because they belong to the same "ethclass" in which ethnic and class interests overlap. However, group solidarity is far less strong for New York Indian medical professionals than for new York Korean greengrocers because the former have not experienced the kinds of intergroup conflict for economic survival that the latter have.

By emphasizing the effects of Koreans' concentration in small businesses on ethnic solidarity, I do not fail to recognize that it also encourages intragroup conflict and competition. It has been well documented that Korean store-owners face strong competition from co-ethnics.[50] However, competition among Korean store-owners, largely limited to the individual level, has never destroyed unity on the community level. Moreover, many Korean business associations in different Korean communities have been established partly to regulate excessive competition among Korean merchants in the same business specialty.

Finally, some readers might quickly point out that the conflict between Korean immigrant proprietors and co-ethnic employees will destroy ethnic solidarity. Several researchers have stressed class conflicts between Chinese business-owners and co-ethnic employees in Chinatown.[51] They have indicated that Chinese workers employed in co-ethnic firms are subject to a high level of exploitation and that Chinese ethnic employees are very conscious of their class interests against co-ethnic employers. However, the Korean community basically differs from the Chinese community in terms of business structure and the socio-economic background of new immigrants and thus it does not have the class cleavages existent in the Chinese community. On the one hand, the Korean community is more entrepreneurial than the Chinese community, as indicated by the differentials in the self-employment rate and the number of firms per 1,000 persons.[52] On the other hand, the Chinese community annually receives a large number of new immigrants from mainland China, who are severely handicapped in employment in the general labour-market and who thus look for employment in the ethnic market. These differences suggest that there is a great demand for ethnic employees in the Korean community, whereas there is an oversupply of ethnic employees in the Chinese community, especially in Chinatown, where most immigrants from mainland China are settled.

Chinatown immigrants are vulnerable to exploitation by co-ethnic firms not only due to their oversupply of labour for Chinese firms, but also due to their lack of resources to avoid starvation ages. Nearly all immigrants from mainland China come here with almost no resources and thus have no alternative to low-wage employment.[53] In contrast, most Korean immigrants bring a certain amount of money to this country at the time of immigration, and a significant proportion of Korean immigrants have started their own businesses with the money brought from Korea.[54] Thus, many Korean immigrants have personal resources that enable them to avoid exploitation by co-ethnic employers. They work in Korean-owned stores mainly to acquire business experience and then move into their own business rather quickly. Most Korean ethnic employees seem to consider their employment as a temporary state to acquire business training and thus approach labour issues from the viewpoints of the owner. A very small proportion of Korean ethnic employees feel themselves exploited by co-ethnic employers, and labour movements are almost non-existent in the Korean community.[55] By contrast, Chinatown workers employed in co-ethnic firms seem to be trapped in the working-class position more or less permanently and thus they are more class-conscious than Korean ethnic employees.

Recent Korean immigrants are interesting to scholars of minority groups partly because they maintain a high level of ethnicity. The vast majority of Korean immigrants speak the Korean language, adhere to Korean customs and values, and maintain social interactions mainly with fellow Koreans. Moreover, they have developed within a short period of time strong ethnic solidarity in protecting their interests against outsiders.

Theorists of ethnicity have emphasized two major factors as bases of ethnicity. First, commonalties in culture and historical experiences that members of a group share provide an important basis of ethnicity. Second, productive activities associated with occupational concentration contribute to ethnic solidarity and group identity. This article has analyzed Korean ethnicity, focusing on Korean immigrants' cultural homogeneity, affiliation with ethnic churches, and economic concentration.

To summarize the foregoing analyses, South Korea is a small, culturally homogeneous country, and Korean immigrants maintain a high level of ethnicity partly because of their strong cultural and historical ties. Other current US immigrant groups such as Asian-Indian, Filipino, Chinese, and Iranian groups are characterized by subgroup differences in language, customs, values, religion, and political ideology, which hinder the development of national ethnic consciousness. Korean immigrants share one language, the same customs and values, and the same historical experiences. These commonalties in culture and historical experiences provide a cultural basis of Korean ethnicity.

The vast majority of Korean immigrants are affiliated with Korean immigrant churches, and their high affiliation with ethnic churches further reinforces Korean ethnicity. Korean immigrant churches first of all contribute to Korean ethnicity by providing places for fellowship and social interactions. They also contribute to Korean ethnicity by helping to maintain the Korean cultural tradition. The Christian religion is not a Korean indigenous religion. However, Korean immigrants have modified the Christian religion in such a way that it fits into their need for Korean ethnic subculture and Korean ethnic identity. Historically, this nationalization of Christianity has occurred to black and white-Catholic ethnic groups as well.

Korean immigrants concentrate in a limited range of small businesses, and their economic segregation also enhances ethnic attachment and ethnic solidarity. First of all, Korean immigrant businesses contribute to Korean ethnicity by binding ethnic members together, as they depend upon family members and co-ethnic members for business operation. Furthermore, Korean immigrants' concentration in small businesses has strengthened ethnic solidarity because Korean merchants have been involved in conflicts with outside interest groups for economic survival. Korean ghetto-merchants have received rejection and hostility from black customers. Moreover, Korean entrepreneurs have clashed with white wholesalers, white landlords, and white labour unions over economic interests. These business-related conflicts with outside interest groups have motivated not only Korean business proprietors but also other Korean immigrants to be concerned about their common fate and marginal status in the USA.

---

[1] Won Moo Hurh and Kwang Chung Kim, *Korean Immigrants in America: A Structural Analysis of Ethnic Confinement and Adhesive Adaptation* (Madison, New Jersey: Fairleigh Dickinson University Press, 1984); Jeffrey Reitz, *The Survival of Ethnic Groups* (Toronto: McGraw-Hill, 1980); Milton Yinger, "Toward a Theory of Assimilation and Dissimilation," *Ethnic and Racial Studies* 4, No. 2, 249-64.

[2] Luciano Mangiafico, *Contemporary Asian Immigrants: Patterns of Filipino, Korean, and Chinese Settlement in the United States* (New York: Praeger, 1988), 174.

[3] Nathan Glazer and Daniel Moynihan, *Beyond the Melting Pot: Negroes, Puerto Ricans, Jews, Italians, and Irish of New York City,* (Cambridge, MA: Massachusetts Institute of Technology, 1963); Milton Gordon, *Assimilation in American Life: The Role of Race, Religion, and National Origin* (New York: Oxford University Press, 1964); Andrew M. Greeley, *Why Can't they Be Like Us?* (New York: Dutton, 1971); Andrew M. Greeley, *Ethnicity in the United States: A Preliminary Reconnaissance (*New York: John Wiley & Sons, 1974).

[4] Edna Bonacich, "A Theory of Middleman Minorities," *American Sociological Review* 37, No. 5 (1986), 583-594; Edna Bonacich and John Modell, *The Economic Basis of Ethnic Solidarity: Small Business in the Japanese American Community* (Berkeley and Los Angeles, CA: University of California Press, 1980); Susan Olzak, "A Competition Model of Ethnic Collective Action in American Cities, 1877-1889," in *Competitive Ethnic Relations,* eds. Susan Olzak and Joane Jagel (New York: Academic Press, 1986), 17-46; Reitz, *The Survival of Ethnic Groups;* William E. Yancy, *et al.,* "Emergent Ethnicity: A Review and Reformulation," *American Sociological Review* 41, No. 3 (1986), 391-403.

[5] Olzak, "A Competition Model of Ethnic Collective Action in American Cities, 1877-1889;" J.R. Bodnar, *et al., Lives on Their Own: Blacks, Italians, and Poles in Pittsburgh, 1900-1960* (Urbana, IL: University of Illinois Press, 1982).

[6] U.S. Bureau of the Census, *1980 Census of Population,* PC80-1-B1 (Washington, DC: United States Printing Office, 1983), 125; "Korean-American Population Has Reached One Million," *The Central Daily* (May 29, 1989).

[7] Antonio J.A. Pido, *The Pilipinos in America: Macro/Micro Dimensions of Immigration and Integration* (Staten Island, NY: Center for Migration Studies, 1986), 95.

[8] Parmatma Saran, *Asian Indian Experience in the United States* (Cambridge, MA: Schenkman Books, 1985), 114.

[9] Raymond B. Williams, *Religions of Immigrants from India and Pakistan: New Threads of American Tapestry* (New York: Cambridge University Press, 1988).

[10] Ivan Light, *Ethnic Enterprise in America: Business and Welfare among Chinese, Japanese, and Blacks* (Berkeley and Los Angeles, CA: University of California Press, 1972); Stanford Lyman, "Contrasts in Community Organization of Chinese and Japanese in North America," in *Canadian Journal Of Sociology and Anthropology* 5, No. 1 (1968), 51-67; Standford Lyman, *Chinese Americans* (New York: Random House, 1974).

[11] Peter Kwong, *The New Chinatown* (New York: The Noonday Press, 1987); Mangiafico, *Contemporary Asian Immigrants: Patterns of Filipino, Korean, and Chinese Settlement in the United States.*

[12] Ivan Light, *et al.*, "The Four Iranian Ethnic Economies in Los Angeles," Unpublished Manuscript (University of California at Los Angeles, 1990).

[13] In-sook Han Park, *et al.*, "Korean Immigrants and U.S. Immigration Policy: A Predeparture Perspective," Paper of the East-West Population Institute, No. 114 (Honolulu: East-West Center, 1990), 31.

[14] Korean National Bureau of Statistics, *1985 Population and Housing Census* (Seoul: Korean Economic Planning Board, 1987).

[15] Park, "Korean Immigrants and U.S. Immigration Policy: A Predeparture Perspective," 60.

[16] Pyong Gap Min, "The Structure and Social Functions of Korean Immigrant Churches in the United States," *International Migration Review* 26 (1992).

[17] Won Moo Hurh and Kwang Chung Kim, "Uprooting and Adjustment: A Sociological Study of Korean Immigrants' Mental Health," Final Report submitted to the National Institute of Mental Health, US Department of Health and Human Services (1988), 63.

[18] Min, "The Structure and Social Functions of Korean Immigrant Churches in the United States."

[19] Illsoo Kim, *New Urban Immigrants: The Korean Community in New York* (Princeton, NJ: Princeton University Press, 1981), 199.

[20] Won Moo Hurh and Kwang Chung Kim, "Korean Immigrants in the Chicago Area: A Sociological Study of Migration and Mental Health," Interim Report submitted to the National Institute of Mental Health, US Department of Health and Human Services, 1987.

[21] Min, "The Structure and Social Functions of Korean Immigrant Churches in the United States."

[22] Ibid.

[23] Pido, *The Pilipinos in America: Macro/Micro Dimensions of Immigration and Integration.*

[24] Mangiafico, *Contemporary Asian Immigrants: Patterns of Filipino, Korean, and Chinese Settlement in the United States*, 74.

[25] Bok-lim Kim, *The Asian Americans: Changing Patterns, Changing Needs* (Monteclair, NJ: The Association of Christian Scholars in North America, 1978).

[26] Steven Cohen, *American Modernity and Jewish Identity* (New York: Tavistock Publications, 1985), 56.

[27] Young Chun Kim, "The nature and density of Korean churches in the United States," in *Koreans in North America: New Perspectives, in Koreans in North America: New Perspectives,* eds. Seong Hyung Lee and Tai-Hawn Kwak (Seoul: Kyung Nam University Press, 1982), 215-30.

[28] Andrew M. Greeley, *The Denominational Society: A Sociological Approach to Religion* (Glenview, IL: Scott, Foresman, and Company, 1972), 119.

[29] US Bureau of the Census, *1980 Census of Population,* PC80-1-D1-A (Washington DC: United States Government Printing Office, 1984), 8.

[30] Pyong Gap Min, *Some Positive Functions of Ethnic Business for an Immigrant Community: Koreans in Los Angeles,* Final Report submitted to the National Science Foundation, 1989.

[31] Pyong Gap Min, "Immigrant entrepreneurship and wife's overwork: Koreans in New York City," Paper presented at the Annual Meeting of the American Sociological Association, 1990.

[32] Min, *Some Positive Functions of Ethnic Business for an Immigrant Community: Koreans in Los Angeles.*

[33] Ibid.

[34] Kwang Chung Kim, *et al.,* "Intra-group Differences in Business Participation: A Comparative Analysis of Three Asian groups," in *International Migration Review* 19, No. 1 (1989), 82-111; Pyong Gap Min, "A Comparison of Filipino and Korean Immigrants in Small Business," in *Amerasia Journal* 13, No. 1 (1986-87), 53-71.

[35] Kwong, *The New Chinatown.*

[36] Min, *Some Positive Functions of Ethnic Business for an Immigrant Community: Koreans in Los Angeles.*

[37] Kim, *New Urban Immigrants: The Korean Community in New York;* Min, "Immigrant Entrepreneurship and Wife's Overwork: Koreans in New York City."

[38] Bonacich, "A theory of middleman minorities." Jonathan Turner and Edna Bonacich, "Toward a composite theory of middleman minorities," in *Ethnicity* 7, No. 2 (1980), 144-58.

[39] Kwang Chung Kim and Won Moo Hurh, "Ethnic Resources Utilization of Korean Small Businessmen in the United States," in *International Migration Review* 23, No. 1 (1985), 82-111; Ivan Light and Edna Bonacich, *Immigrant Entrepreneurs: Koreans in Los Angeles, 1965-1982* (Berkeley and Los Angeles, CA: University

of California Press, 1988); Pyong Gap Min, *Ethnic Business Enterprise: Korean Small Business in Atlanta* (Staten Island, New York: Centre for Migration Studies, 1988).

[40] Edna Bonacich and Tae Hwan Jung, "A portrait of Korean small business in Los Angeles," in *Koreans in Los Angeles: Prospects and Promises,* Eui-Young, *et al.* (Los Angeles, CA: Center for Korean-American and Korean Studies, California State University, 1982), 75-98; Light and Bonacich, *Immigrant Entrepreneurs: Koreans in Los Angeles, 1965-1982.*

[41] Kim, *New Urban Immigrants: The Korean Community in New York;* Light and Bonacich, *Immigrant Entrepreneurs: Koreans in Los Angeles, 1965-1982*, 318-19.

[42] *Sae Gae Times,* "Preparation of six-million dollar litigation," May 24, 1990.

[43] Kim, *New Urban Immigrants: The Korean Community in New York.*

[44] "Koreans' anger roared Fulton fish market," in *Sae Gae Times* (July 29, 1988); "The Slavin sent a letter of apology to the Korean Fish Retailers' Association," in *Sae Gae Times* (November 16, 1988).

[45] Min, *Ethnic Business Enterprise: Korean Small Business in Atlanta*, 112.

[46] Ibid., 114.

[47] *Korea Times of New York*, "Korean merchants forced to open 24 hours," December 15, 1988.

[48] "The Slavin sent a letter of apology to the Korean Fish Retailers' Association," in *Sae Gae Times* (November 16, 1988).

[49] U.S. Bureau of the Census, *Subject Reports, Asian and Pacific Islander Population in the United Staes: 1980,* Section 1 (Washington, DC: United States Government Printing Office, 1988), 465.

[50] Kim, *New Urban Immigrants: The Korean Community in New York;* Kim and Hurh, "Ethnic resources utilization of Korean small businessmen in the United States;" Min, *Ethnic Business Enterprise: Korean Small Business in Atlanta.*

[51] Ivan Light and Charles C. Wong, "Protest or work: dilemmas of the tourist industry in American Chinatowns," in *American Journal of Sociology* 80, No. 6 (1975), 1342-65; Jimmy Sanders and Victor Nee, "Limits of Ethnic Solidarity," *American Sociological Review* 52, No. 6 (1987), 745-67; Richard H. Thompson, "From Kinship to Class: A New Model of Urban Overseas Chinese Social Organization," *Urban Anthropology* 9, No. 3 (1980), 265-93; Bernard Wong, "The Chinese: new immigrants in New York's Chinatown," in *New Immigrants in New York,* ed. Nancy Foner (New York: Columbia University Press, 1987), 243-72.

[52] Min, *Some Positive Functions of Ethnic Business for an Immigrant Community: Koreans in Los Angeles.*

[53] Kwong, *The New Chinatown.*

[54] Park, "Korean Immigrants and U.S. Immigration Policy: A Predeparture Perspective;" Kim and Hurh, "Ethnic Resources Utilization of Korean Small Businessmen in the United States;" Min, *Ethnic Business Enterprise: Korean Small Business in Atlanta*," 80.

[55] Min, *Some Positive Functions of Ethnic Business for an Immigrant Community: Koreans in Los Angeles.*

PART VI

EDUCATING TOWARD CULTURAL PLURALISM

Lorna Gonsalves-Pinto's provocative essay on "Teaching Ethnic Studies" raises many questions relative to curriculum, teaching/learning, and ethnicity/race. She optimistically argues that the ethnic/racial "insider's" perspective can be learned when knowledge about racial and ethnic peoples is taught effectively. In a critique of the process and product of education in the United States, she asserts that sharing such information and perspectives with students has been woefully lacking.

From what she refers to as her "outsider's/insider's" perspective, Gonsalves-Pinto reminds us that the educational system has in many ways mocked the democratic spirit and acculturated against the possibility of an active, multicultural citizenry. Consequently, a nation of functionaries rather than literate and active citizens has been the American curriculum's primary product. According to Gonsalves-Pinto this ill-fated product derived largely from the nation's failure to adopt a multicultural pedagogy.

Gonsalves-Pinto asserts that the significance of ethnic studies is that it "challenges traditional views on race and ethnicity," but this challenge seems to emanate from the marginality of ethnic studies and its responses to Eurocentric theory within the Academy. One wonders, nevertheless, if the marginality and counter response accrue to some extent from the all too frequent exclusion of European ethnics from ethnic studies curriculums. Does this exclusion derive, at least in part, from a white oppressor-non-white victims diatribe? Does the exclusion deter the Ethnic Studies specialist from engaging meaningful class analysis when emphasis centers on a particular ethnic group of color vis-a-vis a white powered elite? Does American education colonize the minds of, what Gonsalves-Pinto labels NAFLAS, by using multiculturalism to pacify them without questioning class factors within ethnic and racial groups? If educators uniformly taught from multicultural perspectives, would classism be eradicated?

Finally, Gonsalves-Pinto offers strategies for teaching about the experiences and perspectives of ethnic and racial peoples in the United States and for unlearning the colonized or "blinders" mind-set. She discusses these strategies and the student and teacher opinions of them in an open-ended way that invites experimentation and energetic discussion.

Teaching Ethnic Studies: "Disturbing the Peace"

Lorna Gonsalves-Pinto
Ethnic Studies Department,
Bowling Green State University

Educational Curriculum in the United States—A Critical Appraisal

Over the past decade much attention has been focused on the issue of educational reform. Goodman, in his historical review of school reform, describes three waves:

> The 'first wave' of school reform was in response to this country's rural, farm-based society; the 'second wave' was established for the industrial age; and currently a 'third wave' of school change is needed for the coming 'information/technology age.' (Goodman 1995:1).

He argues that changes made through each of these waves of school reform have been only superficial and have not transformed the underlying norms, values and structures within educational institutions (1995:2).

At the turn of the twentieth century, schools, which were governed by a "marketplace rationale," trained large numbers of second generation immigrants to be "good workers." Individuals like Cubberley and Bobbitt espoused the idea of training future workers

Reprinted by permission of the author.

(Cubberley 1916: 338; Bobbitt 1924:7-8). On the other hand, there were others, like Dewey who proposed that students should be taught to create their own futures (1976:49). Goodman suggests that "transformative efforts based upon a vision of schooling for democracy offer one example of how our educational purpose can be broadened beyond social functionalism" (Goodman 1995:7).

In the United States, which according to Mantsios (1995:409) is the most severely stratified society in the industrialized world, education has continued to prepare students to become passive citizens and to function in a social system which is viewed as unchangeable (Goodman 1995:7). Pepi Leistyna urges "progressive educators" to play their role in dismantling systems of oppression and building, instead, a democratic and just society (Leistyna 1995:322). The educational system in the United States is situated within a wider social framework, one that, according to hooks (1995:491) is "governed by the politics of domination," and functions to reinforce the social norms and values of this framework (Baldwin 1988:4). Challenging norms that uphold inequality and oppression are met with a great deal of resistance causing those who challenge these norms to live "on the edge of alienation and apart from the security of those who accept the status quo," (Chafe 1995 428) or to be accused of being "anti-American" or "Marxist" (Leistyna 1995:322). Ethnic Studies, as a discipline, questions and challenges traditional views of race and ethnicity. In so doing, Ethnic Studies continues to live "on the edge" and "apart from the security of those who accept the status quo."

In the spring of 1978, writer James Baldwin, then a visiting professor in the department of Ethnic Studies[1] at Bowling Green State University, emphasized the importance of asking questions as he addressed a group of students.

> What education really means is the courage to ask questions, the courage to take nothing for granted, to recognize that every answer has a question. No state, no tribe, no people is really anxious to have that kind of questioning person around called quite accurately "disturber of the peace." (Baldwin 1978)

Much of what has passed for United States history and culture has remained unquestioned by the vast majority of people (Banks 1991:21). Textbooks are read and examinations are taken, and most teachers focus far greater attention on teaching students *what* to think rather than *how* to think. It is rare for teachers to encourage students to question sources of knowledge and to investigate the authenticity of facts presented in textbooks. What students in the United States have been taught are versions of history and interpretations of events from the non-critical perspectives of the dominant European American culture. Lacking from the curriculum has been a critical examination of the experiences of Naflas[2] Americans within the context of power relations in the United States.

The omission of multicultural perspectives from the curriculum has masked the social injustices that many ethnic groups[3] have been subjected to—injustices that have had a major impact on the past and present experiences of these groups. The contributions of different ethnic groups and the struggles and triumphs of these groups as they collide with each other in a system of unequal power relations are essential components of a multicultural knowledge base. Students have a right to this knowledge, but they have been denied this right. Teaching from multicultural perspectives is an educator's obligation, but unfortunately, most educators have not fulfilled this obligation to students. The process of filling this gap in public education is indeed a monumental task and Ethnic Studies has emerged as a major "disturber of the peace." If peace is a positive concept, what does Ethnic Studies gain by disturbing it? The peace that Baldwin seems to refer to is best articulated by Martin Luther King who suggested that a negative peace is maintained through the "absence of tension," but a positive peace is achieved only when there is the "presence of justice." (King 1963) An awareness of the injustices suffered by different ethnic groups provides a disturbing picture of the experiences of these groups in the United States and offers some incentives to work for positive social changes. However, there continues to be a great deal of resistance to unmasking the ugliness of ethnic relations in the United States. In addition, there continues to exist a pervasive belief, on campuses across the nation, that the incorporation of multiculturalism[4] in the curriculum will lead to unnecessary tensions. However, as King states,

> . . . we merely bring to the surface the hidden tension that is already alive. We bring it out in the open where it can he seen and dealt with. Like a boil that can never be cured as long as it is covered up but must be opened with all its pus-flowing ugliness to the natural medicines of air and light, injustice must likewise be exposed, with all of the tension its exposing creates, to the light of human conscience and the air of national opinion before it can be cured (King 1963)

What is the general consequence of masking the ugliness of ethnic tensions? The negative peace, which is generally promoted through the educational curriculum in the United States, reinforces what Griffin (1988:296) refers to as a mass delusion. A pervasive mass delusion[5] in this country is that all people have an equal chance to achieve their full potential. These and other mass delusions have been carefully drilled into the minds of generations of students as they pass through the educational system in the United States. Those who question or attempt to dismantle this delusion do so at the risk of being considered disloyal, unpatriotic and even dangerous. I have found it essential to introduce students to the concepts of "responsible" versus "irresponsible loyalty," which I have developed in order to encourage them to participate in critical evaluations of ethnicity without feeling guilty about being disloyal citizens. Responsible loyalty, refers to loyalty that involves critical assessment and support for action towards positive social change that will benefit the nation as a whole whereas irresponsible loyalty involves passive acceptance of the status quo and refusal to question and confront social injustices that have plagued and continue to plague our nation.

Education in the United States presents and reinforces non-critical values and norms (Kelly, 1988:314). As such, it acts as a gatekeeper of the status quo and restricts the vision of students. Schools socialize students into "becoming American," and during this process, Naflas Americans are placed in the "other" category (Madrid 1993:381). Kelly uses the internal colonialism[7] model as a framework for analyzing the schooling of Vietnamese Immigrants. "In nations where schooling is compulsory, like the United States, education becomes for the colonized the first instance of forced entry into the society and culture of the colonizer." (314)

Here, Kelly compares the "white majority" to the colonizer in the sense that the major decisions regarding schooling and the curriculum are made by this group. The colonized, according to Kelly, are comprised of Naflas Americans. Through the process of education, the cultures of colonized groups are denied and the culture of the "white majority" is emphasized. As far as a critical examination of ethnic issues is concerned, public education, too often, has served to close rather than open minds. James Baldwin in his inspiring article entitled A *Talk to Teachers,* describes the following paradox:

> The paradox of education is precisely this—that as one begins to become conscious one begins to examine the society in which he is being educated. The purpose of education, finally, is to create in a person the ability to look at the world for himself, to make his own decisions, to say to himself this is black or this is white, to decide for himself whether there is a God in heaven or not. To ask questions of the universe, and then learn to live with those questions, is the way he achieves his own identity. But no society is really anxious to have that kind of person around. What societies really, ideally, want is a citizenry which will simply obey the rules of society. If a society succeeds in this, that society is about to perish. The obligation of anyone who thinks of himself as responsible is to examine society and try to change it and to fight it—at no matter what risk. This is the only hope society has. This is the only way societies change (Baldwin 1988:4).

During the sixties, a large number of individuals critically examined society and worked towards broad social and political changes, but these movements have not gained momentum. Instead, we have taken several steps backward. In an era in which many educators themselves have been trained to simply obey the rules, the educational system continues to function as a gate keeper for the status quo. The narrow focus of the traditional curriculum the hesitance on the part of many educators, to critically evaluate their roles and missions as teachers, and the resistance of these educators to change, has resulted in the mass production of passive learners, who in turn maintain the tradition of a negative peace.

Today, a growing number of educators are confronting the biases inherent in the public school curriculum. For example, in an effort to examine the information that is being transmitted to school children, the Council on Interracial Books for Children conducted a survey of history textbooks copyrighted 1980 or thereafter. Several major themes were evident:

> This bland and meaningless voice [of history] will not teach a student to reason sharply think, critically to question seriously, or assume independence. What this interpretation does instead (aside from boring the student) is to inculcate the notion that historical events are inevitable. History is presented as an impersonal force not a product of human activity. Real human conflict and meaningful political strife do not exist. This is the message the U.S. history textbooks of the eighties convey to elementary and secondary school students; if they conclude that history is irrelevant to their lives and struggles who can blame them? (Charnel 1984:4)

Ethnic Studies introduces students to the idea that history and culture are indeed products of human activity and are not abstract concepts that are imposed on society by some unknown force. People create history and culture and, as such, they can be significant agents of social change. Of course it cannot be assumed that all individuals, who are associated, in any way, with Ethnic Studies are willing and/or able to become agents of social change and are willing or able to examine ethnicity as a factor that is linked with unequal power relations in the United States. Individuals who are involved in programs that promote inclusion in the curriculum and/or cultural sensitivity in the work place list a wide variety of motivations for their involvement.

Rationales Behind a Multicultural Focus

Teaching through multicultural perspectives challenges the traditional curriculum and triggers a variety of reactions in the minds and hearts of individuals. Proponents and Opponents of a multicultural focus in the curriculum are equally adamant. There are scholars who feel that it is essential to study about the diverse ethnic groups that make up the United States, and that a multicultural focus should become an integral part of the core curriculum simply because it is more valid than a monocultural curriculum (Hilliard 1991:12). Takaki suggests that a multicultural focus has an "intellectual purpose" in that it allows individuals to perceive events through the eyes of different groups, thereby promoting a more comprehensive picture of United States history (1993:4). There are others who feel that a multicultural focus should not be incorporated because it will somehow displace the traditional curriculum and "teach contempt for the founders of the nation and for everything European and white." (Ravitch 1991:9). Bloom (1987), who is concerned with the new academic permissiveness, and Hirsch (1987), who describes the "tower of Babel" effect, join the backlash against a multicultural focus.

E. San Juan presents an insightful critique of the concept of multiculturalism:

> Despite claims to the contrary the national imperative to include courses on cultural diversity (non-Western material) into the general education core curriculum in many colleges and universities springs from a conjunctural crisis. Multiculturalism may be conceived as the latest reincarnation of the assimilationist drive to pacify unruly subaltern groups. It can be interpreted as a strategic response to the deterioration of the social fabric of the country in the decade after the early seventies when progressive policies and institutional reforms gained by the civil rights struggles of the sixties were severely eroded or wiped out. (1994:62)

San Juan cautions that discussing multiculturalism without addressing hegemonic power relations will only reinforce racial inequalities in the United States and suggests that discussions of multiculturalism must be situated within wider social contexts including the "centralized state and the power of corporate business" (1994:66). These wider sociopolitical contexts are missing from a large number of discussions of multiculturalism. This is due to the fact that multiculturalism, as San Juan maintains, is included merely to "pacify unruly subaltern groups."

In academe, there is a tendency amongst many administrators, faculty members in other departments and students, to reduce Ethnic Studies to a superficial overview of the customs and traditions of various ethnic groups. However, it is impossible to teach/learn about ethnicity and ethnic groups without critically examining the unequal power relations that have placed groups at different social and economic levels in society. At many conferences, campus meetings and other academic gatherings, attempts to discuss the connection between ethnic issues and unequal power relations are met with extreme suspicion and even hostility. Angry voices bemoan the politicization of the curriculum. This is ironic, considering the political role that public education has consistently played in the United States in terms of its efforts to support the status quo.

The rationale for including information about different ethnic groups in the curriculum varies from individual to individual and from institution to institution. From comments of individuals on various sensitivity training planning committees, curriculum planning committees, and comments of my students and participants in cultural sensitivity workshops,[7] I have observed some general motivations for the inclusion of multicultural perspectives.

For many individuals, enrollment in Ethnic Studies courses or participation in cultural sensitivity workshops is just another "requirement." Individuals who study about different ethnic groups simply because they are required to, often view the "requirement" as just another fad. The pre-conceived attitudes of these individuals generally influence their receptivity to information and their participation in discussions. At Bowling Green State University, all undergraduate students are required to take at least one course that examines multicultural perspectives. Interestingly, research points out that despite initial resistance to the requirement, the majority of students felt that they had benefited from the cultural diversity course/courses.

Currently, institutional and organizational personnel emphasize the practical benefits that result from knowledge about different groups. "Learning to get along" is a common goal. According to these groups the ethnic composition of the United States and the increasing diversity within the work force demand that individuals learn how to get along with people from different ethnic backgrounds. In my own experience, this rationale is the most common one and large sums of money are spent on trying to facilitate positive work relations between members of different ethnic groups. Businesses and large scale organizations are increasingly requiring personnel to participate in cultural sensitivity workshops to facilitate positive inter-ethnic relations and to reduce ethnic tensions. This, they feel, will result in smoother operations, greater efficiency, and productivity. An example of an agency which utilizes cultural sensitivity workshops to address and deal with situations associated with changing demographics is the Ohio Association of Chiefs of Police which is turning to cultural sensitivity training sessions in an effort to reduce tensions and violence between law enforcement officials and individuals from different ethnic groups. In the "train the trainer" sessions, in which I participated, changing demographics and practical benefits were presented as the main reasons for conducting sensitivity training.

Many school teachers, and academicians in general, focus on the intellectual stimulation that accompanies an exploration of the experiences of different ethnic groups. These persons are fascinated by the unique customs and traditions that characterize ethnic groups in the United States and present information about different ethnic groups to reduce boredom and/or to satisfy curiosity. Information that is sensational is of particular interest to these individuals. An example is the recent "curiosity" regarding female circumcision, also known as female genital mutilation. Many individuals view this phenomenon from a very narrow perspective, and do not develop a comprehensive understanding of all the factors that affect women's lives in these areas. Some Western women visit such countries as the Sudan and "see" only clitoridectomy, but do not observe the negative effects of multinational corporations on exploited workers, the consequences of western exploitation of many "third world" countries, or other significant factors that affect women's lives in this region (Gilliam 1991:218). In addition, these individuals do not make attempts to learn about the complex and diverse reactions of different African women to the issue of clitoridectomy.

Another rationale for including a multicultural focus is one that views developing and promoting a critical understanding of ethnicity and ethnic issues as the ethical obligation of all individuals. A critical analysis of ethnicity, it is believed, will motivate individuals and groups to learn from past mistakes and take action to dismantle systems of oppression. This rationale is not a common one and I have observed that those who articulate it are subjected to a frenzied attack from those who feel that being critical of power relations in the United States is akin to being a disloyal citizen. Moreover any attempts at engaging in these types of discussions on the part of first generation citizens are met with further hostility complete with a warning to "go home where you came from if you think the U.S. has problems."

While it is difficult to maintain that departments of Ethnic Studies across the nation have just one rationale for teaching Ethnic Studies, I think that a generalization may be made about a common rationale for teaching Ethnic Studies. It revolves around the idea that educational institutions have an obligation to foster a critical understanding of ethnic issues and the historical and current power relations that shape the experiences of different ethnic groups in the United States. The ultimate goal of Ethnic Studies then is to promote this critical understanding as an integral part of all fields of study. In planning and implementing pedagogical strategies used in academic institutions, it is important that individuals clarify the rationale for inclusion of information about different ethnic groups. In many instances individual rationales and institutional rationales are in conflict with each other, and this results in serious clashes during the process of implementation. It is essential that individual and institutional rationales be fully discussed prior to planning and/or participation in classes or workshops that present multicultural perspectives. The rationale for inclusion generally dictates the approach utilized.

James Banks (1991) lists various approaches to teaching multicultural content. The contributions approach which is presently the most common approach is one that includes the names of a few ethnic individuals in the curriculum. Information about these individuals is presented from a traditional eurocentric perspective and the individuals chosen for inclusion are generally those who do not challenge the dominant group in the United States. In such a curriculum according to Banks, Booker T. Washington and Sacajawea would be included whereas Malcolm X and Geronimo would not. In Bank's additive approach a book or a particular unit on an ethnic group is added to the curriculum. This approach continues to view ethnic experiences from a non-critical eurocentric perspective. The transformation approach according to Banks allows students to examine ethnicity and ethnic issues from different ethnic perspectives. Finally the social action approach is an extension of the transformation approach in that it stimulates students to use their critical understanding of ethnicity to motivate them to take personal and social action which is geared towards becoming more aware of multicultural issues as well as becoming involved in projects that address and deal with a variety of multicultural issues.

In schools across the country teachers are more likely to use the contributions or the additive approaches. However those who view inclusion of information about different ethnic groups as an ethical obligation are more likely to use the transformation and/or the social action approach. The department of Ethnic Studies at Bowling Green State University encourages the transformation approach and some faculty members use the social action approach. Through these approaches the classroom becomes an environment which is conducive to the formation of critical perspectives of ethnic relations in the United States. A comparative study of ethnic groups contributes to an understanding of the different experiences of these groups within "shared contexts." (Takaki 1993:10). Students are encouraged to test information, apply it in their everyday lives, and become involved in action projects that address and deal with the issues examined in the classroom. As an Ethnic Studies faculty member, who uses the transformation/social action approach, I find that introducing my students to the *blinders removal* framework sets the stage for an understanding of the goals and objectives of the course.

The *Blinders Removal* Framework: Clarifying the Goals of Ethnic Studies

Traditionally, educators and students have made the assumption that the knowledge presented in classrooms across the country was accurate. Another assumption about education was that it was apolitical. Alongside the movement to diversify the curriculum, has come a serious questioning of the assumptions mentioned above and a push to reevaluate the role of education in the United States. While students in our schools have been taught about different ethnic groups, the information was presented through the context of non-critical eurocentric frameworks (Banks 1991:13). Most of these frameworks did not encourage the questioning of a status quo that supported social inequalities. In fact, a very large proportion of my students report that, in their homes and in their schools, they have never discussed any issue through multicultural perspectives. In order to be effective in teaching students to question traditional knowledge and critically analyze ethnic issues it is essential that teachers re-evaluate their own assumptions regarding teaching/learning through multicultural perspectives. Prior to teaching students through multicultural perspectives, educators need to carefully consider the manner in which students have traditionally been taught to approach the issue of multiculturalism. Teaching strategies may then be developed around assumptions that are based upon common experiences and attitudes of students. A framework which I use to explain the goals of Ethnic Studies to my students is the *blinders removal* framework. This framework has its foundations in a set of assumptions arrived at on the basis of consistent observations of students in several Ethnic Studies courses, interviews with students, and a survey of several secondary and post-secondary textbooks. I am in the process of testing these assumptions with different groups of students, and I continue to find strong support for each one of them.

Assumptions Underlying the *Blinders Removal* Framework:

- Individuals in the United States have been trained to view their world with blinders on—blinders in the form of a non-critical eurocentric perspective (see figure 1a). In this sense, non-critical eurocentrism in public education is not a phenomenon that has occurred by mere chance.
- There is an unquestioning acceptance of the status quo and a fear of criticizing the dominant ways of thinking in the United States.
- The process of unlearning what is familiar and safe, and learning what is new and disturbing is uncomfortable and often intimidating.
- There is a general tendency (more pronounced in European Americans) to keep the blinders on and to resist viewing the world through multicultural perspectives.
- Required exposure to critical multicultural perspectives is the only way most individuals will attempt to remove the blinders (see figure 1b).
    - A multicultural view of ethnicity in the United States can only be obtained if the blinders are discarded and the critical perspectives of different ethnic groups are taken into consideration (see figure 1c).

The *blinders removal* framework is a useful one in that it introduces students to the goals of the class and also provides a basis for developing pedagogical strategies. What the *blinders removal* framework suggests is that Ethnic Studies, as a discipline, aims to assist individuals in the removal of blinders that restrict their understanding of ethnicity and ethnic issues. It becomes clear that teaching/learning strategies in Ethnic Studies develop under very different circumstances when compared with teaching/learning strategies that have been developed with the traditional eurocentric curriculum in mind.

Figures 1a, 1b and 1c.
Moving from Non-critical Monocultural to Critical Multicultural Ways of Thinking—Discarding the Blinders

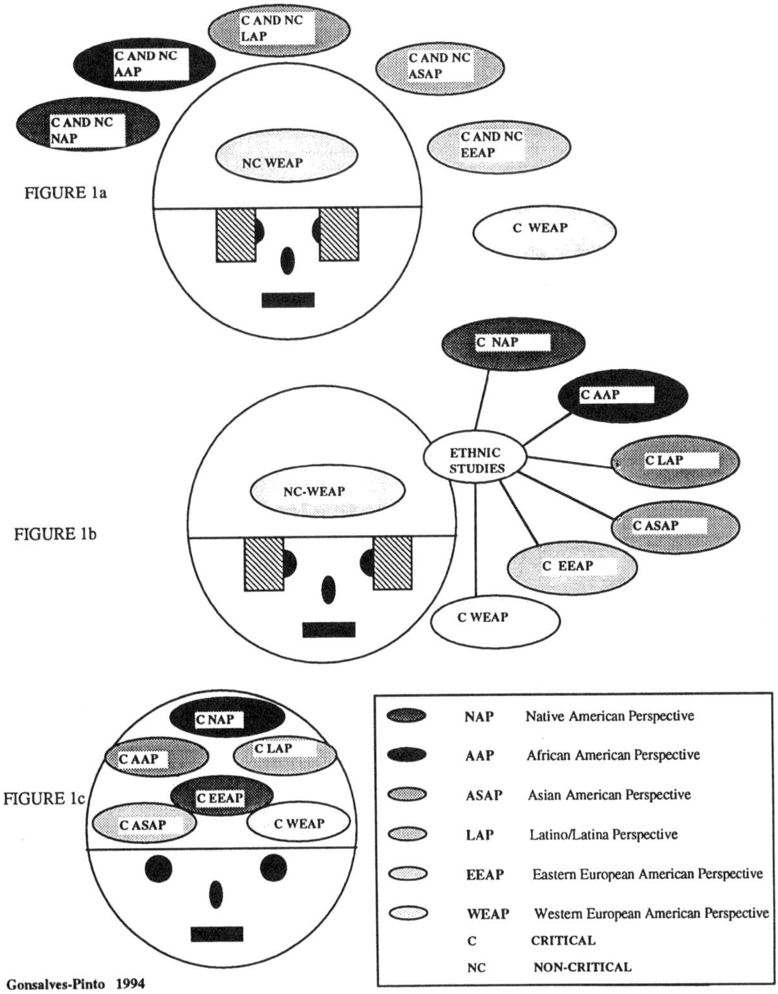

Gonsalves-Pinto 1994

Based upon students' reports, the placement of blinders begins at an early age in the United States. In those homes that maintain a negative peace, multicultural perspectives are not generally presented or discussed. When ethnic groups are discussed, group problems are associated with characteristics that come from within the group rather than from social structures that support economic, educational and other inequalities. In schools, blinders are held in place by educators who, themselves, have a restricted vision of the world. For individuals who have lived their lives behind the safety of their blinders, any attempt to remove blinders is generally met with suspicion.

Prior to assisting students to think critically through the removal of blinders, they need to understand what critical thinking means and what they will gain from it. Colombo, Cullen and Lisle offer the following explanation:

> [Critical thinking] involves asking questions rather than memorizing information. Instead of simply collecting "facts," a critical thinker probes them, looking for underlying assumptions and ideas. Instead of focusing on dates and events in history or symptoms in psychology, she probes for motives, causes—an explanation of how these things came to be. A critical thinker cultivates the ability to imagine and value points of view different from her own—then strengthens, refines, enlarges, or reshapes her ideas in light of those other perspectives. She is at once open and skeptical: receptive to new ideas yet careful to test them against previous experience and knowledge. In short, a critical thinker is an active learner, someone with the ability to shape, not merely absorb, knowledge." (1992:2)

Guiding students through the processes of unlearning intellectual passivity and cultivating active learning presents teachers and students with a formidable challenge. As a faculty member in the department of Ethnic Studies I am well aware of the fact that the simultaneous processes of unlearning and learning in Ethnic Studies courses are usually accompanied by strong emotions. In addition, each student experiences a variety of emotions—emotions that might promote or inhibit individual as well as group learning. Receptivity to information in Ethnic Studies courses varies depending upon several interrelated factors such as whether or not the student's parents/guardians engaged them in critical discussions of ethnic issues, the student's rationale for taking ethnic studies classes, what the student has heard about Ethnic Studies courses in general, and the student's first impressions of the teacher. Students who believe that they have everything to gain and nothing to lose from the maintenance of a negative peace will strongly resist disturbing that peace and will, in turn, resist removing their blinders. On the other hand, students who understand the futility of maintaining a negative peace at the expense of a positive peace will be much more enthusiastic about removing their blinders. Because most students have been socialized in a visually oriented society, with little practice in abstract thinking, I feel compelled to use graphics to ensure a full understanding of a variety of concepts in Ethnic Studies. Projecting figures such as 1a, 1b and 1c allows students the opportunity to "see" what happens when blinders are in place and to "see" what happens when they are discarded.

The *blinders removal* framework can be illustrated by using a simulation that examines views regarding the receptivity to different groups in the United States. Individuals who have been trained to view their world through blinders (as in figure 1a) have a tendency to see the United States as a nation of immigrants (see figure 2). Observe the simplistic perception of immigration with no reference made to the different experiences of European Americans and Americans and sub-groups within each of these categories. Students in my classes generally agree that this is indeed the perception of immigration that has been taught in schools across the nation.

This perception is a commonly held one in the United States and for those who view history through this non-critical monocultural perspective, blinders restrict vision and allow a limited understanding of historical and current ethnic issues and events. A negative peace is maintained by presenting the illusion that within the United States all cultures are allowed to flourish freely and there is equal opportunity for all. Students have not been taught about the exclusionary nature of immigration laws in the United States. An examination of the history of citizenship will make it evident that for 162 years naturalization laws in the United States granted citizenship to European groups but denied citizenship to several Naflas groups (Takaki 1994:27). The illusion of equal opportunity is consistently reinforced, in most institutions, through a variety of spoken and written mediums. For example, a common ritual that school children participate in is the daily pledge of allegiance which refers to "one nation indivisible with liberty and justice for all." The consistent recitation of phrases such as these leads most European Americans and some Naflas Americans to believe that there is actually liberty and justice for all in the United States. A large number of my Naflas American students assert that while they consistently recited the pledge of allegiance, they also knew, from their own experience, that the United States has not generally stood, and does not generally stand, for "liberty and justice for all."

Figure 2.
A Non-Critical Monocultural Perspective of the Receptivity to Ethnic Groups in the United States

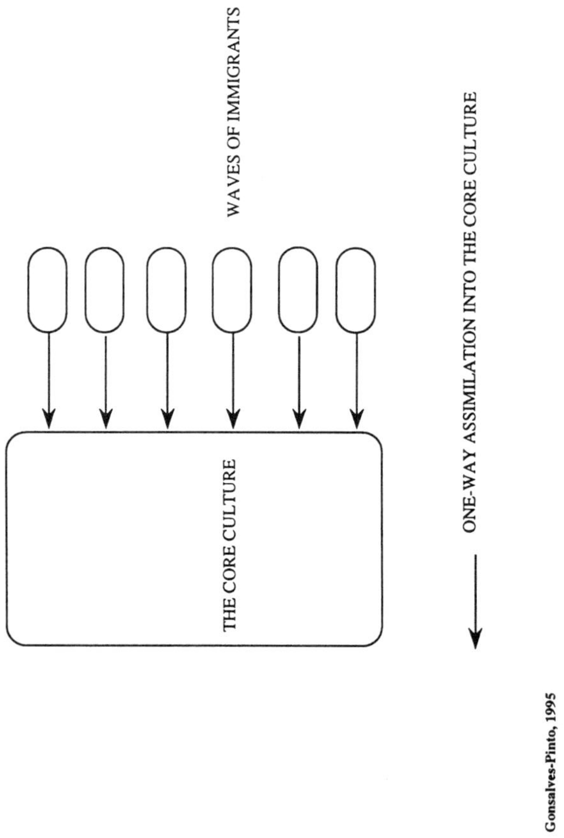

Figure 3.
Critical Multicultural Perspectives of the Receptivity to Ethnic Groups in the United States

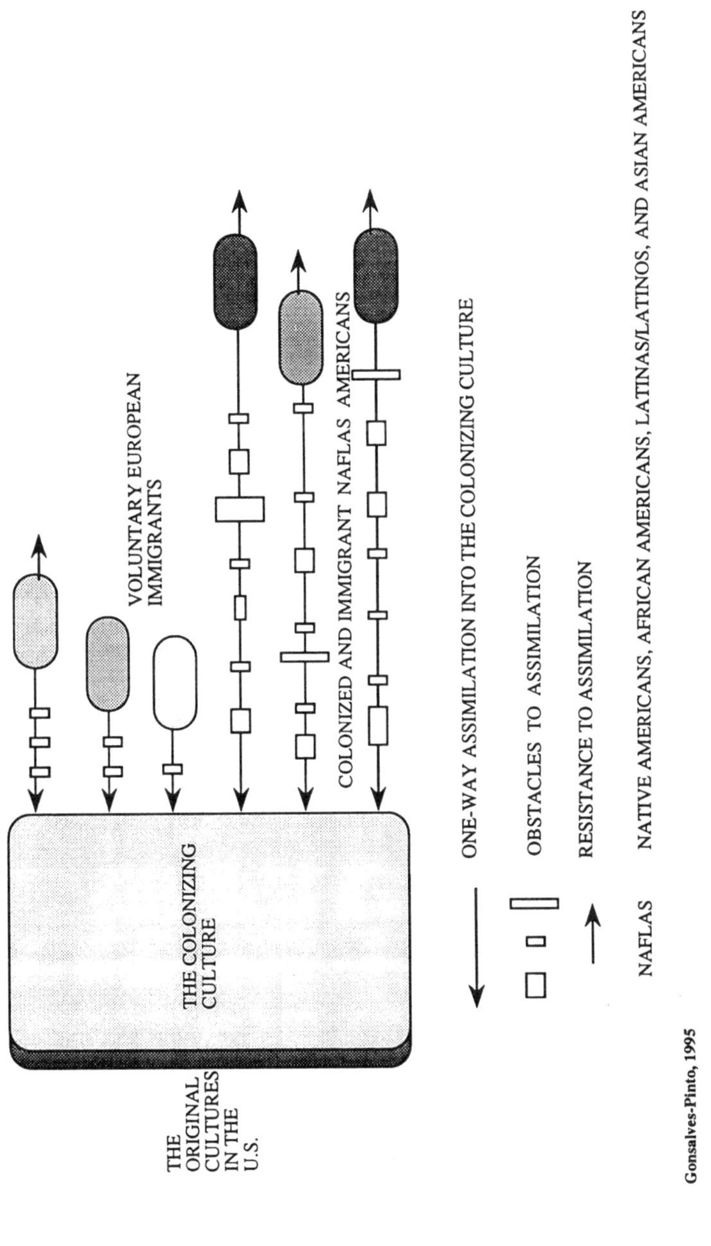

Viewing the historical experience of groups in the United States through multicultural perspectives allows students to understand the authentic experiences of different groups and allows a critical understanding of the social contexts within which individuals and groups functioned and continue to function. Students are thereby presented with opportunities to make a well-informed assessment of ethnic relations in the United States. Figure 3 provides students with a taste for multicultural perspectives of the historical experiences of ethnic groups in the United States. A completely different picture emerges than that presented through a traditional monocultural perspective. Discrimination based upon ethnicity has prevented many ethnic groups from fully participating in society (Wilson 1987). It becomes clear that the original Native American nations in the United States were forcibly suppressed by specific groups of European settlers who established their own culture through physical and cultural genocide, forced re-location, and forced assimilation.

Ethnicity and race were important factors determining the experiences of groups in the United States. Following the imposition of the Western European American Culture, the full participation of voluntary European immigrants, who identified with cultures other than the Western European culture, was blocked by obstacles in the form of prejudice and discrimination. Their one-way assimilation into the colonizing culture occurred at a tremendous psychological cost. These immigrants felt a great pressure to give up their language, reject their traditional norms, and even change their names. *Poplovskis* became *Popes* and *Mabertos* became *Maberts* as cultures of origin were suppressed and later discarded. Ultimately, a large proportion of individuals from European ethnic groups were able to "pass" as mainstream Western European Americans.

There were also specific colonized Naflas peoples whose full participation in society was blocked by such obstacles as enslavement, genocide, relocation and internment. Many of these groups resisted assimilation but were consistently compelled to take on the values and norms of the colonizing culture. While most European Americans have been able to assimilate more completely, most Naflas Americans are still marginalized. Based upon a comparison of monocultural and multicultural perspectives, it is clear that a very large gap exists between the two. This void supports the maintenance of a negative peace. What students traditionally learn does not really equip them with the knowledge and skills necessary in the struggle for a positive peace.

Students are not alone in being laced with this void in their education. Most educators, both European and Naflas American have been trained in eurocentric institutions and have been traditionally taught by mostly European-American teachers (Bowler, Auletta and Jones 1993:60). Many of these educators themselves have blinders on. Their own attitudes toward ethnic issues and the subject matter in multicultural curricula impact their effectiveness in the classroom (Banks 1991:501).

From my own experience as a teacher and a cultural diversity consultant, I have found teachers (as a group) to be one of the most resistant groups. With the move towards inclusion in the curriculum, there is an assumption that once departments or programs have decided to diversify the curriculum, educators are willing and able to effectively present information through multicultural perspectives.

Prior to planning and teaching courses that focus on multicultural perspectives, the following questions need to be addressed: Who assists educators in the blinders removal process? Can educators feel that they have fulfilled their obligation to students by simply using the contributions or additive approaches? What pedagogical strategies can educators use to effectively guide themselves and their students as they move from monocultural to multicultural ways of thinking? Is introspection regarding personal perspectives on ethnicity and ethnic issues an essential component of teacher preparation? As teachers, we too struggle, as we confront our own biases, and try to make room, in our minds and hearts, for multicultural perspectives of our world. Paulo Freire, in *The Pedagogy of the Oppressed*, cautions:

> the true focus of revolutionary change is never merely the oppressive situations which we seek to escape, but that piece of the oppressor which is planted deep within each of us, and which know only the oppressors tactics, the oppressors' relationships (1970)

Preparing to teach Ethnic Studies humbles us as we remove our own blinders and shed non-critical eurocentric ways of thinking. As faculty members who teach Ethnic Studies or those who incorporate multicultural perspectives in their respective fields of study, we are in various stages of the blinder removal process ourselves. As teachers, we are called upon to shed yet another set of blinders—blinders that have prevented us from reaching beyond traditional pedagogical strategies that support passive learning. Teachers who choose to use the transformation or social action approach to teaching ethnic studies invest a great deal of time and energy in the development of unique pedagogical strategies which recognize that students are *un-learning* and *learning* simultaneously. Teachers need to proceed with caution since removal of the blinders might initially be blinding as students are faced with what seems like a limitless expanse of new knowledge—a panorama of perspectives. Teaching Ethnic Studies requires careful planning as students move through a sequence of un-learning and learning processes.

In my own classrooms, I have developed several strategies in an effort to enhance learning in what could otherwise be a veritable battle field. As I look back to the first Ethnic Studies class that I ever taught, and compare the learning environment and student accomplishments in that class with those in my current classes, I am convinced that specific pedagogical strategies have made a positive contribution to teaching/learning in my Ethnic Studies courses.

The importance of preparatory work must be emphasized. Students who are not accustomed to critically examining ethnicity and ethnic issues are al ten surprised to discover how they think and feel about ethnic issues. As they progress through various stages of learning, they should be encouraged to experiment with different ways of communicating their ideas and interacting with their classmates. The strategies described in this paper will focus upon tile development of communication skills as students move from basic self reflection to formal presentations on ethnic issues. To obtain a feel for the impact of various strategies as they are applied in the classroom, refer to the sample of students' comments (verbatim) and teacher's insights presented in the appendix section.

Strategies for Assisting Students in the Removal of Blinders:

There is a wide variety of strategies that faculty members in Ethnic Studies can use to assist students in the removal of blinders. Each faculty member might use strategies that work in conjunction with her/his teaching styles and goals. The strategies described in this section have been utilized with success in several sections of courses, i.e., *Introduction to Ethnic Studies, Ethnicity in the United States, Ethnic Women in the United States,* and *Cross-Cultural Perspectives on Women*; which are electives in the required cultural diversity component of general education at Bowling Green State University. The success, or lack thereof, of these teaching strategies is measured in part by my own observations and in part by student responses to each of the strategies. While the overwhelming majority of students found these strategies effective, though sometimes intimidating, there were a few students who did not feel that they were effective in the blinder-removal process. In the Appendix, find that samples of student comments (verbatim) regarding each strategy are listed below the specific strategy so that the reader can obtain a glimpse of student reactions.

Teaching Ethnic Studies or teaching any discipline through multicultural perspectives requires teachers/learners to pay due attention to the content as well as to the process of learning. Every attentive teacher knows that what we teach and how we teach it are both important issues for consideration. It is imperative that teachers spend a significant amount of time preparing themselves and students for the removal of blinders strategies. Students in general have difficulty articulating their views on race and ethnicity. The sequence of strategies outlined below provides students with opportunities to make steady progress in interacting with the teacher and with each other on the topic of ethnicity.

As part of the preparatory phase, I find **interactive processes** most useful. Interaction between students and between students and teachers assists in several ways, but one of the most important is that the discussion of responsible versus irresponsible loyalty is a major stepping stone to critical thinking for a large number of students. Introducing the concepts of responsible and irresponsible loyalties is an important part of preparing students for the removal of blinders. A discussion of these concepts allows students to break down the first of many barriers to communication regarding multicultural issues. At different stages of the blinders removal process, students are both challenged and reassured as they hear the comments of their classmates. As with any new experience, students will learn better if they feel that they can move at their own pace and have control over the removal of the blinders. Students are not generally accustomed to the processes of questioning the source of knowledge or critiquing what they view as established assumptions and theories. Consistent interaction between students and between students and the teacher can facilitate these processes. When it comes to sharing ideas regarding ethnicity students will have a variety of reactions.

To facilitate the process of blinders removal it is important for the teacher to consistently monitor the pulse of individual students and the class as a whole. **Course Journals** provide the means to accomplish this task. Student journals reflect their understanding of the subject matter, their reaction to it and ways in which they apply the knowledge in their everyday lives. Special notes to the teacher may also be included. Students are required to record a dated and titled journal entry for every class period, for each and every reading and for every outside activity. Reactions to the subject matter rather than mere summaries are the focus. Students are encouraged to express themselves freely and students will sometimes draw a picture or write poetry to make a point.

Sharing reactions to new subject matter regarding ethnicity can be very intimidating. **Anonymous Share** has generally been a most popular and productive activity. Students are asked to reflect, in silence, on how they feel about a particular class discussion, article, issue, or the course in general and are asked to write down (in capitals, to ensure legibility) their ideas on scrap paper that the teacher hands out. Students are asked not to mention any names in their notes. The notes are collected, shuffled and re-distributed. Students then read aloud the comments that appear on their note, and the entire class records responses in journals. When questions are posed in the notes, students write down their responses to these questions. There is no specified sequence of readers, and students read their notes as they feel like it. The teacher needs to remind students that all notes must be read and that long breaks between readings will allow less time for discussion. When all the notes have been read, students hand them over to the teacher who tears them and throws them in the trash. What follows is an open discussion, revolving around the anonymous comments.

An essential skill in Ethnic Studies is to learn to listen to different points of view on controversial topics and to assess the validity of these points of view. **Debates** are a vehicle for practicing this skill. The class is divided into two groups that are further divided into three sub-groups (see table 1). Each sub-group selects a spokesperson and an introducer. Once the main question (For example: Should All Students be Required to take Courses which Emphasize Multicultural Perspectives?) has been presented each sub-group develops three main ideas that they will share with their class mates. The atmosphere is formal but friendly and students are presented with the option of taking on the identity of any character of their choice. The first two sub-groups present opening statements, the next two sub-groups present rebuttals and the last two sub-groups present closing statements.

Table 1. A Suggested Format for Ethnic Studies Debate

Example Question:
Should All Students Be Required to Take Courses Which Emphasize Multicultural Perspectives?

Yes—they should be required.	No—they should not be required.
Sub-group 1 Opening Remarks	Sub-group 2 Opening Remarks
Sub-group 4 Rebuttal	Sub-group 3 Rebuttal
Sub-group 5 Concluding Remarks	Sub-group 6 Concluding Remarks

Class discussion of the content and process of the debate

Students experience a variety of emotions as they attempt to remove blinders and, in some cases as they decide to keep them on. To affirm the validity of each student's position, it is important to allow them the opportunity to share specific ideas about ethnicity that they feel strongly about. **Oral Presentations** provide this opportunity. Students select a topic that they feel passionately about and deliver a five minute presentation on this topic. Guidelines are provided for the format of presentations and students consult with the teacher during the planning process. Each student is evaluated by a panel of peers on the content and form of the presentation. (Peer evaluations do not influence students' grades.) Students are asked to present their comments in a non-threatening and constructive manner. A brief overview of "dos" and "do nots" is presented.

An important phase in the blinders-removal process is learning to perceive in stereo. Students find it difficult to set a monocultural perspective aside, so they perceive issues from their original monocultural perspective while simultaneously attempting to perceive issues from multicultural perspectives. Upon completion of a segment or discussion of a particular ethnic group, students are asked to write **Identity/ Switched-Identity Narratives** about their views on a particular issue. They then write another narrative about their views on the same issue, except that in this case, they assume the identity of an individual from another ethnic group. Students then volunteer to share their stories with the class.

Poetry and Music are also very useful as aids in the removal of blinders. Listening to first hand accounts of people's lives, and how they feel about a variety of issues, through poetry and song is an experience that stays with students for a very long time. Many students have never explored the creative works of different cultures, and the messages delivered through this medium are simple and clear.

The above strategies are a sample of those that I use in my Ethnic Studies classes. Students have provided me with consistent responses that have allowed me to retain what is effective and modify what is not. As I read students' critiques of pedagogical strategies which I use in my classroom, I am convinced that to teach Ethnic Studies effectively, teachers must move beyond traditional pedagogical practices and engage students in active learning processes which stimulate them to question traditional views of race and ethnicity and which equip them with skills to critically examine and articulate their own views on race and ethnicity.

Looking to the Future:

As Ethnic Studies departments across the country establish themselves, it is important that they play a significant role in moving beyond curricular reform to institutional transformation. Goodman in his article entitled *Change Without Difference* suggests that: "many school reform proposals and projects, while making technical changes, actually reinforce the underlying values, power relationships, and learning experiences embedded within the conventional ways of educating children" (Goodman 1995:3).

It would be a mistake to focus on curricular reform without planning and implementing procedures for critically examining and changing the very structures within institutions in an effort to democratize an otherwise centralized power structure. In other words Ethnic Studies has the potential to steer institutions, as Goodman puts it, beyond "ameliorative" to "radical" changes (Goodman 1995:2). Ethnic Studies teaches students what bell hooks describes as "the difference between education as a practice of freedom and education that merely strives to reinforce domination" (hooks 1994:4).

Within our institutions mass delusions of equality are so deeply rooted and so consistently reinforced that attempts to address the realities of racism and the other "isms" that operate in the United States are met with adamant resistance. Identifying cues to resistance is a skill that needs to be developed so that students and teachers can address and deal with specific factors that underlie this resistance. Students will relax once they realize that the teacher's goal is not to strip the blinders off but to encourage students to control their own removal of blinders.

> Often initial resistance fades as the semester progresses and the years pass. New information is acquired, new perspectives considered, new voices heard, and new experiences with stratifying institutions gained. Lessons from our classes may not be learned until long after our students are no longer our students (Davis 1992:233).

Many students report that perceiving specific ethnic issues through multicultural perspectives trains them to broaden their perspectives on a variety of social issues. The move towards the institutionalization of a multicultural curriculum tugs at the blinders and stirs the conscience of students and educators alike as the negative peace is disturbed. Memories of another era, in which the negative peace was disturbed, come to mind. The sixties ushered in a wave of critical thinkers who discarded their blinders and worked for a positive peace. Educational reform was viewed as an important first step. Although the seeds of educational reform were sown they did not take root.

> The acid test for ethnic studies was, unfortunately, economic. Although the students of the sixties and early seventies flocked to

> such courses, the downturn in the economy by the mid-seventies made such courses anachronisms: minority students, like others seeking a piece of the American corporate pie, switched to management and business administration courses. (Deloria 1994:99)

Today, an increasing number of students are majoring and minoring in Ethnic Studies. Building a strong inter-disciplinary base, training students to apply their knowledge and skills in their every day lives, providing them with internships, and ensuring their placement in institutions and organizations are essential. Aside from receiving rigorous academic training, young scholars in Ethnic Studies need to also develop marketable skills. Ethnic Studies graduates are entering the work force in increasing numbers and are playing a significant role as ambassadors of a positive peace. Through their representation, the mission of Ethnic Studies is extended into many communities and work spheres. Grant and Sleeter outline some societal goals that are an extension of the academic goals of multicultural education: "to reduce prejudice and discrimination against oppressed groups, to provide equal opportunity and social justice for all groups, and to affect an equitable distribution of power among members of the different cultural groups." (1991:5)

On many campuses, dedicated scholars have succeeded in institutionalizing Ethnic Studies as a discipline. As an increasing number of Ethnic Studies majors and minors graduate and make their mark in their various fields, the move towards the establishment of a positive peace is gaining momentum. Indeed, for those who prefer to maintain a negative peace these are troubling times, but for those involved in the struggle for a positive peace, these are truly exciting times. For both parties there is no turning back.

---

1 Ethnic Studies, as a discipline, includes the study of all ethnic groups and is not restricted to the study of African Americans, Native Americans, Latinos/Latinas, and Asian Americans. In addition, ethnic studies scholars generally agree that a thorough study of ethnicity and ethnic issues can be made only if due attention is paid to the intersections of ethnicity with gender, class, sexual orientation, physical ability, age, and other such factors.

2 In an effort to move away from using "white" as the standard and "non-white" as "the other" I developed the term NAFLAS to refer to **NA**tive Americans, **AF**rican

Americans, **LA**tinos/**LA**tinas, and **AS**ian Americans. In the United States, the term Naflas Americans substitutes the term non-white Americans, and globally, the term Naflas people substitutes non-white people.

3 Generalizations about ethnic groups do not discount the wide range of "within group" differences in attitudes, behavior, and experiences. Generalizations about groups are made only in situations where a very large number of individuals from a particular group share similar attitudes, behavior and/or experiences. For example, in the United States race is a major factor that has been, and continues to be, used to accord differential treatment to groups.

4 When I refer to multiculturalism I refer to more than an overview of the experiences, norms, traditions and values of different ethnic groups. I refer to the critical examination of these factors within broader historical, social and political contexts. In such a study of multiculturalism, unequal power relations between different ethnic groups comprise a most significant component of analysis.

5 A set of ideas that distorts reality and is shared by a large group of individuals (Griffin 1988:296)

6 ". . . by this definition, Blacks, Native Americans, and immigrant communities are internal colonies in the United States. They are internal colonies because their relationship to white, Anglo-America is analogous to that of overseas colonies to the metropole" (Kelly 1988:314).

7 Cultural sensitivity workshops have been conducted for such groups as: school faculty and administration, university faculty and administration, social service agencies, law enforcement agencies, and students groups.

Works Cited

Baldwin, James. "A Talk to Teachers," in *Multicultural Literacy*, editors: Rick Simonson and Scott Walker, St. Paul: Graywolf Press, 1988, 3-12.

Banks, Jams A. "A Multicultural education: For Freedom's Sake." in a special edition of *Educational Leadership* entitled *Whose Culture?* Volume 49, No. 4, December 1991/January 1992, 32-36.

Bloom, Allan. *The Closing of the American Mind: How Higher Education Has Failed Democracy and Impoverished the Souls of Today's Students*, New York: Simon and Schuster, 1987.

Bobbitt, F. *How to Make a Curriculum*. Boston: Houghton Mifflin, 1924.

Bowser, Benjamin, Gale S. Auletta and Terry Jones. *Confronting Diversity Issues on Campus*. Newbury Park: Sage Publications, 1993.

Chafe, William. "Sex and Race: The analogy of Social Control." In *Race, Class and Gender in the United States: An Integrated Study*, third edition. Paula Rothenberg, editor. New York: St. Martin's Press, 1995.

Charnes, Ruth. "U.S. History Text Books: Help or Hindrance to Social Justice." *Interracial Books for Children Bulletin*, Volume 15, 1984, Number 5, 3-8.

Colombo, Gary, Robert Cullen and Bonnie Lisle. *Rereading America: Cultural Contexts for Critical Thinking and writing*, second edition. Boston: Bedford Books of St. Martin's Press, 1992.

Cubberly, E. *Public School Administration: A Statement of the Fundamental Principles Underlying the Organization and Administration of Public Education*. Boston: Houghton Mifflin, 1916.

Davis, Nancy. Teaching About Inequality: Student Resistance, Paralysis, and Rage. *Teaching Sociology*, Volume 20, July 1992, 232-238.

Deloria, Vine. "Identity and Culture" in *From Different Shores: Perspectives on Race and Ethnicity in America*, second edition, editor: Ronald Takaki. New York: Oxford University Press, 1994. 93-102.

Dewey, J. *Experience and Education*. New York: Collier Books, 1976.

Freire, Paulo, *Pedagogy of the Oppressed*. New York: Seabury Press, New York, 1970.

Gilliam, Angela. "Women's Equality and National Liberation" in *Third World Women and the Politics of Feminism*, editors: Chandra Talpade Mohanty, Ann Russo and Lourdes Torres. Bloomington, Indiana: Indiana University Press, 1991.

Goodman, Jesse. Change Without Difference: School Restructuring in Historical Perspective. *Harvard Educational Review*, Volume 65, No. 1, Spring 1995. 1-29.

Griffin, Susan, "The Sacrificial Lamb" in *Racism and Sexism: An Integrated Study*, editor: Paula S. Rothenberg. New York: St. Martin's Press, 1988, 296-305.

Hilliard, Asa G., III. "Why We Must Pluralize the Curriculum." In a special edition of *Educational Leadership* entitled *Whose Culture?* Volume 49, No. 4, December 1991/January 1992, 12-14.

Hirsch, E.D., Jr. *Cultural Literacy: What Every American Needs to Know.* Boston: Houghton Mifflin, 1987.

hooks, bell. "Feminism: A Transformed Politic." In *Race, Class, and Gender in the United States: An Integrated Study*, 3rd edition. Paula Rothenberg, editor. New York: St. Martin's Press, 1995.

hooks, bell. *Teaching to Transgress.* New York: Rutledge, 1994.

Kelly, Gayle. "The Schooling of Vietnamese Immigrants." In *Racism and Sexism: An Integrated Study*, editor: Paula S. Rothenberg. New York: St. Martin's Press, 1988, 313-323.

King, Martin Luther, Jr. *Letter from Birmingham City Jail*, written on April 16, 1963.

Lestyna, Pepi. Editor's Review of Teaching to Transgress: Education as the Practice of Freedom by Bell Hooks, *Harvard Education Review*, Vole 65, No. 2, Summer 1995, 322-330.

Madrid, Arturo. "Diversity and its Discontents." In *Experiencing Race, Class and Gender in the United States.* Mountain-View, California: Mayfield Publishing Company, 1993, 381-386.

Ravitch, Diane. "A Culture in Common." In a special edition of *Educational Leadership* entitled *Whose Culture?* Volume 49, No. 4, December 1991/January 1992, 8-11.

Rothenberg, Paula S., editor. *Race, Class and Gender in the United States: An Integrated Study*, second edition. New York: St. Martin's Press, 1992.

Ryan, William. "Blaming the Victim." In *Race, Class and Gender in the United States: An Integrated Study*, second edition. Editor: Paula Rothenberg. New York: St. Martin's Press, 1992, 364-373.

San Juan, E. "Problematizing Multiculturalism." *Melus.* Volume 19 (Summer 1994), 59-84.

Takaki, Ronald. *A Different Mirror: A History of Multicultural America.* Boston: Little, Brown and Company, 1993.

Takaki, Ronald. *From Different Shores: Perspectives on Race and Ethnicity in America,* second edition. New York: Oxford University Press, 1994.

Appendix

Interactive Processes

Students' Comments:

- "This is the first time I have ever talked about ethnicity with other students. It makes me feel weird, but I also think that it is necessary."
- "We never really talked about prejudice, but I learned a lot from my parents' expressions about how they felt about certain groups."
- "_________ and I discussed how when we were young, we never thought very much about difference. As we grew up, we talked more and more about the 'bad' part of town where 'they' lived."
- "In high school, we had social studies, but we never learned about social relations or the lack of social relations between groups in America."
- "In our last ethnic studies class, I learned a lot from class discussion."

Teacher's Perspective:

- Students learn to recall how and when ideas about ethnicity were introduced into their lives.
- They look inwards to discover what ideas regarding ethnicity they have accumulated over the years.
- They learn to deal with the frustration of sorting through issues that they never addressed before .
- They compare ideas with classmates and discover that there are similarities and differences among them, depending on their backgrounds and experiences.
- They learn to evaluate critically their own ideas about ethnicity.
- They learn to analyze critically the subject matter.
- They learn to leave the mind open to modifying or discarding old ideas and accepting new ideas.

Course Journals

Students' Comments:

- "I like how we write notes to each other. You know how I feel without my saying it in front of the class."
- "When I was angry, I just wrote in my journal. Now I can say what I used to write."
- "Journals are too much work, but I do remember things when I write them down."
- "My journal is a souvenir of my course. I can share it with my kids."
- "I do not like keeping a journal because it takes too much time and it gets boring to write reactions to every thing I read."
- "My journal is my punching bag."

Teacher's Perspective:

- Journals provide a medium of communication for students who are not accustomed to one-on-one communication with teachers. Often, I invite these students to stop by the office to discuss specific journal entries.
- Teachers can keep track of students' struggles and triumphs as they attempt to remove blinders.
- Proactive rather than reactive measures can be taken to avoid pent up anger and frustration.
- Journals encourage reflection on the subject matter and indicate student reactions to the same.

Anonymous Share

Students' Comments:

- "I like to hear how others feel about racism. It is not something we talk about."
- "People are more honest when they do not have to look at you."
- "I guess I am not the only one who feels angry, frustrated, embarrassed and silly. So many of us just never thought about these issues before."

- "It feels strange to hear my comments through someone else's voice."
- "I wish we had more time to discuss each person's note."
- "We need more Anonymous Shares."
- "I do not like it when some students smile at my comments. It makes me feel stupid."
- "I wish people would be more honest and and say how they really feel about blacks and quit saying what they feel they are supposed to say."

Teacher's Perspective:

- Students learn that they are at different stages in the blinders removal process.
- Students learn that there is a wide variety of reactions to the new perspective that unfolds before them.
- Students become collectively involved in the learning process by sharing their feelings about their new perceptions.
- Students reflect on their personal responses to the topic under discussion.
- Students record these ideas in writing.
- Someone else's statement is read through the voice of another.
- Students listen to their statements in someone else's voice.
- At later stages in the course, each student gauges her/his progress and that of the entire class.
- Students realize that each person has a unique way of interpreting and dealing with new insights.

Debates

Students' Comments:

- "It was hard being in the negative group and arguing against the cultural diversity requirement when I am for it, but I got to understand why some people would not want it."
- This was a fun way to listen to different points of view."
- "Jesse Jackson was great, but I did not like it when people laughed out loud at his comments."

- "I never really knew what multiculturalism meant until today."
- "I was terribly nervous to speak in front of everyone especially after I heard ________'s comment regarding 'ignorant whites.'"

Teacher's Perspective:

- Debates provide a forum for the free expression of ideas on a variety of topics.
- Students invariably have an opportunity to argue on the side that contradicts what they actually believe.
- Students learn to listen to two sides of an argument with respect for each debater.
- Students learn to present ideas with respect for all those present.
- Regarding the specific question provided in Table 1, students have an opportunity to share rationales for inclusion of multicultural perspectives and to suggest approaches for incorporating these perspectives.

Oral Presentations

Students' Comments:

- "I was scared, but once I got up there I really got into it."
- "I learned a lot from presentations. I have never heard other students discuss ethnic issues, and I was surprised at how good they were."
- "I liked the ones where students told their own stories best."
- "We should have presentations in every course. Teachers can learn from students too."
- "I didn't think that racism still affects so many people today. I felt awful when I heard about _______'s experiences."
- "I liked the suggestions from the panel of students who evaluated me."
- "Students should have an option to present or not to present."
- "I did not feel that I had enough time to conduct research on my topic. We need more time."

Teacher's Perspective:

- Oral presentations open up the class to student generated themes and information.
- Organizing oral presentations early in the semester provides all students with the opportunity to share their ideas with the class and challenges hesitant students to take the first step in sharing ideas about ethnicity.
- It provides the teacher with the opportunity to identify special topics that students might like to discuss.

Identity/Switched-Identity Narratives

Students' Comments:

- "This was a lot more difficult than I thought [it would be]—even writing my own narrative [was difficult]."
- "I just guessed what someone from another ethnic group might think. I usually . . . judge people from my own perspective, so trying to think through their perspective was hard."
- "I never before thought about how a Native American would look at Columbus. I was even angry when I was writing from this perspective."
- "I found myself defending positions that I would usually make fun of."
- "I thought this exercise was not fair to me or to the group I was representing because I was stereotyping them."
- "I was uncomfortable at how I as a white man looked at Columbus as a hero when I as a Native American man saw him as evil."

Teacher's Perspective:

- Writing narratives facilitates introspection.
- Students practice perceiving the same issue or event with and without blinders.
- As each student struggles to enter a frame of reference which is foreign to him/her, they recognize the rigidity of their perspectives but they also recognize that they are capable of rationalizing different perspectives.

- Many students realize that they do view the world through blinders.
- Students become aware of their own stereotypes regarding different groups.

Poetry and Music

(Regarding "Ella's Song" and "I'm Gon' Stand," performed by Sweet Honey in The Rock)

Students' Comments:

- "The words and voices were beautiful. The women seemed so determined."
- "I guess it is true that we cannot rest until the killing of black males is as important as the killing of white males."
- "I would love to choreograph a dance to this song." (This particular student did actually choreograph a dance to Ella's song, and it has been performed at many university events.)
- "I felt myself singing again and again—'we will not bow down to injustice.' It was kind of eerie."
- "I have never heard this kind of music before. It really makes you think"

Teacher's Perspective:

- Reading poems allows students to shed blinders and to step, even though very briefly, into the minds of individuals from different groups.
- Students are encouraged to present their own artistic expressions on the themes of ethnicity as it intersects with class, gender and other factors.
- Students often share poems with friends and relatives.
- Students hear about issues in the authentic dialects of ethnic groups.
- The passion of the artist comes through and stirs the audience.